Acclaim for AMAN

The Story of a Somali Girl

"A direct, heartfelt autobiography. . . . This revelatory first-person narrative puts a human face on the country we have come to know largely through bewildering photo ops on the evening news."   —*Elle*

"In this memoir of her early years, Aman reflects on life, lineage, and community. She interweaves the story of her own struggles with the cultural and political evolution of Somalia."   —*Ms.*

"A riveting story of survival."   —*Publishers Weekly*

"An extraordinary story . . . shockingly real. Not only is the book an extraordinary glimpse of a country undergoing violent political and social change, it's an engrossing personal saga."   —*Vancouver Sun*

"A lyrical first-hand account of a complex and charismatic modern-day African heroine. . . . [A] unique and rich account of life in a fascinating and troubled land."
                    —*Kirkus Reviews* (starred review)

"A lively and rare oral autobiography from Africa [that] deepens our understanding of a distant culture."
                    —*Toronto Globe and Mail*

AMAN

The Story of a Somali Girl

Aman is a pseudonym that means"trustworthy"in Arabic.

AMAN

The Story of a Somali Girl

As told to Virginia Lee Barnes
and Janice Boddy

Vintage Books

A Division of Random House, Inc.

New York

FIRST VINTAGE BOOKS EDITION, SEPTEMBER 1995

The Library of Congress has cataloged the Pantheon edition as follows:
Barnes, Virginia Lee.
Aman: the story of a Somali girl/as told
to Virginia Lee Barnes and Janice Boddy.
p. cm.
ISBN 0-679-43606-5
1. Aman. 2. Somalia—Biography.
3. Women—Somalia—Social conditions. 4. Girls—Somalia—
Biography. I. Boddy, Janice Patricia. II. Title.
CT 2208.A43B37 1994
967.7305'092—dc20
[B] 94-6745
Vintage ISBN: 0-679-76209-4

Manufactured in the United States of America
10 9

For Mama, Grandmama, and Lee

and all my friends who helped me, and

anybody who has helped my people

FOREWORD

*audience,
participation*

Like a realistic novel, an oral history allows us to witness the
sweep of time and transformation through the everyday experiences of ordinary lives. This is history "close up", portrayed by
someone fully immersed in the events she describes, whose words
expose the hidden framework of culture, religion, and morality
that shapes her own and others' acts. Aman's narrative, the story
of her life and family in Somalia, begins long before her birth and
ends shortly after her flight to Kenya, then Tanzania, at the age
of seventeen. It is at once a striking account of rapid social change
in arid northeast Africa and a candid, intimately personal story of
a young girl's struggle to "come of age", of her strength of will
and remarkable resiliency in the face of tremendous social odds.
And it is a tale that is beautifully, at times wrenchingly, told.

Virginia Lee Barnes, the anthropologist with whom Aman
originally worked to produce this memoir of her youth, noted in
a scholarly paper months before her early death that she had
long sought a Somali woman who would tell the world her life.
Lee wrote: "I knew that if I found such a woman, she would tell
a wonderful story, because Somali culture has its own high narrative tradition; Somalis are known throughout the world as a

nation of poets—a people who are masters of the verbal art."
Like others who have grown up in a largely oral culture, Aman
has impressive powers of recall. Societies with oral traditions
cultivate the art of memory, and when coupled with dramatic fi-
nesse, the outcome can be rivetting. Stories, of course, are imagi-
native translations of life-as-lived into life-as-told. And memory
is naturally selective: no recollection of the past is wholly untem-
pered by present circumstance or understanding. Yet traces of
Aman's adult self in this story of her youth are muted; her biography reverberates with the themes and concerns of Somali culture as it was when she was growing up in the 1950s and 1960s,
and continues, in sadly disrupted form, today.

As I write, in early 1994, Somalia is very much in the news.
In the throes of a bitter civil war—"brutal anarchy", as some re-
porters describe it—exacerbated by a terrible famine that the war
partially caused, Somalia today is a tragic country, a land of death
and refugees. Some 30,000 displaced Somalis currently live in the
Canadian city where I teach. Aman herself now resides abroad.
Yet her story allows us to turn the clock back to a more peaceful
time, when Mogadishu, the capital city, was hailed as the safest
city in East Africa—*relatively* safe, that is, if you were a young girl
on the run; safe once you knew how to handle men. Aman's tale
of hardship and triumph, of "learning"—becoming street and
socially wise—allows us privileged insight into the world of Somalia's most vulnerable citizen: the female child. This is one
girl's story; it does not apply to all. But it counters media images
of Somalia as a land of starving, uncared-for children and inhu-
mane, marauding "warlords".

Positioned beyond the halls of power and wealth in colonial
and postindependence Somalia, Aman describes her country's
social arrangements as one who lives them, without undue
theoretical rationalization. English, the language in which she

recorded her tale, lacks Somali's fine-grained distinctions for different categories of kin. Despite this difficulty, her story describes a system of family and connection far different from European forms, but similar to those found elsewhere in Africa and in the Middle East. In Somalia, as Aman puts it, "Father is your main blood." Descent is traced exclusively through the father, back several generations to a common founding patriarch. Descendants in this paternal line make up a lineage—a patrilineage, to be precise—that is named for its founder. Larger groups form by tracing even deeper into the past; these Aman refers to as tribes, though "clan" and "clan-family" are terms more often used in the Western press. And beyond that still, Somalis hold to the belief that they are all descendants of a small number of ancestors who were sons and grandsons of a single father, the mythical Samaale. Whether near or remote, each descent group is a political association as well as a unit of kin. But where anthropologists and, no doubt, Somali clansmen grapple with the political intricacies of the system, Aman speaks refreshingly of people: "sisters", "cousins", "relatives". Though "Father is your main blood" and determines political affiliation, Somalis acknowledge relationship with maternal kin: members of their mother's, father's mother's, and mother's mother's descent groups. These relations lack the political authority and intense obligation of patrilineal kin, but are nonetheless important sources of support; so too are relatives by marriage. Aman frequently relies on such support when fleeing from her father's sons. The mother-focussed family she grew up in contrasts with the Somali ideal: she does not reside with her father and his other children; and her maternal half-brother and half-sister with whom she does, both belong to lineages other than her own. Yet, as the novels of Nurrudin Farah affirm, in southern Somalia Aman's household is hardly unique.

Aman is equivocal about her culture (she calls it that), cherishing some aspects of it, despising and railing against others. In all these things her account provides a welcome corrective to the notion that culture fully determines the person, and a challenge to Western conventional wisdom that Muslim societies are rigid and homogeneous. Too often it is assumed that social ideals of male authority and female subservience go unquestioned by Muslim women themselves. Such views deny women political acumen and rob relations between women and men of their delicacy and tension, for they overlook the realities of women's power and contribution, the subtle ways they can apply or subvert the "rules" in their quest for self-realization.[1] But if Aman resists some of her society's practices, she does not extricate herself from its values and concerns. She is ambivalent about her rebellion, defies those who chastise her for flouting expectations, but is ashamed and embarrassed when she fails to meet them all the same. She has internalized her culture's constraints, as all of us implicitly do, and seldom reflects upon them as such: "That was how it was," she says, "that is how it is."

How Aman *came to be*

This book has been a collaborative enterprise from the start. Its words are Aman's, but how they came to take the shape they do merits comment.

Virginia Lee Barnes was an American anthropologist who did fieldwork for her doctorate (University of Hawaii) among the Lugbara in northwest Uganda. Prior to that, she had been with the Peace Corps in Somalia between 1965 and 1967, and she returned there in 1981 as a volunteer aid worker in a refugee camp in the south. In 1982, Aman was living in Italy, where she met and married an American serviceman. Shortly after that she came to the United States to live, and three years later Lee and Aman met. They became close friends. In their frequent conversations the story of Aman's life began to emerge, and the anthropologist in Lee was intrigued. The two began to talk with a tape recorder running. Lee would then transcribe Aman's narrative and read it back to her, for clarification or change, when next they met. At first Aman was reluctant to allow even the name of her country to be known. As work progressed she became less reticent, disclosing towns and cities, but disguising the identities of individuals, lest they be dishonoured by her revelations—a dishonour that, given the close alliance between Somali politics and kinship, could have distressing results. Work on the manuscript ended in 1989, when Lee became ill; she died the following summer. At the time of her death she had completed a draft, started the introduction, and made some inquiries of potential publishers.

After her death, Martin Buss, a friend of Lee's and a professor of religious studies at Emory University, took up the task of editing the manuscript for consistency and repetition. Martin, with Penny Orr, Lee's sister and executrix, and John Middleton, her academic mentor and a professor emeritus of anthropology at Yale, resumed the search for a publisher and cast about for someone to introduce the text. On the latter point, John contacted me, and I provisionally agreed. I had met Lee at a couple of conferences, where we'd spoken together of our common interests in northeast Africa, the last time in November 1989, when she was unwell. Later, when I met Aman, I learned that Lee had given her my name and phone number, with instructions to ask me to continue efforts to publish the story in the event that something happened to her. Although my involvement was initiated otherwise, Lee's wishes have been fulfilled: Aman and I were, it seems, fated to see this through.

In the winter of 1992 I read the manuscript, and was immediately captivated by this snapshot of a society in transition, as seen through the eyes of a girl. When I completed researching and writing the anthropological Afterword, I approached Louise Dennys, publisher of Knopf Canada, who had expressed interest in my work with African women. Knopf Canada were immediately drawn to Aman's direct voice; her brave and unapologetic telling of her story, even when it deals with matters that so often are taboo; the vitality that set her on a course that turned her into a runaway street kid; and the courage that led her to escape by night from a Somalia in turmoil after the military coup. But they felt, and I agreed, that there were some gaps in the story as it stood. Ultimately this led to my going to Aman's city to interview her in the summer of 1993. We got along well and worked intensively together for the better part of a week; the transcripts of our taped conversations ran to several hundred pages, providing much valuable material, almost a new book, a richer, more reflective voice.

I corrected and provided an index to the transcript, but by now the university term had begun, and the task of integrating this material with the original text fell principally to Rebecca Godfrey, an editorial assistant at Knopf Canada with a degree in cultural anthropology. Together Louise and Rebecca and I discussed and edited the manuscript page by page, scene by scene, careful to follow as closely as possible the chronology that Aman had established. We felt it was crucial to honour Aman's convention of addressing her friend Rahima (Lee), so as to preserve the immediacy of the telling in this text of her conversations with Lee and, later, myself. Then, before we were finished, Aman was flown to Toronto, where, in the boardroom at Knopf Canada, she was read the manuscript over a period of several days. She corrected the text, which she had not heard since before Lee's death, and approved or improved upon it.

Aman's first language, Somali, is poetic and richly nuanced. She has become fluent in English only recently—and she neither reads nor writes—yet her narrative sense is undiminished. In transcribing her words to written text, her expressions and the rhythm of her voice were maintained. But the space restrictions of a single book meant that some details had to be left out. We were aided in the editing process by her younger, educated cousin, who helped enormously with Somali spellings and terms. (In deference to readability, however, we have sometimes used forms most commonly employed in the international press—for place names such as Mogadishu, and personal names such as Ahmed, in place of Axmed.) As we worked, Aman chose pseudonyms for people whom she had originally identified only as "my sister", "my cousin", "my boyfriend"; those whose reputations could be hurt by her account remain unnamed.

While Aman's story stands by itself as a work of eloquence and drama, for readers unfamiliar with Somalia I have written an Afterword that furnishes historical and cultural context for events and customs described or merely alluded to in her text, where Somali social relations, and women's perspectives on these, are addressed in greater detail. My own anthropological interest, resulting in a book published in 1989,[2] has been focussed mainly on northern Sudan, a desert region of north Africa similar to Somalia, but separated from it geographically by the culturally and religiously distinctive Ethiopian highlands. For the better part of two years I lived in a village on the upper Nile among women who, like Somalis, are Sunni Muslims and socially organized by patrilineal descent. Although there are many social and historical differences between Aman's society and that of the Muslim Sudan, which I know best, in important ways the two are alike. Salient here are the controls intended to discipline women's lives; like the women in this book, northern Sudanese girls are "circumcised"—undergo clitoridectomy (excision of the clitoris and inner labia) and infibulation (paring and surgical closure of the outer labia); women's marriages are, for the most part, arranged; women and men, in different ways, abide by an honour code comparable to those found throughout North Africa and the Islamic Middle East; married women are liable to be possessed by capricious spirits and to participate in a cult called *zar*. On the basis of such resemblances between the women with whom we worked and whose societies we have both respected and ambivalently admired, I took pen in hand to help complete Lee's task.

Putting together *Aman* has been an exhilarating co-operative process, the labour of many who believe it is important that the voice of this Somali woman be heard.

Janice Boddy
Toronto, Ontario
February 27, 1994

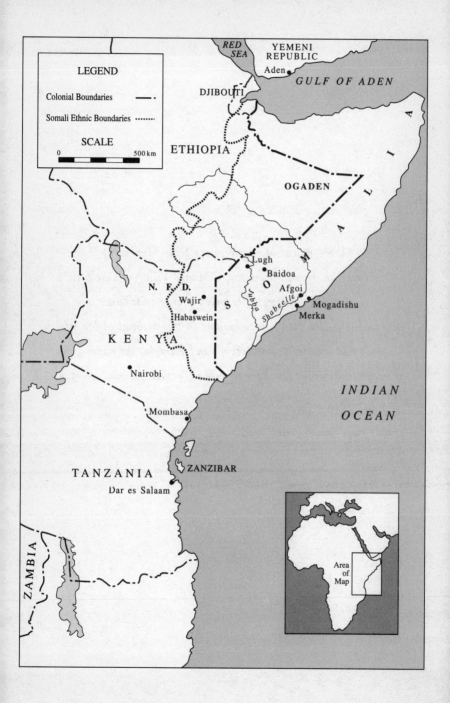

LEGEND

Colonial Boundaries — · — · —

Somali Ethnic Boundaries ·········

SCALE

0 — 500 km

RED
SEA

YEMENI
REPUBLIC

Aden

GULF OF ADEN

DJIBOUTI

ETHIOPIA

OGADEN

S
O
M
A
L
I
A

Lugh

Baidoa

Afgoi

Mogadishu

Merka

N. F. D.

Wajir

Habaswein

Jubba

Shabeelle

S
O

KENYA

Nairobi

INDIAN

OCEAN

Mombasa

ZANZIBAR

TANZANIA

Dar es Salaam

ZAMBIA

Area
of
Map

*All the names of people in the book—including
the name of Aman's home town, Mango Village—have been
changed to preserve the privacy of individuals.
Aman has chosen all the pseudonyms in this account of her life.
Aman means "trustworthy", and Rahima, the name
she gave to Virginia Lee Barnes, means "compassionate".* — J. B.

CHAPTER

I

B'ism Allah, ar-Rahman ar-Rahim

MY NAME IS AMAN. I AM GOING TO tell the whole world my story, but especially my friend Rahima, who is listening here. It is also my grandmama's and my mama's story, so I'll start with my grandmama.

My grandmama had brothers—I don't know how many there were—and sisters and a number of cousins. She came from a big family. There was a king who was head of the whole area where her family was living at the time. And it happened that there was a big tribal war—in those days, different tribes used to fight each other—and my grandmama's tribe lost the war. The king's tribe was bigger, so they won. When they won, they captured a lot of the men in my grandmama's family and kept them alive. Back then, people didn't kill women and children captured in war, so the women and children who had been captured were alive too. The young boys were still alive, because they usually only killed the men and the big boys—the ones who were over fifteen. But it so happened that my grandmama's father and her brothers were all dead. Even her mother was dead—she had died accidentally in the shooting. You see, the king's tribe had guns, but all my grandmama's tribe had were the traditional weapons of our people: short, curved, double-edged knives, bows and arrows, and spears.

Anyway, all my grandmama's family was dead except for her three sisters and three of her cousins—all girls. When the battle started, the seven girls climbed a tree to get out of the fighting, and after the battle was over they came down again and went to their house and found the bodies of my grandmama's father and mother and her brothers and her close cousins. They buried their dead relatives, and after they finished burying them, they decided to leave that area, because they had lost everything—all their cows and goats had been taken away, and they had nothing to eat. They had to go and find something to eat, somehow. Besides, they couldn't stay where the battle had taken place because there was a lot of blood on the ground and many dead bodies lying around, and it would have been dangerous to stay there because wild animals like lions and leopards would come and eat the bodies.

And so my grandmother and her three sisters and three cousins ran away from that place. But the grown men from their tribe who had been captured by the king were kept alive, and when they asked what would happen to them, the king replied that he wanted to see how many days a human being could survive without food. The king built a strong house out of stone for them and put them inside and sealed up the house so that it had no door, and left only little holes through which he and his men could look each day and watch the men die. He watched them until he saw the last one die. When they saw all this happening, the few people that were left in the area became frightened and ran away. In the end, nearly everyone ran away.

My grandmother was one of the oldest in the group of seven girls. In those days, if you were a girl or a woman and you fled out of the territory where you'd been living into another tribe's territory and you met a man, the first thing he would do is ask you what lineage you belonged to—whose daughter you were, and who your father was. When he found out exactly who you were—that you were only running away from danger and you weren't from an outcast or slave tribe—then he might ask you to marry him. No women would say no, because they all wanted a place to live. Most of the grown women used to end up being married to somebody, no matter who he was.

My grandmama and the others just headed west as far as they could go. At the first place they stopped to spend the night with a family, some of them got married, and at the next stop some more left their little group. In this sort of situation you just travelled nonstop until you found someone who knew your family or who was the same lineage. My grandmama told me that some men, when they saw women in that kind of trouble, would act vulgar—they wanted to look you over as if you were an animal they were going to buy. They would look at your teeth, at your hair, and then tell you to turn around so they could look your whole body over. If you wanted to get married there, you would go through all that.

This is how my grandmama ended up with my granddaddy, who had a whole lot of animals, especially cows and camels. My granddaddy was one of the powerful men. He was rich for that time, when people were rich if they had a lot of animals. My granddaddy liked this girl, who was beautiful, even though she was begging, and so he fed her and then asked her to marry him. He said she could keep her younger sister and cousin with her, and that was when she decided to say yes to him. She told me that he was a hard man, but she couldn't find anyone better, so she got married to him. My grandmama never married a man from her own tribe. Only my granddaddy. He was the first, and he was the last. He gave her a hard time, but she put up with it.

My grandmama had five children altogether—three boys and two girls. She also had two miscarriages, so she was pregnant seven times. Most of the children in those days were at least two years apart, because people had to breast-feed their children.

My mama was the first girl. She told me that when she was growing up, her daddy had everything. Her daddy was very rich and very powerful, but he was mean too. He was not giving, giving, giving. At the end of his life he took his family away from all the other families, and they lived by themselves in a big, big land, like this old man named Gurgati in a story my grandmama used to tell.

Once a long, long, long time ago Gurgati lived out in the countryside with his family. He needed water for all his animals —goats, sheep, camels, and cows—so he told two of his older sons to go look for water. They had never done that before, so they said, "Daddy, what should we do if we can't find any water and we get too far away?" Their daddy told them, "Go farther on, until you find some. Follow the rain." Then they said, "What if we can't find anything to eat or drink and we finish what we are carrying with us?" Gurgati said, "Anything can happen when you go on the walk for water—you have to be careful. If it's hot, walk early in the morning and then stop when it gets hot and sleep, and start walking again in the evening when it gets cool. If you see anything you can eat, even if it's a dead animal, maybe one that another animal killed, and you are really hungry, you may eat it, but eat just a little of the meat—enough to keep you alive. Don't make your stomach full, and don't take any of the meat with you—leave the rest of it there. And when you come to a place where you can get water and food, before you do anything else, throw up what you have in your stomach and wash yourself. Make sure there's nothing left in your stomach, because that animal was *baqti*—dead. Because we're Muslim you should have a knife to kill an animal, and you have to say the name of Allah before you kill it." So they said, "All right, Daddy," and they set off on their journey.

They travelled for days and days, and finally they finished all the food and water they had with them. At last, just as their daddy had told them, they found a dead animal. They were both hungry, so they ate some of the meat. The elder one ate as much as he could, but the younger one only ate a little bit. He said to his elder brother, "Eat just a little. Remember what our father said? Don't eat so much!" But the elder one didn't listen; he ate and ate. And then he cut off some strips of the meat to take with him. His younger brother said to him, "No, don't take any. Don't you remember what our father said?" And the elder brother said, "No. I don't want to go through again what we have just been through these past few days. I'm going to take some with me." And he didn't listen to his little brother; he took the meat with him.

While they journeyed on, looking for water, the elder brother was eating the meat. The younger brother wouldn't touch it and he was angry with his brother. Finally, they found a family camped near some water. The younger brother said, "Come on. Let's do what our father said. Let's go throw up." The elder brother said, "No!" The younger one went and threw up, and when he came back he washed himself with water.

The family offered them some food on one big plate. But the younger brother refused to eat with his elder brother. The people in the family asked him why, and he told them the story of what his brother had done. He felt his brother was dirty, because he hadn't done what he had been told to do. So the family gave the elder brother a separate plate.

And from that day on the brothers were separated. The younger brother always considered his elder brother to be unclean because he hadn't done what his father had told him. What he had done was against our religion—he broke the Law and he broke his father's command. So he was very low.

When the two brothers came back home and told their father what had happened, their father couldn't keep his elder son, because it was shameful. People were very proud and they didn't want anyone who was disgraceful or shameful within the family, so they kicked him out. And that's how he became an outcast—going from place to place, place to place.

Eventually the older son had children, and his children did the same thing. Now his descendants, the Midgaans, are everywhere. Most of them are poor, but they are working people, labouring people, and they work for the other people, in the city and in the country. They are good people. Even though I'm descended from Gurgati's younger son, we Somalis are all brothers and sisters—we all come originally from the same blood, but we separated because of what the elder brother did.

When she told this story, my grandmama would say there are many people that life makes low—people make them low, the system makes them low, and it's terrible. She believed that since all of us Somalis have one language and one religion, we should all be equal, even if many people don't see it that way. Life is hard, she said, and one person can't survive alone. Everybody needs help. We should love each other and care for each other and help each other, so Allah can help us.

CHAPTER

2

M<small>Y MOTHER GREW UP IN A TOWN</small> by the sea. She was very pretty and very strong. She was fifteen when her father decided she should get married.

It was in the 1930s, just before the big war started, and the Italians were already fighting in Ethiopia. There was a lot of damage and a lot of killing. Women were getting raped by the white men, who were forcing Somalis to do what they didn't want to do. The men were told: Bring me your daughter, give me your wife. My mother told me that and my grandmama told me that. It was bad for my people then, very bad.

My granddaddy gave my mama away fast, before the Italians could grab her. It was important to get her married so nobody could mess with her. He gave her in marriage to a *sharif*—a descendant of the Prophet. This man also had a big name: a little power, from a good family, and everyone respected him.

When the *sharif* came to ask for my mama, my granddaddy couldn't refuse to let him marry her. But after my mama had stayed with him for a couple of months she began to feel lonely, because she was young and he was old. She pleaded with him for a divorce. If she had run away from him she would have lost her father's name, and because her husband was a *sharif*, if she had made him angry, he could even have cursed her. So the best thing she could do was beg him for a divorce. And he understood, and gave her a divorce.

Mama went back home to her family after she got her divorce. And then another big man asked for her—an *imaam*—an old man my mother's whole tribe had chosen as leader; a man they listened to and trusted. He was the best man in the whole area, so her father couldn't say no. He was the kind of man her father wanted for his daughter. In those days, they married for the name; they were all selling their names. So her father decided he would have her married to this second old man, and even though she wanted to refuse, she had to say yes. This old man had two other wives. Her first husband had also had two other wives—those big men always had three or four wives… well, at least two or three. We know men want more than one woman…we know that. And under Islam, you can have more than one wife, so you don't have to do the wrong thing. Our religion says don't make love if you're not married to the woman —you have to marry her. This way any child conceived won't be a bastard; the baby will have the father's name and be *halal*— legal. A man can have four wives at one time if he can support all of them equally. It's hard to do, but if you don't you'll get punished, later. After death.

Soon Mama became pregnant, and for that reason too she had to stay with him. She gave birth to a daughter who died as soon as she was born, and after she lost the baby she began to refuse her husband. He couldn't oppose her, because it wouldn't be good for his name. Besides, he didn't want to be enemies with her father; the two of them were friends and both of them were old and big men from the same tribe. Her husband looked at the situation from both sides and decided to let her go.

She hadn't liked either of these men, and she'd let them know it, slow and nice. No harm done. She decided not to return to her daddy's, now that she had ended two marriages he had arranged. She didn't want her father to become her enemy—and she didn't want to get stuck with another husband he chose. She had a cousin on her father's side who lived in a town, so she went there to visit her cousin and live with his family for a while.

She met a Somali officer in the Italian colonial army, and he wanted to marry her. He was a friend of the cousin she was living with. He had a name and a good family, *and* he was in the military. When he asked her to marry him, she said to herself, Why not? He didn't have any other wives, and he was living in the same town; she needed a change, and she didn't know the area she was living in, so....She didn't really marry for love—she just wanted to choose a man for herself and see how that was, for a change.

He gave her everything. She was married to him for a long time —four or five years—and during that time she grew up. Her first marriage had been when she was only fifteen, and she had been married for only four months. After she was divorced, she had to stay home for three months to make sure she wasn't pregnant. If she was, in our culture, she would have to stay married to that husband, at least until she had his child. So about seven months after her first marriage, when she was sixteen, she married the second man. When she married the third man, she was only seventeen.

But this time she had married on her own—nobody had given her to this man. It was a happy marriage. She liked him, you understand. It wasn't that she was in love—it was because he gave her everything. Everything a woman could get, she got: a good house, clothes, everything.

When her husband got transferred, they moved to a town near the Ethiopian border, where they stayed for a couple of years. By this time my mama wanted babies. The man she was married to had been married a lot of times—six or seven times —and he had never had any children, although he was in his forties or fifties. Now, the only thing my mother wanted was children. A woman usually had children by this time in her life —if you got married at fourteen, fifteen, or sixteen, by the time you were sixteen you had to have had your first baby, at least. And my mother loved children. She said she used to suffer a lot, hiding her jealousy from the other ladies who had children. She talked with the older women who lived beside her in the military compound. They told her the same thing: "Look how many times he's been married. He's never had children. He never will." She knew that she could have children, because she had a baby already, so she realized it was time to end this marriage. She said she used to pray to Allah all the time.

One night she had a dream. She had finished her dinner and was lying on the bed. And two very beautiful tall women in long white dresses came down and they spoke to her. They stood at the foot of her bed, one on one side and one on the other, and they called her by name: "Why are you crying all the time? Why don't you let us sleep? You cry every day, night and day, all the time. Why are you doing this?" She told them, "I want a baby so much. I want a baby." They told her, "You're going to have a baby. Tonight, rest and sleep. You need to sleep too, because you have cried so much. Don't worry so much. Trust in Allah. Be quiet, and trust yourself." She said, "I will." One of the women put her hand on my mama's forehead, and the other put her hand on my mama's stomach, and they said, "You will have a lot of babies!" And then they were gone. My mama said her eyes were open, and suddenly nobody was there. She didn't know if it was a dream or if it was real, but she believed it was real. She believed in it because she was a religious person.

About a week from the day that she had this dream, something happened. At that time she had three men, all of them from the military, working for her in her house as servants. One bought the food and prepared the meals; one cleaned the house and washed and ironed the clothes; and the third one was a watchman who worked outside the house, guarding it and letting people in and out of the gate. Besides these three men there was a hired woman who was Mama's companion. She could send her to the shops in town when she wanted something; the woman would go with her when she went out; she was a servant just for Mama, to keep her company.

So what happened was that her watchman got transferred to another town, and another military man came to guard the house. This one was young and handsome. He had to be introduced to her, because she was the lady of the house. When he greeted her, her heart was beating fast. She liked him from the first minute she saw his face. As he was saying "It's nice to meet you," her eyes met his eyes. They both felt a shock, and they looked at each other for about a minute. She had never felt that way before. She explained to him about his job and told him that if he wanted anything to eat or drink he should just ask the cook.

It was hot in the place where they lived, and in the afternoon the watchman used to sprinkle the garden with water to make it cool and to keep down the dust. My mama and her husband used to sit outside in the evening and drink tea. They used to offer their new watchman tea, because he sat right in front of them by the gate. He knew she liked him and she knew he liked her, they knew they liked each other, but there was nothing they could say to each other. But she began to think about how she could get out of that house—out of that marriage. Finally, she decided to tell her husband the truth. To do anything else— to go home to her family, stay a couple of months, and come back again to the same problem with the same man—didn't make sense. So she told her husband that she wanted a divorce. She was afraid she might get beaten, even though he had never beaten her yet. He was the kind of person who gives you everything, but he was a tough man—that was why the Italians kept promoting him in the army. He was the kind of person who gives you orders and scares you.

When she told her husband she wanted a divorce, he was lying on the bed after they had made love. I guess he wanted to make love, and she had to go along with it—if she was ready to get divorced, I don't think she'd have wanted to make love. After she told him, he got up and walked around. He asked her if she was sure, and she said, "Yes, I'm sure." He said, "You're not happy, are you?" She said, "No, I'm not happy." He asked her why she wanted a divorce, and she told him the reason. He said, "Oh, that! I should have known." He hated her answer, because he knew he couldn't make children. But my mama had told him the truth. She told me, "I stayed with him for a long time, because he was so kind, so nice to me, and respected me so much. But these things wouldn't help me. I wanted a child, and he couldn't give me that. So I said to him, 'Let me go. I'll pray to Allah for you. When I have children, I'll bring my children to you and you can treat them as though they are your children.'" He told her to think about it and said they would talk again in the morning. They went to sleep.

In the morning, he asked her, "Do you still want a divorce?" And she said, "Yes." He was too proud to keep a woman who didn't want him, so he said, "If I divorce you, you won't get anything except the clothes you have on. Do you still want a divorce?" My mother said he couldn't believe she would ever agree to that, because there was so much to lose. She said, "Yes." He said, "Are you sure?" She said, "Yes." He said, "Is that what you want?" She said, "Yes!"

He got up, got dressed, and left the house. He came back at noon with the divorce paper in his hand. In my culture, divorce, like marriage, is pretty easy to do. Your husband could come back from work and say, "You're divorced! Go!" And you'd leave. He has a witness come over to hear him say a *dalqad*: "I divorce thee." If he says it twice, that means there's a chance they'll get back together—it's like a separation. But if he says it three times— that's it!

There's a lot of divorce because there are a lot of reasons to bring a divorce. The husband wants to get married again, and he has too many wives and can't support them all. We feel, if the marriage doesn't work, why stay and suffer? We just get divorced and try the next one. You get divorced, you're not on your own, because you can always go back home. We support each other: brother give, sister give, uncle give, Mama give, cousin give, Daddy give. We all help each other. If you're a year old or a hundred years old, it's the same. You always have your home.

Divorce is easy—for the man. For women, if your father and brother have chosen your husband and you find you can't stay with him, that's a problem. Our religion says a woman can only divorce a man if he comes at you from behind, if he's impotent, or if he chokes you. If it's just that you don't like him, then you have to give him a hard time until *he wants* to divorce you. You run away, you disrespect him, so he gets tired and says, "Hey" —because he knows he can always get another wife. But my mother didn't even need to do that. She said she couldn't believe he would divorce her that easily. And he couldn't believe she

[handwritten marginalia: divorce / oral renunciation of marriage / by witness]

would give up everything she had just because she wanted children. So they ended up divorced, and she left empty-handed. He called a military car with a driver to take her back home to her family, and she didn't take anything with her except the clothes on her back. She was eager to tell the watchman what had happened, because she was really in love with him. But the car and driver were ready to take her home, and her husband was there, so she couldn't say anything to him before she left.

But the watchman was still working at the house and he found out everything, and after a couple of weeks he came to visit her. In our country everyone knows everyone's family by name, and he was able to find her just by asking around. My mama had to stay at home with her family for three months to make sure she wasn't pregnant, but after four months she and the watchman got married. They went back to the same town near the Ethiopian border that she had lived in with her former husband, because her new husband was still the watchman at her former husband's house! The difference was that now she lived in the lower-class section of town, while before she had lived in a walled compound with the military commanders. Now she lived in a one-room mud-and-wattle house that she and her new husband rented, instead of a big fancy stone house provided by the military. She enjoyed it, she said. She didn't miss all those things she had had, because she was in love with this man. Besides, she had brought her younger brother with her from home so that she would have someone from her own family for company. She said she was happy, very happy, even though she didn't have the kind of life she had before. She felt wonderful. And after a couple of months she was pregnant!

Now the British and the Italians were fighting over Ethiopia, and my mama's ex-husband, out of spite, told her new husband that the army needed him to fight, and he would have to move to where the fighting was. Mama went with her husband to this new town in Ethiopia, and she took her little brother with her. One day there was aerial bombing on the town, and everyone ran. My mama's brother had been at Qur'anic school when the bombs had fallen, and after the air raid was over they couldn't find him. People said he was dead. Mama looked for him all over the place, but she couldn't find him.

Mama told me that somehow she knew her brother was still alive. For weeks she looked and looked for him, but she couldn't find him anywhere. Then she received word from home that her father had suddenly died. Her elder brother had already died, quite some time before, and only her mother and the younger children were left at home. So she went back to take care of her family. Besides, all the military wives and children were being sent home, because the war was getting worse.

When the war slowed down again, her husband sent word to her that she should come back to where he was stationed. But she wouldn't leave her family—her mother was still in mourning, and Mama was supporting her. In our culture, when a woman's husband dies, she has to be in mourning for four months and ten days. She has to wear all white clothes and stay at home; she can't touch a man's hand—Islam forbids it. She can't touch grease, or oil her skin, or take a shower, or wash her hair, except for once or twice a week, and she has to save all her hair combings and nail cuttings. At the end of the time of mourning, you invite several *sheikhs* to your house. *Sheikhs* are men devoted to the Qur'an. Not only when someone dies, but whenever something goes wrong, a *sheikh* helps people. He reads the Qur'an, and explains it. We all try to do what the Qur'an says.

When the mourning ends, several *sheikhs* come with two or three religious women, and the women go into the bathroom with you and wash your body and your hair, and dress you in new clothes of your favourite colour, with all your gold if you want. Then they go and bury the hair combings and nail cuttings you have been saving. The *sheikhs* pray for you and your dead husband, and read the Qur'an. After that, everyone eats and there is a big celebration, and your mourning is over.

Since my grandmama was in mourning and couldn't go out of the house, my mama wanted to stay with her and help her. She sent word to her husband that she couldn't come and join him. Her father's cousins were coming to take her father's animals, and she had to stay there to protect the property. She said that since he was the one who was alone, he should come and live with them; that they had everything they needed there because her daddy had left it all to them—animals and houses and land—and that they would move to his family's territory as soon as her mother's period of mourning was over. Finally, she said, he was the one in the middle of a European war—why did he want to stay there and die?

But he didn't want to come back to her. He didn't want to leave the military. So he married another woman, who lived in the area where he was stationed. By the time Mama found out, she had already moved herself, her mother, her brother, and most of her father's animals to the place where her husband's family lived. She had also had his baby girl—my elder sister Hawa. She was angry and jealous, and told him he should give her a divorce—so he sent her one.

Mama was happy that she had a little girl, but she was also in pain because she had lost her father, her little brother, and the man she loved. But she had to go on with her life, and anyway, she was still young and beautiful, with a big name from her father, and all the animals—the cows and the camels. Everybody loved that woman—she was beautiful. She had lots of men courting her then—men with big names wanted to meet her.

But she had sworn to herself that she would never again be dependent on a man, never again put all her property together with his, stay in his house, and just wait on him. That is what she used to tell all the men who were courting her, and they were amazed, because she was the only woman they knew who acted like a man.

Anyway, she finally married another man, on her own terms. But after two years they divorced, because even after she had his baby, she refused to move in with him and leave her mother and the rest of her family. This time Allah had given her a boy, and she named him Hassan. She was having a great time with the new baby. Besides the baby, she had her mother and her sister and her brothers. Even though her youngest brother was still missing and everyone said he was dead, she knew he was still alive; she used to pray every day and every night about him.

After that she stayed single for a couple of years, then married another man and had a baby girl who died, and got divorced again. Finally, when her kids were growing up, she met my father.

My father was the son of a chief. When his father died, the people voted for my father to become the chief. He was like a policeman—he went wherever there was trouble. He took care of problems in his tribe or between tribes. He was young—well, not really young. My mother had been through all these marriages and divorces, and she must have been over thirty, and my daddy must have been thirty-seven or thirty-eight—something like that—when they got married. They were comfortably middle-aged, both of them. My daddy was handsome—a tall man, dark—not too dark, like chocolate. He was a slim man, with high cheekbones like me. Very beautiful features he had—a nice smile, nice eyes—everything was nice about my father. He was very intelligent. Even before he became the chief he had children and wives, because his father had started him marrying when he was young. When he married my mama, he already had sons and daughters who were around twenty years old. He liked pretty women, and Mama was beautiful. She had light-brown eyes and brown hair. And so they got married. He had two other wives, a house in a village, and a lot of places in the interior, where he kept his wives and children, with cows and goats and sheep and fields of maize and beans; and he had many camels that his eldest son and his younger brothers were herding in the interior, because camels can't stay in the wetter areas near the cows and fields. They were a big, rich family, compared to other people. My mama's family had enough to be comfortable too.

Now, my daddy was the kind of man who, when he married a woman, took her into his house and she stayed there. If he got tired of her he would divorce her, and she would go back to her family. The woman had no power. Like I told you, my mama had decided when her father died and the man she loved divorced her that she wasn't going to be dependent on men any more. She had her property, and her husband had his; if she got married, her husband would come to her house, because that was the way she wanted it. She didn't want to leave her family, because she was the only strong person in the household— Grandmama had asthma and was sick all the time, and was too sweet a person to defend herself and the children and keep the relatives from taking their property. Besides, if she went to live with her husband, she would have to cook and keep house for him and take care of the children of the wives he had divorced, plus all his animals, plus the farming. But if she spent all her time looking after his children, who would take care of her mother? So Mama refused to live with him. She had everything she wanted—her mother and brother and sister and her two small children, and all the property her father had left—and she was trying to take care of it all, as her father would have done.

People respected her because she had a rich name and was powerful. She wasn't about to give up all that for a man, because the love she had in her own family was bigger than the love of just one person.

Daddy understood why she wanted arrangements the way she did when my mama explained to him that she had lost her father and her brother, and all her husbands had divorced her, and her mother was from another tribe, and she had a younger brother to look after. But after they had been married for a while, he really wanted her to come and live in his house. Mama said no again. My daddy told her she could bring her children with her to his house. But she still said no, because Grandmama wouldn't have been able to take care of everything; my mama was the strong one, and she wanted to stay in charge of the household.

So my mama flatly refused to move in with my daddy. At first he couldn't believe it, but he let her stay at her place for a few months. After four months she became pregnant, but still she didn't want to move in with him. Then he knew she really meant it. And he said, "Unh-unh." Even though he loved her, he wanted a woman in his house. So he married another, younger, woman. Mama became a bit jealous, because when a man gets a new wife, his old one becomes less important—it's like she's no good all of a sudden. She told him she wanted a divorce because she knew he was going to spend more time with his new wife anyway. He didn't want to divorce her, but to satisfy her and make her hold her peace, he agreed. All she would ever say to him in her loud, strong voice was "Give me a divorce. Give me a divorce." So he said, "You've got one!" He didn't really divorce her, but my mama thought she was divorced. She moved her household and set up house with some people farther away so she wouldn't have to see his face—she was that angry with him. By that time she was already pregnant with me.

CHAPTER
3

MY MAMA AND GRANDMAMA HAD been travelling for a couple of days, walking miles and miles with their animals, searching for water. Mama was nine months pregnant. When you live out in the bush with animals—goats, sheep, camels, cows—you've got to find water and grass for them. So people go where water is or where rain has fallen—you have to follow the rain. We call that *sahan*: the look for water. It can take days and days, sometimes, just to find where there is water.

Mama and Grandmama stopped for the night, and made breakfast in the morning. They were on the move again, when her labour pains started. I was on my way. It was late in the day —the time when the heat of noon is gone and the land looks beautiful in the long, low rays of the afternoon sun. My mama knew her labour had begun, but didn't want to stop because there were a lot of people travelling together. My grandmama had already seen her holding her stomach, and my mama had told her that her labour had started. As the sun went down, her labour pains began to be closer together, but still she didn't want to stop. Finally, after the sun went down, they reached the place where they had planned to set up camp for the night. Mama told Grandmama to set up the house quickly, because it was time, she was about to have the baby, and besides, it was nearly dark. So they put up the bush house fast—in about half an hour, because women in the same group help each other. They made a big fire outside the door of the house so that the light would shine inside and they could see while the baby was being born. Grandmama had helped Mama give birth to all her children, and there were two other women to help. When the baby was ready to be born, the two women held Mama under her arms, in a standing position, and Grandmama sat between Mama's legs with a knife to do the cut with and to catch the baby when it came out. About half an hour after they got everything ready, I was born.

In the morning they were on the move again, with Mama bleeding. She had a little girl! That's how she had me—while they were on the move. It was beautiful.

The next day, they reached the place where the water was. The women and the children were tired. They saw a nice big thorn tree, and they stopped beside it. They let the camels sit and drink, to relax a little bit. And then it began to rain. When it rains in the desert, everything smells good. When you look around—everywhere—the plants begin to grow. A lot of different flowers were there, flowers that nobody planted—Allah planted—white ones, red ones, purple ones—wildflowers all around them. Everything turned green and life was back to normal.

When he heard about me, my daddy sent word to Mama that she wasn't divorced—because she had a baby now. Men talk nicely when there is a baby involved. My mama and my daddy were still married after all, and that's how, after a year, my sister Sharifa was born.

My mother still refused to accept what my father wanted, which was for him to be the boss. He wanted to put her animals together with his animals—everything together. My mother didn't want that, and that was the reason they finally did divorce. My daddy was in love with her, but he had his pride. Everyone respected him and he didn't see why she couldn't respect him too, after having two of his children.

My daddy said that if she wanted a divorce he wouldn't give her anything, or give anything to me or to Sharifa. He said he wasn't going to support us unless we came and lived with him. Always, when he divorced, he kept the children. That's how it is in our culture: you belong to your father's family. You take your father's given name, and his father's given name, so you don't lose your history. You know where you come from. It's not about what country you come from, but what father. A tribe is a large, large, large family, so you can go back a thousand fathers, and that's still your roots. You belong very little to your mother's side. Father is your main blood.

So my father was angry, and he said, "If you want the children you can take them with you, but I won't give you a penny." And Mama said, "Fine. I'm not going to leave my daughters with you the way your other women did, and risk that your wife will whip them and not feed them right, unh-unh. I want my children—that's all I want." So they promised each other—"I won't give you anything" and "I won't ask you for anything"—and they kept their promise.

Now, if I look back, I think my mama loved my daddy and he loved her. They loved each other. But my mother was hard and jealous and Daddy was after a lot of women. He was in control, and Mama wanted to have control. So they lost each other.

But Mama loved him, I know. Otherwise, why did she cry? I remember she cried a lot. And my daddy loved her, even though Mama was the only wife who took his children away from him.

To make matters worse, after they had been divorced awhile Mama's brother, who was next to her in age, died of malaria.

When I first remember things, I remember being out in the bush. We were not staying in one place, we were moving, moving, moving. I would wake up and see Mama taking our home apart, and the camel sitting there for her to put the house on. Everybody was doing the same thing. Because we're a group, we move as a group, not as a family—maybe eight families, ten families, fifteen families…we all move together. When we were ready to move, the women would break their homes up. They tied the camels together by their tails, and they all walked in a line, with one person leading in the front. All the camels have a rope around their necks and the first person in the line just holds the rope and pulls, and the camels *galug, galug*…they have a bell around the neck, and we walk along, with just that sound: *galug, galug, galug.*

You have to keep moving your animals in the country, because cows eat a lot of grass and camels eat the leaves off the trees. After they eat everything, you have to move them to the next place where the grass is not touched yet. We move along, and even the camels seem small, because the flat land seems to stretch out forever—as far as your eye can see—it reaches out to where the sky begins. We walk along over the dusty, dry, sandy land until we find somewhere nice and green. When you're moving from place to place, everything you have has to go on one camel. So those houses in the country have to be easy to move. When you get to where you plan to stay, you dig a hole, making a design with your feet, making a circle as big as you want your home. You have a frame made of long branches bound together and curved, like a beehive, and you cover that with woven mats made of straw or grass. You hang an old cloth at the front and that's the little door. You can get in and out and it's nice and cool. You put a mat or sheet inside, and you sleep. Since you don't have a suitcase, you keep your belongings and clothes wrapped up in a bag, and you use that as a pillow. Or you might even grab a sack of beans or corn—anything you want—just to hold you. It's a simple life.

And in the morning you hear *chickee, chickee, chickee, moo*, and *aaa*, and it's beautiful. Everything comes alive. Everything gets up one at a time. Early in the morning they milk the cows, the goats. Then it's breakfast-time. We have milk with hot grits or popped corn with milk—they burn the corn in the fire—*bup, bup, buppa*: popped corn. If we have sugar, we make tea. The older boys take the cows and goats away to find something to eat. The young children go with their mamas, or with the girls who are going to watch the small baby goats or the small baby cows. In the evening, everyone comes back together and we cook a big meal. We eat meat that the women have dried and we put beans and white corn together and make a dish we call *amboolo*.

After the meal, if they want, the big boys and girls dance. I was about four or five when we were in the country, but I re-member I went with the big boys and girls. We'd collect a lot of wood in the evening so we could have a big fire. Most of the time we'd sing and talk. With the fire and the smoke, the flies and mosquitoes go away. We sit around the fire. We're just wild kids, in this beautiful place. We dance and we have fun. That is my first memory.

I also remember—I don't remember it really well, but I re-member one evening I was with the girls who were watching the sheep and goats close to the house. I was playing with the little lambs and children, when a ram butted me in the chest. I fell down. I got up and he butted me again. Every time he hit me and I fell and got up, he hit me again. When I fell down he would go away, and then I would get up and he would come back, running, and hit me in the chest again. I was crying and in so much pain, and I didn't know enough to stay lying down so he wouldn't hit me again. Finally my mama heard me crying and came with a big stick and hit the ram in the head a couple of times and he ran away. But I got sick. My mama said that that night I had a high fever. She said that I had blood in my mouth too, and that I cried a lot. I think now that I must have had a broken rib, but nobody knew that then. In the night, when I got very hot, Mama held me on her lap naked, outside, so that the air could keep me cool. And then she got tired of doing that, because I rolled off her lap a couple of times when she fell asleep, so she took a whole cowskin, and dug a hole in the ground and lined it with the cowskin and filled it with water, and made me sleep there so my body could cool. I was very hot because I was very sick. Mama said I began to have trouble breathing. I was panting, breathing really fast, and coughing. Some people said I had asthma.

Mama called a man to come and look at me. He said I had signs of pneumonia and he was going to give me a treatment to make me feel better. He put one of his special sticks in the fire until it got red-hot, and then burned me with it three times, on each side of my chest, and on my back. He was a specialist. This was how our medicine treatment was done in those days. So he did that, and I felt a little better.

From then on in my life, I remember everything. I played a lot with my younger sister when she was four and I was five. The ground would get hot in the middle of the day, and Sharifa and I would jump—aa-aa-aa-aa! We'd run to where the grass was—no shoes—and we'd rub our feet in the grass. The grass was rough. It pinched us, and aaaah! When it rained, we'd bury our clothes in the ground to keep them dry, and we'd take a shower naked and run naked, and when the rain stopped we'd dig and get our clothes out. And shake them and wear them again! It was nice!

Sharifa was four years old and she was beautiful. One evening Mama was praying, and she ran to Mama and said, "Mama, Mama, I'm cold, I'm cold." Mama had a shawl around her shoulders, and she covered my sister with it and put her on her lap and rubbed her and said, "What's wrong with you, Sharifa, what's wrong?" My sister said, "Mama, I'm cold." She wanted some milk, so Mama gave it to her. And then Sharifa started to moan, "Unnnnh, unnnnh," and her fever got higher and she began to shiver and have chills. Since my father was a chief, we had some blankets, and my mother brought her inside and covered her up with them. But my sister began shaking all over and moaning louder—"Unnh…unnh…unnh…." My father wasn't there. He and my mother were already divorced, and to walk from where we were staying in the interior to the town where he was took twenty-four hours. It would be a long way to carry a child as big as Sharifa. So my mama sent some men to look for Daddy, to tell him to come back and drive his daughter to the hospital in the city. Sharifa was sick for about four days. On the fourth day my daddy came, as the sun was going down, and soon after he came, she died. They buried her the next morning. And I remember being alone.

Daddy came to the funeral with another man. My daddy and my mama talked, and he told her to leave everything with my grandmama and to come into the town of Mango Village for a while, until she got over being sad. She told him that she wouldn't come until the rains ended, because she still had all her animals and they needed to be fed. But after the rains ended, she would come then. My daddy stayed around for about three more days, and then he left.

After we had stayed for a month longer in the interior, my mama and I came to Mango Village. It was a large village—maybe several thousand people. It *is* a mango village. Fruit grows everywhere, and it's always green there because of the river. There are many canals, so the farms can have water. They grow all different vegetables and fruits. Different foods grow in different soils. The soil closest to the river is black. If you walk a little bit, you see other kinds: one is red, one is fine and white like sea dirt. What can grow in the black soil cannot grow in the red or the white soil.

Around Mango Village there are farms where sugar grows, and there was a sugar factory nearby—the only one in Somalia. So it was perfect. There was one river and only one short road.

Daddy had houses in Mango Village, but Mama didn't want to live in one of them. He said he wanted her to come and be his wife, and she could have one of his houses all for herself, but she refused. She wanted to get a house on her own. She had a relative in the village, and we stayed at his house while we looked for a house to rent. Soon we found a nice house near Mama's cousin. During this whole time she was very sad.

Altogether we stayed in Mango Village for about three weeks, before going back to the interior. I was very sick now, so I went to where my father lived. A village doctor came, and he covered me with sheep's blood—he poured it all over my shoulders—and he burned me with a red-hot stick the way they did when the ram hit me. It was painful, but I felt better. My daddy wanted me to stay with him until I was healthy again.

In my father's camp, there was a man named Abdi. Years ago another tribe had come to my father's land, begging, trying to find something to eat. He gave them something to eat and at night they slept outside his home. They left a child. I think they felt safe with my father, as though they were part of his tribe. He took on this baby, he raised him like his own. Abdi was a grown man now and he took care of my daddy's cows.

In the morning, the cows have a lot of milk—that's when they have the best milk, it's still warm and it's sweet. Abdi woke me up and took me with him to milk the cows. He gave me a big wooden bowl and filled it with milk, hot with foam. My daddy's new wife came over and she wanted that milk for her children. She asked Abdi why he was giving me all the best milk. Abdi said, "Well, she's been very sick. She needs hot milk." I kept drinking, and he whispered down to me, "Drink, drink." I raised the big wooden bowl to my lips, and drank as quickly as I could. She stood next to me and she looked at me. I was looking at her, and she was looking at me. She said, "Look at that. She finished everything!" And then I just threw up. I felt a pain inside, like somebody was twisting me, and I couldn't stop myself from throwing up. Abdi said to her, "See, witch, look what you did."

I said, "What made me throw up? What made me sick?"

And he took me in his lap and told me, "Her eye makes you sick. *Qumayo*—that witch gave you the evil eye."

That's when I really understood how good it was that Mama had fought to keep us with her.

After a while, when the rains stopped in the interior and it was the dry season, Mama came to get me. Some kind of disease had begun killing the animals in the place where she was. Everyone was saying, "My cow died," "My camel died," and "My goat died." As the animals started dying, we children had less and less milk to drink. Healthy animals caught the disease because they were grazing on land where animals had already died. People lost many animals, and in those days, if you didn't have animals, you had nothing—even if you lived in the city with a beautiful big house, they would still call you poor if you had no animals. My mother really believed in animals, because her father had always believed in animals. She loved them, and her animals were all dying. You can't stay where there are dead animals because of the danger from hyenas and jackals and lions. You have to move. I remember when Mama came to get me—she was very, very sad. She had lost everything—almost everything—that she loved: her brother, her daughter, and most of her animals.

So she left the camels that hadn't died with my father's people, and she left her sheep and goats with Grandmama, and brought her children and cows back to Mango Village. We went back to live in the house that she had already rented. When we left that house in Mango Village, she had just put a lock on and left—and when we came back she paid the rent and everything was fine. But her sheep and goats were still dying, and Grandmama was tired of running after them. Since there was no water anywhere in the interior, Mama decided that she should sell them before they died from the drought or from the disease. So one day she brought them to the big market in the town and sold all of them. And she hired somebody to watch the cows.

With the money she got from the sale of the sheep and goats, she bought the house we were renting in Mango Village. The houses there are built of mud and wattle. People chop up grass and mix it with dirt and cow dung. They add water to that and mix some more. They make a frame out of wood, and one person goes inside the frame and another person stands outside. Then they take big pieces of the mix and just throw it onto the frame: you throw from the inside, and I throw from the outside. Then you take water and smooth the walls and then we plaster them. On round houses, the grass roofs are peaked like cones. On square houses, we put zinc panels on the roof so water can't come through. The houses are very neat, very regular. They're cool, the way the bush house is, but the houses in Mango Village are permanent.

We had four of those houses, two square and two round, and a latrine, all arranged around a courtyard—the *daash*. The *daash* is where you cook, where you keep water, where you sit when people come—it's like a living room. Some of them are open to the air and some of them are covered so rain cannot come through. If you can afford it, you cover your *daash*; otherwise it's open. Around the houses and *daash* is a low fence of woven branches.

Mama rented out two of our four buildings to a relative.

Mama was still very, very sad. She didn't like it in Mango Village because she came from close to the sea, and she didn't like the river. She was over six feet tall, big-boned and so strong, especially to me, because I was little. But she became sick because she had lost so many people. Her elder brother had died before he had even grown up; her father had died; her little brother had got lost in the war and everyone said he was dead; three of her daughters had died; and her last living brother had died when Sharifa was born. Her sister had married and moved into the interior with her husband's people and her twin baby boys had both been eaten by hyenas in the same week. And now most of Mama's animals had died. It was a real disaster. She became very sick and stayed in bed for months. But we had enough money, and at that time everything was very cheap. We survived, and slowly Mama got better. They told me she was sick for six months. I know she was sick for a long time, and everything was going down, down, down.

But when she began to get better, I began coughing all the time. You remember that the ram hit me in the chest, making me cough? I had just kept on coughing and coughing. Hawa, my mother's daughter from her husband the watchman, was living with us again, and she took me to the big city, Mogadishu, to have an X-ray. They said my lungs had a hole—TB had just started—and they would have to put me in the hospital.

It was morning when they took me to the hospital. My mama couldn't take me because she was still too weak to come to the city, and my daddy wouldn't come. So my sister took me. Italian nuns were there: white ladies wearing white headdresses, long white robes, and white shoes! They had necklaces—big wooden crosses or small little beads. When the nun showed me where my bed was, I had never seen that kind of bed before: blanket, sheets, pillow, and a nightstand. I said to her, "Are you sure this is my bed?" When we lived in the interior we slept on mats on the ground, and when we moved into town we slept on wooden beds. She said, "Yes, it's for you. Get comfortable, put your basket in the nightstand. Lunch will be ready in a couple of hours. Go out and play and meet some new friends." But my new friend was my bed, because I really loved it. I started to sit on it and just jump; it went up and down, soft…. And the nightstand…I opened it, I looked in it and said, "What do they use it for?" They used it for things like toothpaste and soap and the few clothes you had brought with you. They didn't have a big wardrobe; whatever clothes you had you kept in the nightstand or else under the mattress. I only had two little dresses besides the one I had on, in a little basket. You had to buy your own soap, and I hadn't known that, so my sister had to bring me some the next morning. For cleaning our teeth we used sticks, and I had brought my little stick with me, so I didn't have any problem with that.

After I had played with the bed for a while, I went out to meet some new friends. Girls look at you strangely when you're new, you know, so they looked at me and laughed at me. It didn't bother me. I was used to girls like that back home; they used to call me names because I was sick and skinny, coughing a lot. I just looked at these girls in the hospital and laughed inside and said to myself, I know what's going on. You're sick too. Some of them came up to me and talked to me and asked me where I came from—who I was—what my name was. I talked to them nicely. I was tough too, but they didn't know that. I was only seven, but I was a real fighter. But I wanted to be careful here because I liked everything.

I especially liked the food. After we had played for a while, there was a bell—*gong! gong!*—it was twelve o'clock, and time for lunch. That was the first time I ever ate at a table. The food was delicious—soup, and meat, and bread, and vegetables. Everything was different.

After we had eaten, the nuns put us in our beds and gave us medicine. We woke up around four o'clock in the afternoon and took a shower. And the showers! At home I used a cup to pour the water over me. I loved water! I was always bathing, but Mama would get angry because water wasn't cheap. You had to pay someone to bring it to you. Water from the well, the water that was the most expensive, we used for cooking. And river water, it didn't cost as much, so if you didn't have a lot of money, you used that. But here I could stay and use the water until I decided to turn it off.

After the showers, we had tea with milk and biscuits, and then we could play. One day while we were playing, a girl asked me if I wanted to go and see the crazy people, and I said yes, so we went to find them. You could see them in their compound through the gate. It was terrible—a lot of the people I saw were naked, and they threw stones at us and yelled at us. Every day I explored a new part of the hospital, until I learned all about it.

The hospital was really big and had so many different sections. You could even get lost in it, it was so big. It had all the dangerous diseases in it—syphilis, TB, crazy people, people without hands or without legs from disease, without eyes or noses, with nasty faces, scary people—a lot of different diseases. Leprosy too. I learned all about that after I had stayed in the hospital for about a month; in spite of the rules, I used to go and visit some of the people with those diseases, and I became friends with them. I used to help them get things that they needed from outside the hospital; they would give me money and I would buy food or cigarettes for them when I went out. But I never got close to them or touched them, because I was afraid to, even though I liked them.

You could go out of the hospital once a week, and every week I went to visit my brother's cousin and her family. Mama was still sick, so they would also come and visit me because she told them to look after me. After a while, though, I met some other girls, bigger girls who were eleven and fourteen, and they went out every day. There was a high wall around the hospital, and tall trees beside the wall. These girls used to climb the trees and jump the wall. Coming back inside was no problem because the main gate was open for everyone to go in and out, unless you came back after eight o'clock, when visiting hours were over and the gate was closed. So I did the same thing the older girls did— jump over the wall and come back before eight—because now I felt much better. I had grown and gained weight because of the medicines. The doctors told me, "You'll be leaving this month."

A week before I was to leave, a friend of mine and I were playing ball. I don't know what happened to her, but the next thing I knew she had slapped me. Maybe I hit her with the ball—she didn't explain. Anyway, the ball shouldn't have hurt her because it was made from old rags that I had sewn together. But I didn't

wait to ask what had happened—I just hit her back. I hit her
with my head and grabbed her by the hair and hit her against
the wall, and she lost two teeth. There was a lot of blood. She
was still fighting—she was scratching me and hitting me and biting me, so I had to fight back. Even though she was older than
me, she couldn't beat me up, because I was strong too.

People came and separated us, and the hospital called her
family and the police. The police took us to the police station,
and I told them to call my chief in that city. He and my daddy
were third cousins. I knew where he lived and what his name
was, and his father's name, but I had never been to his place.
The police went to get him. The girl's chief arrived with her father, and the three of them talked to the police, and the police
told them what had happened. The two chiefs and the girl's father went out and talked and reached an agreement that my
family would pay her family four camels and two cows. That's
how it is in Somalia. If you make a mistake, or kill somebody,
or knock teeth out, or do any physical damage, there's a payment. You have to pay for the damage you did. If somebody
broke your window, you'd want the window fixed, right? If I give
you a big ugly cut, you become ugly, I've damaged your face, so I
have to pay for that damage, at least something. We have rules
for everything. And you have to go by the rule.

The chiefs decided on four camels and two cows because the
face is an expensive part of your body. They have a value for
each part of your body. If I break your arm or leg, it's not such
a big payment because they'll mend. The most value is for your
teeth because you can never have your teeth back. The face is the
beauty of the body.

In those days nobody stayed in jail more than twenty-four
hours, because after your chief and the other chief reached an
agreement, the police would let you go. That's what they did.

They talked, and they agreed. She went with her father, and I went with my uncle. I spent the night at my uncle's house. The next morning he took me to where I could catch the bus, paid the fare, and sent me home to Mango Village. It had been almost seven months since I had gone into the hospital.

CHAPTER
4

MAMA BEGAN TO SELL FRUIT AND vegetables in the market because her cousin had fields and orchards and had told her she could take a wheelbarrow full of produce every day and sell it so she could buy food for the children.

In the morning she would go to the market, and everything was there. Around the market were some bungalows: little shops and butchers. In the market were all the best fruits: different kinds of oranges, different kinds of bananas. Everything's fresh! The sellers sat outside in the sun—there were maybe forty or fifty of them. They sat on the ground, and we'd walk around, buying what we wanted. I remember this is how people sold milk: You had stacked tin containers with a handle. You'd take them to the women and men selling milk and say, "Let me taste your milk," and if you didn't like it, you went and tasted some other, as much as you wanted. When you found the best milk, they'd fill as many tins as you needed. You'd say, "Put some more! Put some more, fill it up!" There were different tribes, and one tribe were kind of dirty little people, and Mama would always say, "Don't buy milk from them!" It was nice spending days in the market. I'd stay there with Mama until seven, until it closed.

Other days, I stayed with the older women. In my culture, the grandmothers take care of the babies. They're beautiful, they're lovely, they care…they spoil the babies! Grandmothers on your mother's side, or your father's side, or just relatives, it doesn't matter. There is no charge; it's free. Everybody who's elder—they watch the children, they look after everybody. If they see children doing wrong, they spank them and tell them not to do that. So all of us children behaved well! They fed us—very few grandmothers would tell you to go home.

In Mango Village you could go to anyone's home, and they'd let you sit and eat with them. That's how it is. I myself had a lot of places I used to go. I even had my chosen favourite food—I even knew who made the best food! And who didn't! Sometimes I used to choose where to go while my mama was working at the market.

One day, I remember, Mama had left to work and I was walking to see an elder lady I liked, and my father passed by. A friend of his, like a brother, had died, and my daddy had raised his son. So he goes to this son's house. When he passed by, in front of our house, all the kids came to tell me: "Hey, your daddy pass by here, yah, yah, your daddy's here." And I wished he would stop and come in. I wanted all the kids to come and see my daddy come by, I wanted them to know he loved me, I just wanted to be proud of him, and for all the kids to know I had a daddy. But he didn't go to my house, he passed by, and I would have had to go to this son's house to see him. And that hurt.

My sister Hawa was old enough to get married now. She was light-skinned, and not only that, she was pretty, pretty, with so much beauty in her. Big lips, her teeth were superwhite, and her gums were black. Very beautiful eyes and nose, soft hair—everything about her was beautiful. Lighter-skinned girls like that—they keep them in the house because they are afraid that someone will put the evil eye on them. People are jealous of girls like that, so they have to be kept inside. They have to wear a *shuko*, a big, long-sleeved black dress to cover themselves. Because the evil eye will make you sick. You can get a rash, bumps all over your body; you can get a fever; you can get all kinds of diseases. Then a *sheikh* will have to come and read the Qur'an to you, pray for you, and give you water to drink. He'll write a part of the Qur'an on a piece of paper, which you'll wear to protect yourself.

I asked Mama why my sister was light-skinned. And she said, "I bathed her with hot water." I thought, aahaa! So when Mama left to milk the cows—I was little, but I put a big pot in the fire, and I filled it with water, and added more wood to the fire, until the water began to boil and boil. My mama came back and found this big pot with water boiling. She asked me, "What's this water for?" I said, "I want you to bathe me, Mama. I want to become light like my sister." My mama cried! She said, "I'm glad you didn't bathe yourself, because I was teasing you. This is a creation from Allah. See how everything is different, animals are different, humans are different. It's not something you can do."

After a few months, a drought began, and the river dried up. There weren't enough vegetables and fruits to sell. But my mother was strong, strong. Very strong. A lot of women were very strong, and I can say that truly Somali women are the brain of Somalia. Tough women, very smart. I got so much from them. I was trying to be there, to replace my daddy, to help my mama, to show that if she didn't have him, I was still there to help her. I was young, but next to my mother, right there.

The money she had got from selling our animals was nearly gone. She couldn't even earn little bits of money, because there wasn't any rain. She was upset every day. Finally she decided to sell the house and move to Mogadishu, the big city by the ocean. Besides, Hawa was getting married, and was moving to Mogadishu soon. Mama thought we would move and see if things were better there.

The place where we were going to stay was the place I had been going to visit every weekend when I was in the hospital. Hassan's cousin had a lot of land, so she gave us space where we could build a house and keep the cows too. In the city they keep the cows fenced in the household compound, and tie their legs at night. That way they can feed them and sell the milk. After Mama sold the house in Mango Village, she used the money to buy more cows. She was now doing pretty well. She hired a man to go with my brother to drive our cows to the city, because it was a three-day walk. We went to the city in a car. In our new place Mama built one round mud-and-wattle house—for me, my grandmama, and my brother, Hassan. Mama and I slept side by side on a wooden bed. There was only one sheet, and she always made sure she covered me with it. It was no problem. But some nights, I thought of the spring bed I had had in the hospital. If people had money, they bought those. They could also have tables and more dishes, with maybe a radio, and everything clean. I wanted that. But we didn't have it and it didn't bother me. I was happy with what we had. I knew we were poor.

And we liked the place. It was clean, and the city had a lot of things we didn't have back in Mango Village. I liked the smell of the village better though, the fresh breeze—it smelled like flowers. In the city, it smelled like the food they cooked. In the morning, I could smell spices.

About ten days after we were settled, things began to get bad. First my grandmama got sick, and right after that, our cows started dying. My mama used to get up early in the morning, before sunrise, to pray, and then at sunrise she milked the cows. Before she prayed though, she would go and look at the cows, to make sure they were all right. That morning, when she went to look at them, two of them were dead, and she couldn't believe it. She called some men to help her drag the two dead cows somewhere—they hadn't begun to stink yet, so they had to drag them somewhere and bury them. And every day it was like that—more cows died. Mama couldn't even sleep at night; she had to stay outside and watch them dying one by one. Some of them she killed with her own hand, so people could eat the meat. They kept on dying until only about four were left.

This was not a very common thing, and it was becoming a terrible disaster. My mama thought it was *qumayo*—the evil eye. The part of Mogadishu where we had moved, it was a poor area, and not many people had all the cattle we had. My family, when we arrived from Mango Village, we were all pretty, fresh, and good looking, healthy looking. People there had very little, and they were surprised to see us…healthy kids, healthy cows, healthy family. So Mama thought they were jealous, and had put the evil eye on us.

My mama had a woman relative who lived about thirty miles outside the city. She had a little farm there, and some cows and goats and sheep. So Mama and Grandmama and I took the four cows to that place, and Grandmama stayed there when Mama and I came back to the city because it was healthier there.

I was young, but I saw the pain in Mama's face. I thought, I'm just like her. I loved my mama and I felt the same pain too. Because she slept next to me, I knew when she cried, I knew when she was troubled, I knew when she didn't sleep, I knew all this because she stayed awake, praying softly beside me. But no one else ever knew, because the next day she was in the market or with her animals, working and laughing. No one else could ever tell what she went through. But now she had changed—she wasn't the same woman. She didn't even wash her clothes. Sometimes she would go out and just walk for miles and miles, thinking about what to do, until she came to a decision. And I couldn't even go with her, because I couldn't walk that far.

I wanted to give Mama more than she had because she had already done so much, and she fought so hard to keep us with her. I wanted to show my father she was right—we could do it without him. I wanted her to rest.

Sometimes I used to climb up in a tree so I would be closer to Allah. I would pray and beg him to please help us, send us some money. I looked up to the sky. I thought he might leave money in the clouds.

Hawa tried to get some help for us from her husband. She brought us a little money, but it wasn't enough. When she asked him for more, because she knew how serious our situation was, he said that he had married her but not her whole family, and he wasn't responsible. So my sister asked him for a divorce, and he gave her one easily, and she came back to live with us. Now things were even worse, because we had one more mouth to feed. And Mama felt responsible for their divorce, so she felt more pain.

There were a few mornings when we didn't have anything in the house except water. So what we did was, we went to the houses of some families who were Mama's lineage. We knew they would be cooking lunch. They didn't know we were coming; we just went and stood there, and they invited us in and gave us food, and we ate. We had never done that before; we were too proud. But we did it for a couple of days. Sometimes we slept with empty stomachs, and sometimes Mama would come back late with a little sugar, and we would cook tea and drink that for dinner and go back to sleep again.

Mama used to go out early every morning, as if she had something to do, just the way she used to before. One morning she came back with a little tea, and we drank the tea that evening, and the next morning she was about to go out again. I said to her, "Mama, where are you going?" She said, "Come on, come with me." Hawa still had to stay home so she wouldn't get the evil eye. But Mama said to me, "Let's go." Mama and I walked for half an hour, until we came to a big white church with a big crowd of people sitting in front of it waiting for something. I asked Mama, "What is this place? What are you waiting for?" She said, "This place is where people who don't have anything to eat can get something to eat." I asked her, "Are they going to give us meat?" She said, "No, they'll only give us rice, or maize, or beans." I told her, "Wonderful! So we're going to eat today!" And she said, "Yes, thank God, we're going to eat something today."

We had come to that place at about seven in the morning, and the people in charge didn't show up until nearly noon. There were a lot of people there—a lot of women with children crying. It was hot. Hot! There was no water. Empty stomach… the sun killing you…the children crying—small children—because they didn't have anything to eat. When the men finally showed up, everyone wanted to be first. Everyone was hitting each other—piling up on top of each other and fighting. My mama was doing the same as everyone else, because that was the only way you could get any food. They might finish passing out all the food before everybody could get some, so everybody wanted to be first. Guards came to stop the fighting, and they began beating people with their nightsticks. One of the guards hit my mama two times on the head with his nightstick. She felt dizzy, she almost fell down, but that didn't stop her. She went right on up to the front, with me along, and we got three big cans full of rice—Mama got two, and I got one. We went home and cooked the rice, and had a big celebration. That day, my cousin—whose husband had given us the land to put our houses on—gave us some sugar. We cooked the rice in water, and we had rice and tea. And it was delicious, delicious because I hadn't had a decent meal in three days.

The next day Mama's head was swollen where the guard had hit her. She couldn't even pray, because every time she sat up she felt dizzy. She fell down once, and after that she stayed lying down until she felt better. She stayed in the house for three days. She became convinced the place where we were staying was un-lucky, so she went to see another cousin, Habib, to see if there was any way he could help us. She went to ask him for some help—for some money—and I went with her. She told him the situation, and he told her we could all move into one of his one-room round houses in four or five days, as soon as he could get his tenants to move out. He also said he was going to talk to an-other cousin who had a little shop, and see what he could put together to help us. He gave us twenty shillings that same day, just for our living, to get ourselves a meal. So we had twenty shillings, and Mama went to the market and bought some meat, and some of everything else we used to eat—bananas, fruit, oil, sugar, milk—everything!

We took the bus in the morning, and we brought some of the food to Grandmama. We brought sugar, coffee, fruit, rice, and spaghetti—meat they had, because the woman my grandmama was staying with had chickens. We took all we could to her.

I called the other lady "grandmama" too, because she was old. Two of the cows were pregnant, and they had fresh grass and clean water. We spent two nights there, eating and talking, and it was beautiful.

Then we came back to the city. We moved into the house Habib had given us. Habib could help us a little bit, because he had the rent from his other three houses and he had a job besides. The little bit he helped was a lot to us. And another cousin said he would lend us some money to get Mama started in whatever business she wanted—if she made money she could pay it back, but if she lost it he didn't care. That was more than enough. Mama couldn't believe it. Wonderful! Remember how I prayed to Allah? This was like a gift that he sent to us. It was a huge relief.

My cousin brought fifty shillings to us the next day. Mama took it and went into the bread-selling business. She would go to the bakery, where they made the bread early in the morning, and take a big bag and some cloths with her. When you're a bread-seller, you go to the bakery with your bag and your cloths and give the baker the money for the bread and then wrap the hot, freshly baked bread up in the cloths and put it in the bag, and then you go out and start selling. You call out, "Bread! Bread! Bread for sale!" and people come out of their houses and buy as much as they want. After you finish selling one bag, you can go back to the bakery again, but mostly you only sell bread in the early morning and in the evening—people only eat it for breakfast and for dinner. So Mama used to go two times—once in the morning and once in the evening. She made a couple of shillings a day—sometimes as much as three. In the evening, if there was any bread left over, she would bring that, and we would cook some meat and sauce to eat with it. If there wasn't bread, we would cook maize-meal porridge or rice and beans. At least we had a meal to put on the table.

I didn't stay at home either. Habib's wife knew a woman who was working for an Arab family, who told her she knew of another family that needed a little girl to work for them. I told Habib's wife, "Yes, I want to go to work for them." She said I could come on Friday, because on Friday my mama didn't sell bread. On Friday in our country most of our people don't work because it's the holy day—the day to stay home with your family. The next Friday we met the family, and they told me they were going to treat me like their daughter. They were a husband and wife, and because the wife was Arab she didn't go outside the house, which was why she needed me—to go to the shops and to do a little work inside the house too. They said they could pay me twenty shillings a month and give me a place to stay, with food and clothes.

Mama left me there and said she would see me the following Friday. The first night the woman made me sleep on the floor, on a thin little mat. I couldn't sleep because the floor was so cold. So I took the cushions off the couch and put them in a row on the floor and went to sleep on them.

In the middle of the night the Arab woman went to the bathroom and saw me sleeping on the floor on the pillows. She woke me up and told me, "Don't ever do that again!" and made me put the pillows back on the couch. It was my first night, and I couldn't tell her that the floor was too cold to sleep on. I wouldn't have minded if it had been a dirt floor, but it was cement. I had never slept on cement before in all my life. I was frightened, so I was quiet, and when she was gone I lay down on the floor. I still couldn't sleep. I got up and sat in one of the chairs and slept. But she wouldn't even let me lie down on the chairs, because she said my feet were dirty. She didn't give me any sheet to cover myself with. I had only a little small piece of cloth and one dress—that was all I owned in the whole world. I needed a sheet to cover myself with, but I had to wear my dress in the morning. So what I did was, I wore my clothes at night and covered my head with the little piece of cloth so the mosquitoes wouldn't get me. And I became sick, with coughing, a cold, and fever.

The woman made me work like a big person, although I wasn't even eight years old yet. She made me work hard, hard, until I washed the last glass, the last spoon. Ah! Sweep the house, mop, make the bed—work like I was a big person. Sometimes I couldn't wash the clothes—when they got wet, they were heavy, and I couldn't lift them, so I just stirred them with my hand.

When I became sick, she didn't do anything about it. At night, when it was cold, I would cough and sneeze and my body would have chills and then be hot as a fire. The next morning I had to wake up and work. Even if she only wanted water in the middle of the night, she would wake me up and make me get it.

She wasn't feeding me right—I was hungry all the time because she would only give me leftovers. In the morning her husband didn't eat breakfast. He would have a glass of milk and then go to his shop. But when she woke up she would make herself an egg or fried meat with flat bread; she would eat what she wanted, and give me what she couldn't eat, maybe one of her four pieces of bread. At lunch-time, if her husband came home, they would eat together. I had to wait until they were finished. Then, to what was left over on their plate, she would add one or two more spoonfuls, and bring me the dirty plate they had eaten on. If he didn't come home, she would send me to his shop with his plate of food. I liked that, because as soon as I was around the corner I would eat some of his meat, and wipe my hand and my mouth with the sand from the street so he couldn't see that I had been eating his food. I still dream that

I'm always hungry and she is scolding me about the couch and saying, Never do that again.

I thought my mama would never come back to get me. I didn't know how to go home. I didn't know where my family was. For seven days she slaved me...she did. And when my mama came, I cry, I cry. I'd begged Allah to bring back my mama. Rahima, the day she came I couldn't believe it. When I opened the door and saw her, I cried and I held on to her so tightly, as if I'd never let her go again. She asked me, "What happened?" I cried, "She made me sleep on the floor, she made me wash the clothes, she screamed at me, she didn't treat me right..." and my mama began to cry too.

That morning was Friday, and the husband was at home. Mama got angry; she wanted to grab the woman and break her neck. She could have done it, she was so tall and strong, but the husband was there. He held her back and talked to her nicely—he told her to calm down and asked her what had happened. Really, he didn't know what had happened. When I told him what his wife had done to me, he got angry at her, and he said to me, "Why didn't you tell anybody? Why didn't you tell me?" He apologized again and again. The agreement that my mama had had with them was that they would pay me twenty shillings for a whole month, so what he did was, he gave me the twenty shillings for the one week, to compensate for what his wife did to me.

I went with my mama and stayed at home until I felt better. Now Mama had my twenty shillings to add to the fifty shillings from Habib, besides the little money she was earning—she was making a couple of shillings a day. She was getting back the face that I used to see. And one day soon after, she took us to the store and bought us all clothes, because at that time clothes were cheap. My brother got new pants and a shirt. I got a new dress—we wore one piece of cloth, which we tied around our shoulder and wrapped around our waist. I chose one with a bright-yellow pattern, and Hawa chose a pretty one too. Mama also bought us rubber flip-flops. She bought a dress and sandals for my grandmama, and some food, and took the stuff out to my grandmama and spent the night with her.

When Mama came back from visiting Grandmama, she said she had made a decision to stop selling bread and to start selling milk. She had met some other women who were selling milk, and they had told her how much money they were making —more than the little bit she had been making selling bread. She decided to buy a milk container, because milk you can sell every day, all day long. People need it all the time—morning, lunch, and evening.

Now she left the house early in the morning, at about sunrise, after she had prayed, and she would come home after sundown. She would sell four or five containers full of milk a day. When she had sold a whole containerful, she would go back to the market and buy another one. She didn't come home during the day to eat. When she did get home in the evening, she would eat a little fruit, and inside the milk container would be lots of food. Some days, though, she was so tired that she fell into bed and went to sleep as soon as she came home, and sometimes her feet would get swollen because she had to walk so far with such heavy loads. We had such respect for her—she was a real fighter—and I used to rub her feet in the evening when she was lying down.

When it came time for her to come home in the evening, we were all excited—especially me, because I was younger and I loved bananas and she used to bring some for me every day. So I would be outside looking for Mama, and everybody else would come out too, because she always brought them a little cake or something sweet to eat before dinner was ready. Then we would cook a big meal to eat at nightfall. We used to eat rice a lot, and pancakes and flat bread, with meat and vegetables. One night it was spaghetti, the next night rice, the next night maize-meal porridge, the next night flat bread, and the next night pancakes.

Hassan began to work too—he would go to the market with Mama in the morning and carry things for people, so he was bringing home a little money. After a while in the milk-selling business, my mama made good money—she was saving an average of four or five shillings a day, and that was after she bought our food, because back home you shop every day for everything, fresh. We were doing really well. We started to cook a bigger meal, so Habib and his family could eat with us—because they had helped us out and been so kind to Mama. One day they would cook, one day we would cook, or else we would all cook together and then eat outside, all from the same plate. We were one big happy family.

But even though Mama was saving money, she knew Mogadishu wasn't for us. She loved animals, and she had decided to go back to Mango Village after we saved enough money. I wanted to help her, so what I did was, I began to sell flat bread and pancakes. When I asked Hawa to help me bake the flat bread, *muufo*, she said, "No—unh-unh!" She didn't want to have burns and scars on her arms. So Habib's wife was the one who showed me how to make it. You grind corn, grind it till it's flour. Then you make bread, you slap it with your hands until it's flat like pita bread, slap, slap. And then you put it in a clay-pot oven where the wood has burned to charcoal. The oven is big, it can fit twenty pieces of *muufo*, three or four rows across, but the hole where you put it in is small and hot. You can feel the heat on your face and chest. You have to have a long arm to reach inside without getting burned. I still have scars on my arms from burning myself on the mouth of the oven. But I learned—sometimes I used to save half a shilling or a shilling a day. We were eating our breakfast for "free", because I made the pancakes, and sometimes dinner was free too if I couldn't sell all the bread and we had some left over. I began feeling better and better, because I was learning better and better how to make the *muufo* and pancakes, and I was selling more because my *muufo* and pancakes looked better. So we made money—my mama, and my brother, and me.

One day when Mama was selling milk, she met her third husband—the officer, the one who couldn't have children—in the street. When she saw him she felt ashamed because she looked so draggled and tired. She had wanted to go and ask him for help many times, because she knew he was living in the city, but she was too proud to ask. And now he was seeing her like this! They talked for a while, and he offered her some help. She refused, but he insisted. He told her, "At least take my help for your children." She told him where we were staying, and one evening he brought us about ten pounds of sugar, a big container of cooking oil, and big bags of rice, tea, and coffee. And he gave Mama some money. He used to come and visit us now and then, and he would bring me candy and cookies. He liked me, and I used to wish that he was my father, because he was such a nice man.

We stayed in Mogadishu for eight months. By then the two pregnant cows that Grandmama was looking after had had their calves, so we had six cows, and Mama had enough money saved for us to go back home.

When we got back to Mango Village, Mama started doing a little business again. This time we kept our cows in town; there were many other people who did the same thing. They hired someone by the day to take the cows outside of town for grazing in the morning, watch them all day, and bring them back in the evening. She had to pay money for that, but people put their animals together and hired one man to watch all of them. She did that, and she sold the cows' milk, and she was selling eggs too. Once again she had started something new.

CHAPTER
5

WE MOVED WITHIN MANGO VIL-
lage a couple of times. The third place we lived was the same
house that Mama had sold when we went to Mogadishu, because she really liked that place. Mango Village, that's where
paradise is: water and trees and grass and oh, it was good to be
back there. Outside it was dirty, dusty, and hot, but inside the
houses it was always cool. We painted flour sacks white, red,
blue—whatever colours we liked—and we put them under the
zinc roof to keep out the heat. We painted animals, flowers, and
trees on the walls and it made our house look really pretty. We
would lean over the fence and talk to our neighbours: "Do you
have any sugar?" and they would call back, "Sure," and hand us
some. We didn't need to go to the store; if we needed something,
we'd just ask a neighbour.

One of my aunts on my father's side and her children were
living in the group of houses we moved back to. She had three
daughters—one was about my age, one was younger, and one
was older. Her two younger daughters hadn't been circumcised

yet. So my aunt and another aunt were planning their circumcision, and they asked my mama if she wanted to have me circumcised on the same day. But my mama said no, because she didn't have enough money or time. You have to invite a lot of people and cook a lot of food for them, so you have to have money, even though the people you invite bring you money too. My mother didn't want to take money from anyone—she wanted to do it with her own money, invite people to eat, have the party, and let them leave without giving her money. She was a religious person, and our religion doesn't allow you to take money because it would be as though you were selling your food, and that's no good. So she told my two aunts that they should go ahead and do it just for my two cousins.

But my aunts said to themselves, "No, that's not fair. We're leaving Aman out by doing the other two. It's not good for our name—our brother's name. And besides, she's the oldest and it's shameful to do the younger ones and not her." So they decided to do me too, without letting my mother know. They knew that Mama had to go milk our cows before sunrise and that she wouldn't be back until midmorning. When they do circumcisions, they do them early in the morning, before it gets hot and before your blood gets hot and begins to run—early in the morning, as soon as you wake up.

They invited *everybody*. They killed one bull, two goats, and a sheep, and cooked the whole night. The next morning my mama left to go and milk the cows. My aunts and their friends had spent the night over at our houses, and they had to get up early in the morning to cook tea and coffee and a big breakfast for all the people who would be coming. That's when they woke me up. They were giving a shower to my two cousins, and they told me to go take a shower too. I asked them why, and they asked me if I wanted to be circumcised as well. I told them yes,

I wanted to—all the girls my age wanted to because it's shame not to—but I was afraid, and besides, my mama didn't want me circumcised today.

They talked to me nicely and let me know that they were going to do it whether I liked it or not, so I should be good and take a shower and come back. I went with my cousins, and when the three of us were finished with our showers they wrapped us in the old scarves that women wear around their shoulders, and we each had a new piece of cloth—they cut us each a big piece. They shaved our hair, and two *sheikh*s read the Qur'an over us. They told us that there was no pain and that we had to be good, and that they were going to give us a lot of gold and a lot of money, and the one who was the best would get the most. You know, they were deceiving us children. They were mainly telling me, because I was going to be the first one, because I was nine— the eldest. So I told them, "All right." Outside, the women and children were already singing and dancing. They do the circumcisions outside, with a lot of clapping and singing so people won't hear you cry. They were going "Lulululululululu" and singing my father's name and my lineage's name, saying that they were the best. I was so proud when I heard all this. I said, Yes, why not? to myself. They put gold on me everywhere, and money everywhere, and they took me outside under one of the tall trees in the yard.

There was a big woman there who holds the girls while they are being circumcised—a strong woman. They gave her a low four-legged stool. There was another tall, skinny, black woman named Fatima to do the circumcision. The big one grabbed me by the hand and held me. I told her, "You don't have to grab me hard, I'm not going to run." She said, "Oh, you're a good girl! I've never met one like you before. You're a big little girl, aren't you?" I said "Yes!" She said, "Are you sure you're not going to run away?" I said, "No, and I'm not going to cry either. And you're not going to tie me," because I knew they usually tied the girl's legs. And she said, "Good. I like that." She made me sit on the ground, on some dry grass that she had laid down. She told me to take off the piece of cloth I had on. The way she did it was, she sat on the stool and spread her legs and put me on the ground with my back to her, with my legs next to her legs. Usually she would tie the child's legs to her legs and then spread her legs wide and the child's legs with them, and she would also hold the child's arms so she couldn't move. But I told her, "You don't have to tie me," because I wanted everybody to be proud of me. If she had tied me, it would have seemed as though I was frightened, and I didn't want to do it that way. She said, "All right." She trusted me, she really did; she didn't tie me, but she wrapped her legs around mine and held me that way, in case I jumped. I sat there, and she told me what was going to happen. She said, "It's not a big thing, it's not that painful." She told me to be strong the way I had said I would be: "Don't let your family down. Don't let yourself down. The children will laugh at you tomorrow if you cry today." I told her I wouldn't cry—I was going to be strong. And I was.

She put a small white container with charcoal ashes in front of me, between my legs. And now the other woman, Fatima— she was a beautiful woman—came towards me. She told me her name, and told me how calm she was. She talked to me nicely so I wouldn't feel pain. She said that if I was bad she could be bad—and while she was talking to me like that, she was getting out her knives and all the other equipment and wiping them to make them clean. Then she took some of the charcoal powder between her thumb and forefinger and started playing with my clitoris, pulling on it so that it would become bigger as she kept on talking, and I was talking to her too, asking her questions—

when was she going to do it?—and she answered me, even though she was lying. After she got everything ready, that was the time she told me to close my eyes. I asked her, "Is this it?" She said, "This is it. This is it. It won't take a second. Close your eyes. When you open them, the pain and your clitoris will be gone." I told her, "All right!"

This time, she even pulled out the knife—a little knife, shiny and sharp, with a little hook on it. Now she pulled harder on my clitoris, and this time I turned my face away and told the other woman, "Hold me tight," and gritted my teeth. And then my God, Rahima, everything happened. My body was gone in a second, just as they had said. I could hear *shuuu*...like the sound when they are slicing meat—just like that was the way she sliced my body. She cut everything—she didn't cut the big lips, but she sliced off my clitoris and the two black little lips, which were *haram*—impure—all that she sliced off like meat. Oh, Rahima, I thought I was going to die. I opened my eyes and looked down at myself, and the blood was coming out. Part of me was bleeding heavily, and in the part where she had peeled the flesh off, the meat was white.

Rahima, my God, it had only just started. I asked her if she was finished, and she said no, she was going to do it again. Again she said, "It won't take a minute," and I believed her. And everybody who was watching began putting gold and more money on me—on my head, on my legs—and they were singing. Every time I wanted to cry, I looked around to see if someone would help, but I just saw smiling faces, and I felt shy again and I opened my mouth and pretended I was laughing, but I was dying inside. She sliced the top off my big lips, and then she took thorns like needles and put them in crossways, across my vagina, to close it up. She put in seven thorns, and each time she put one in she tightened them together with string. When she was finished, she put on some black paste to stop the bleeding and make the wound dry up fast, and then some egg yolk to make it feel cool. Then she took some cloth and wrapped it around my legs, from my ankles to my hips. And they wrapped me up in my cloth again and carried me inside to the room they had ready for us. And that's what they did to the other girls.

Afterwards I was sick and had a fever. And when I peed, it felt as though it would kill me. It felt like fire! Or like alcohol when you put it on an open wound. It was hot, that pee, and I cried. They had to cover me up and my teeth were chattering and I was shaking all over my whole body when my mother came back. She was angry. She didn't say anything though, because a lot of people were there. They were giving me some soup when she came in. She was furious, but she went out for a while and came back after she had calmed down. She was trying to control herself, but she was really angry, because they hadn't respected her wishes. They had let her down and treated her as if she was nothing, and she hated that. I think everybody was a bit afraid of Mama, but they all stayed calm and nobody said anything. And she controlled her anger.

I talked to her. I knew she was angry, but I was proud, so I told her to be happy for me. I said, "They did it because they love me. Why didn't you want me to have it done with the other girls? I don't want you to have a fight with them, because you're both my family. I love them, and I love you." She understood how I felt, but she was still angry.

I kept the thorns in for three days. Then the woman who did the circumcision came back and took them out. All that time your legs are tied, even when you pee. You don't drink much so you won't have to pee much. You don't eat a lot so you don't have to doo-doo—they give you only a little soup, with vegetables in it, and dry bread, because they want your body to get dry fast. The more liquids you drink, the more you pee and the more that place gets wet, and they don't want that. Every time you pee it stings, so they pour warm water with salt in it over your genitals while you are peeing. The salt is a disinfectant, and the warm water eases the pain. After you pee, they dry you off and take you outside. Out in the *daash*, they have dug a hole in the ground and put in some lighted charcoal covered with ash. They put incense on it. They have you sit over the hole, still with your legs tied, leaning against a woman sitting on a stool. Smoke from the fire with the incense makes you smell good and the heat makes your wound dry. After three days of doing that every morning and every evening and every time you pee, you heal up fast when you are a little girl.

After the woman who circumcises you comes back to take out the thorns, she examines your circumcision to see if your hole is small or big. She uses a stick about the size of a round toothpick and puts it into the hole. If your hole is much bigger than a toothpick—maybe because you peed too fast—she puts in another stitch with a thorn to close you up again. If not, if your hole is all right, you just rest for seven days with your legs tied together a little more loosely. They give you a walking stick, and you walk slowly and sit slowly and lie on your side with your legs tied together. And in six or seven days, you're all right, and you can go where you want.

I was all right in seven days, but one of the girls who was circumcised with me—the one who was nearly my age—she had to be circumcised all over again, because when she first peed after her circumcision she felt the pain, and then she didn't pee at all for three days. So when the woman came to take the stitches out, she shat and peed at the same time, and opened her hole up wide. Fatima had to stitch her again—the girl had more pain and had to stay in the house almost a month.

The reason they do that extra stitch is so that when you get married, your husband will know you are a virgin. If he sees you have a little bit bigger hole, he'll think you played around. So the women—your mother and the woman who circumcised you— have to make sure your hole is the right size. That's why they do all this stitching and sewing. The other kind of circumcision is *sunna*. They don't cut anything off and they don't sew anything, they only make a little cut or just a pinprick so blood will come —a little blood. It doesn't even feel like a pinch. These days a few people say, "Don't cut it. Make it *sunna*." But then, people preferred it the old way, to make sure their daughter didn't play around, and the husband preferred it so he could make sure his wife is a virgin. Many people still prefer the old way.

A girl who is sewn won't play around, because she is scared of the pain, and she's scared her family will be able to tell when they check her every week. When one door is closed and one door is open, which one is easy to get into? A thief doesn't go to a locked door.

The people your parents invite to your circumcision arrive around two or three in the afternoon. The party is only for women and children, with a couple of *sheikh*s to read the Qur'an. You take all the furniture out of two or three rooms and lay mats and cushions on the floor. Before people go in, they take off their shoes. They come in groups of relatives or friends, and they usually sit together with the people they came with. You bring two bowls of warm water, one with soap in it and one without, for them to wash their hands before they eat. Then you bring the food. Each group has a big plate of rice, meat, and salad, and fruit that you bring on another plate. After they eat, you bring them the bowls of warm water again, and they wash their hands again because they've eaten with their hands. You bring them a cloth to dry their hands with, and perfume to take away the smell of the food. After that, they drink coffee, and have sweets and dates and tea and soft drinks. You bring incense for everyone to smoke their hair with, and then strong perfume for their hair, and after that they have to go, because other people are waiting to sit down and eat in their place. People are waiting outside, singing and dancing, because you may have only two houses, and one house is taken up with the *sheikhs* reading the Qur'an and with a couple of young boys waiting on them, who ask them if they want coffee or tea.

Before each group of women leaves, the women who have been serving the food collect the money. Each woman gives some, no matter how much. And the serving woman has to remember how much each person gave so that she can tell the woman who is giving the circumcising party. Because if you bring five shillings, next time when I go to your place I have to give at least five shillings, or more. It's a payback system—I don't know what to call it exactly, but it's a good system. The only other time they do this is when a woman marries. You collect all the money, the women leave, you clean the room, and another group comes and sits until eleven o'clock at night. At the end of the night, you wash dishes and clean up, and count the money—you know what you spent for the party, and you know what you made afterwards—and then the circumcision party is over.

CHAPTER
6

Now I was a big girl, and Mama put me in school. She bought me tennis shoes! Most of the time I went barefoot, but now I was starting school. The rains were so heavy the water came up as high as our knees. We wore tennis shoes so the glass on the ground wouldn't cut us on our way to school, and when we got to school we washed the shoes, and sometimes we couldn't get all the mud out. We just painted them and made them new. We wore the shoes over and over, and every time they got dragged through the mud, we painted them again.

When I was in school, I loved it; I was so excited. I was happy, you know. For the first year, I was the best student. Many of the teachers were white nuns, and they were kind. I learned Italian fast. A Somali man taught Arabic, and at first I thought he was nice too. I loved learning things in school. But the girls—all the children—started to call me names. They said I had TB and that was why I had stayed in the hospital for seven months—in those days, having TB was like having AIDS—people wanted to stay away from you. They also said that my family had turned poor and we couldn't afford to eat well, and that we had run away to the city and then had to come back.... They told me my story over and over again, and I hated to hear it. I got angry with these children and began to fight with them. Every day. I was lonely. I hated everyone. Now I hated the town.

escape The only thing I liked was to go swimming, so I would skip school to go to the river. A lot of people told us not to go there, it was dangerous. Some people went to swim or to get water for their cows and they were killed. Many of the children in Mango Village died in accidents there: crocodiles got them, or they didn't know how to swim and the water took them. It was like the train—the train that went through the village, taking sugarcane to the sugar factory. Every time the train passed through Mango Village, it rang a bell—*vee, vee, vee*—so everybody could get away, but sometimes we ran to the train, hoping to get some sugar. The train was up on a hill, above the river, and it's going so fast you have to run, and you're a little short child and you try and reach in, and your feet slip, and you fall under, and *phht!* A lot of children lost their arms or their legs, or even got killed. People said it was dangerous, but we didn't listen. And the river was the same for me—one side safe, one side not safe. The safe side had a dam to block the water from being so strong, and it kept out the hippos and crocodiles. That's where we washed our clothes, and that's where we got drinking water, cooking water, and that's where I loved to swim. There was no danger on that side, and when I hated all the people, I went there instead of school. Water was my favourite. If I wasn't swimming in the river, I took three or four showers at home. A day. Every time I felt hot, I went to the latrine—*shuh, shuh, shuh*—quickly, and come out, then go back again. Mama said, "Don't finish the water! You are like a fish!" But I liked to be clean. I was very clean.

The other thing I loved was the movies. The cinema was open to the sky, with a big white wall around it, and there were long pews like they have in a Christian church. Children sat downstairs, and men sat upstairs, big men who didn't want to hear the children's noise. They were white movies, a lot of movies with John Wayne and American cowboys speaking Italian. We didn't understand the language, we just understood the action. When the cowboys and Indians fought, we always wanted the Indians to win; we always took their side because they looked a bit like us and they fought like we did.

We were not supposed to go to the movies; our parents said going to the movies is no good, watching what they do is no good, seeing a naked woman is no good, her dress is no good, they don't cover their hair—and they're kissing!—it's no good! Everybody's family said the same thing. It wasn't only that, they said it wasn't good for your eyes, wasn't good to see something that's not right to see. But I loved the movies! I used to go every night. The movie has to start when the sun gets dark, because the screen is outside. Sometimes we would stand up in front of the theatre and we'd ask the people, "We penny short, Auntie. Can you give me, Uncle, can you give me penny?" The ticket was eight cents, so we used to beg the big people who could pay: "Uncle, take me inside, hold my hand. Uncle, hold my hand! Auntie, hold my hand!" If we didn't get in, since the screen was out in the open, we'd climb a tree and watch it from up there. Sometimes there were Hindi movies, but I didn't like them—the men cried too much. But I liked the songs, and all the dancing.

I stayed in school, dropping out and going back, for almost three years. I was mean now: I used to fight and scare the other girls—I was strong too. I became friends with the boys, and I became more bad because I was with the boys. I knew I was different. The other children had better clothes, they had better shoes, they had better houses, they had a father who was with them, they had everything I wanted and didn't have.

A man from my grandmama's lineage was the District Commissioner. He had just been transferred to Mango Village. My grandmama had never met him, but anybody could go and see him, and my mama and my grandmama had been talking about going. One morning I got sent home from school because I was late. I was feeling nervous and lonely, angry with everybody. The District Commissioner's office, his house, and the school were all in the same area, and as I went past his office I began to remember his name. I looked at the building. It was a beautiful white building. I thought to myself, Why don't you go and talk to him and tell him who you are and ask him to help you? There were two policemen by the gate, and I told them who I was and said I wanted to talk to him. Because they knew my father, because he was the chief, they let me in and they went and told him I was outside his office—a little girl whose father was So-and-so. That's how I got in to see the District Commissioner.

I told him about my mother's side, and who my grandmother was, because he and my grandmother were the same lineage and those people, they love lineages. I told him about my mother and what had happened to us, how we had come back from Mogadishu, and how I was having trouble in school. He looked at me and said, "You're a tough little girl, and I like that. I can tell you have blood—our blood. See how strong you are? That's the way you have to be…strong blood." I was proud then.

I told him about my problems in school, and how I didn't get along with anybody. I told him the Arabic teacher was cruel to me, he had even started to whip me. And I told him I needed a job, because I really just wanted to help Mama. He asked me why my father didn't help us, and I told him that my mama and my daddy didn't get along. I told him about their agreement: either don't ask me for anything or else bring the children back —"I won't give you anything" and "I won't ask for anything." My parents had kept the agreement. I told him everything.

He said he would see what he could do. I told him where we lived, and he said he would come to visit us. I told him, "I'll be waiting for you!" I went straight home and told Mama all that had happened. And on the fifth day after I had been sent home from school, he came. It was late in the afternoon—about five or six o'clock, tea-time—the time everyone usually goes around visiting. Everybody has tea or coffee and sits around relaxing and listening to the radio. The elder people will sit outside every evening, and clean and sweep, and pour water so there won't be a lot of dust. The children sit around, and the ones who went to the movie explain to the ones who didn't what happened so it's just as if you went. All the people sit out there, have tea and talk and say "hey" to each other. When the elder people talk, the children sit around them on the ground and listen, or they play and run around. If you are thirsty, you go and knock on the door—"Auntie, give me some water"—and you get water and she asks you, "You want to eat too?" It's open door everywhere. I don't know if it's still the same.... It's nice, a very nice culture. We have the best country, I believe it's the best country. Elder people teach you how to behave well and how to respect others. You don't have to go to church to get that. There, they preach to you outside. Elder people are like your parents—you have to respect them in the same way, call them "auntie", call them "uncle" or "brother".

I saw the District Commissioner's car, with a couple of children running after it, and I ran to meet him and bring him over to our house. We were all sitting around on four-legged stools. Everybody in our neighbourhood was watching us and talking about us, because they knew his car—he had a government Land Rover.

We brought him tea, and listened to the radio, and talked. He and Grandmama talked *a lot*. They were both from the countryside and knew about the different lineages, so they talked about their lineages and their families. I really enjoyed his visit.

He left around eight in the evening. Before he left, he told us he and his wife had a little boy who was about seven months old and she needed help with the baby. He had two people who worked for him, but his wife wanted someone just to help with the baby. He told me to come to work the next morning at his house. He said I could go from there to school, if I wanted to. But I was angry with the Arabic teacher; I told him I wasn't going back.

Oh, and he gave Mama some money to help her and Grandmama. He gave me thirty shillings to buy some new clothes—he could see we were poor—and he told me I could start work the next day. I was so happy—I kissed my mama and my grandmama, and jumped up and down. I was proud we still had good people and we were showing the neighbours we were still good people. When you are in the government, you don't go often to people's houses, especially poor people's houses. He showed a lot of respect for us, and I wanted to respect him too. And I was pleased I was going to work like his daughter in his house. This was good for me, and I knew I could make life easier for Mama, because he was the one who gave the orders for the whole town.

I couldn't wait for morning to come. I woke up in the middle of the night and asked my mama what time it was. She said, "Go back to sleep!" I was too excited! I got up at sunrise, took a shower, put on the best clothes I had, and off I went. I walked to their house. There were people walking, going to work, many people around, so I wasn't scared. Some of them asked me where I was going, because it wasn't school-time yet. I told them I was going to work for the District Commissioner and he was my uncle—I had started to call him "uncle" out of respect. I told them I was going to stay in his house, and they said, "Wonderful!"

So I arrived at his house. I met his wife, and she was beautiful, and so was his little boy. There were two other people working for him—one man and one woman. I liked the house—it was a big, big, lovely villa. It had seven rooms: two living rooms, a dining room with a fireplace, and bedrooms off a long corridor—a real old European house. My bedroom was one of the guest rooms. It had a bed that was much more comfortable than the beds in the hospital—it was lower and wider, with a headboard. And there were sheets—two sheets, with a blanket on top, and pillowcases. Everything was white and clean. There was a nightstand with a lamp on it, a wardrobe, and a dresser with a mirror. I didn't have clothes to put inside the wardrobe, but every night I used to open it and look in and think, One day I'm going to fill it up full of clothes.

Every evening my uncle used to go out to a movie or to the government hotel to meet with all the other big men and drink coffee and tea and talk about politics. I stayed home and kept his wife and the baby company, because after the two servants left in the evening she and the baby would have been all alone if I hadn't stayed.

I didn't see my family more than once or twice a week, which wasn't enough. I wished I could see my family. So one day, when I had finished my work and put the baby to bed for a nap, I asked my uncle if I could ride with him when he went to town. Our house was only a twenty-minute walk away, but I wanted to ride with him. I wanted the children in Mango Village to see me with this important man in his big car. He said, "All right, you can get a drive with me." I began to ride with him all the time. I would go see my mama, or I would go to the movie with him—me downstairs, him upstairs—and meet him outside after the show. But sometimes that uncle would drive out to the country-side, stop the car anywhere, and ask me to come out of the car. He would pick me up and put me against the car, and hold me against the car like that, his hands against me, take my wrap-dress up, pull my underwear down holding my leg and putting his...and he was doing things. He was touching me and using me. I didn't like that. He didn't try to go in or anything. It was the first time anyone had done that. I was just staying there quiet and still because he wanted it. If I refused, I thought he would stop helping my family. But it was not right. We would never talk about it, never mention it, but we both knew it was wrong. I never told anybody.

Then his wife began to get angry with me. She didn't say any-thing at first, but she began to say, "No, you don't need to go downtown, you don't need to see your mother every day, you have to stay with the baby." She was a sophisticated woman—young, beautiful. Her husband had a good position, and she had people working for her—she thought she was a queen. I talked to her as though I were a grown-up. I told her I had every right to see my family after work, because that was what her husband had told me. She began to call me names, because she was jeal-ous of me. He had started telling me to take sugar and rice from his big storage room, which was full of food in containers. He told me, "Take some of that food home, so your family can eat." He was getting it free—the government was paying for it. But his wife didn't like that. She told me that the only day I could go and see my family was Friday. She was rude to me and called me names. She called me *saqajaan*—it means nasty girl.

Finally I went to my uncle and told him I was leaving. He said, "You're right. I didn't know how to tell you she wants you to leave, so I'm glad you decided it by yourself. But I'm going to help you anyway—tell your mother and grandmother not to worry about anything. Any time all of you need anything—food or money or any kind of help—just come to my office." I think he liked me, but why didn't he want his wife? She was beautiful, and she was open. He told me to go back to school, and he said he would talk to the Arabic teacher and tell him not to whip me, even if I was a few minutes late or made mistakes in my schoolwork. I told him no, I wanted to stay out of school for a while and think things over. I was confused and angry with everybody—with my father, with the world, and with myself.

In school, I had a friend, Fatoun, who was suspended around the same time I was. While I was working with my uncle's family, she had been working for a white family as a maid. We used to see each other at the movies. Her mother had died when she was young, and her stepmother had treated her badly. She was lonely too, in the same way that I was. She was the only one I got along with, and I was the only one she got along with.

One day when we were talking she asked me if I wanted a job like hers. I told her no, there was no way I could work for white people, because of my family. For many reasons, it was shameful to work for white people. I remember on Independence Day, 1960, when we were supposed to sing and dance because of the holiday, I said, "What are we doing this for?" And they explained to me, we're getting freedom! I said, "Freedom from who?" They said we were colonized by the Italians—they killed people, they raped women, they took everything from us, they were not good people—they liked to be the boss, bossing people around and making other people, especially black people, very low. And no religion allows that. Our religion says be equal and even and leave other people alone. Get along with them; if you don't, live alone. They said it was good we had independence, because white people liked to command the blacks. I don't know if it's because they consider us stupid, but they're wrong. I didn't know all that then. I knew my mama had to hide from whites when she was a little girl, but I thought they'd gone. I didn't see anybody beat us or colonize us. I loved everybody and I thought everybody was equal and normal and should be at peace together. But that day I found out we were colonized, we were not even free—and I had thought we were free!

So I said I couldn't work with white people. Fatoun said, "That's fine. I like it. I'm doing it." But I liked the idea too, because she had a lot of new things. She had new clothes and shoes. One day she had a bicycle, and she already knew how to ride it. I asked her where she had got it, and she said that the lady she worked for had given it to her so she could get to work earlier in the morning. I asked her, "Who taught you to ride it?" She said, "The lady I work for and two white children taught me." I said, "You've got white girlfriends?" She said, "I've even got a white boyfriend!" I didn't know what a boyfriend was. She was older than me so she told me, "'Boyfriend' and 'girlfriend' means you love him and he loves you. You don't go with anyone else and he doesn't go with anyone else." I still didn't understand it, but I was curious. "Oh? You've got more white friends? I want to meet some." She said, "You want to meet white people?" I said, "Yes, I want to meet some, and I want to learn how to ride a bicycle too."

Fatoun said she was going to teach me. But the only place she could teach me was inside the white people's compound. Mango Village was divided in two. The Italians—the sugar factory bosses, engineers, and mechanics, and some other bosses—

had their own village they called a compound. It had a gate around it and police watching it and a lot of protection outside, and everything they wanted inside: stores, telephones, movie theatres, restaurants, bars. You name it, everything they wanted was there. I knew if I wanted to ride a bike I'd have to go inside there, because in the village it was shameful for any girl to ride a bicycle. People worried that a girl might split open her circumcision. Only boys could ride. When Fatoun rode her bicycle, children stoned her and called her names, but she didn't care. She was crazy, and she was learning. I wanted to learn too.

I went with her inside the compound. She told the guard at the gate I was coming to do some work with her. He let me in. I started learning to ride a bicycle, but I still hadn't seen her friends. I saw many white people, big ones and children, but they weren't her friends. Then one night she said, "Why don't you come over early? We're going to my friend's house, because his parents are going to the movies." I said, "All right." I left home around four and went to the place where she worked. She was ironing clothes with a charcoal iron. I washed the dishes and wiped off the table, she told the lady goodbye, and then—whoosh!—we were gone! We both rode the bicycle to the boy's house. I waited outside the house while she knocked on the door. She knocked again, and they opened it.

There were three of them—three boys. They were older than us, about fifteen. The tallest one—I liked him. When I saw them—I looked at them in a second, all three of them—the tall one was...beautiful! He had black hair parted on the side like Elvis, and at that time all the girls loved Elvis. My heart was going boom! boom! They all came out and paid attention to me, all three of them. My friend told them my name, but she didn't tell me their names. She knew the white people's language, because she had been working for that lady for a couple of months. Besides, she had learned Italian in school. I knew a little bit from school too, but I was shy—I didn't want to say something the wrong way, something bad.

The tall one came over and said, "*Ciao,*" and I said, "*Ciao.*" They invited us inside. They had music. I had never heard music except for a radio, but they had a record player, and they were playing records—small records, forty-fives, going round and round—and singing at the same time. I had never seen such things before, my mouth was, wow…open, you know.

They started dancing. I had never danced this kind of dance before. It was a Beatles record. I was just watching, but then the tall boy asked me to dance, and I told him I didn't know how. He said he was going to teach me—I didn't understand everything he said—my friend told me what he had said, later on. He said to me, "Do you want to go out and talk? We can go out and talk a little bit." We were afraid that if we went out in the street, someone would see us, so we went out behind the house. He was talking a lot—you know, as if he already knew me. And I kept on saying "Yes" and "Uh-huh", because most of the things he was saying I didn't even understand.

He talked and talked. He told me his name was Antony. He asked me if I was working around there, like my girlfriend, and I said, "Oh, no," as if it was shameful. And he said, "Oh, I'm sorry. Don't be offended. I didn't mean to get you upset." I asked him, "Do you know my name? Do you know who my father is?" Every white man had to know my father's name, because he was the chief of the town. I said, "I am the daughter of the chief." He said, "Oh, excuse me. I didn't mean anything. I didn't know who you were." He called the other two boys and said to them, "Do you know who she is? My father knows her father." Now that he knew who my father was, he treated me with more respect.

They offered us orange juice, and we drank it. We stayed a few more minutes, and he tried to teach me how to dance. But I couldn't, I was too shy. I wanted to, but I was too shy. That was my first white person around my own age...talking to me... though I had a white teacher, and a white doctor in the hospital. This was my first time with white teenagers, and I was shy.

As we started to go, he held my hand. "When am I going to see you again, daughter of the chief?" Like children playing. I was too shy to say anything, because I was thinking I might not say it right and he might laugh at me. So I only said, "Uh-huh," "Uh-huh," "Uh-huh." He knew why I was saying that, so he just said goodbye, and I said goodbye, and the two of us left.

Rahima! I couldn't sleep that night. That boy was always on my mind—everywhere I went he was with me, every minute he was with me. I was always thinking about him, I was crazy about him. I started going to talk to Fatoun for hours and hours. I would go early in the morning to talk to her, because there was a chance I might see him in the street. I would do anything to see him. I was so sick—I was so in love.

I told Fatoun that now I wanted a job with a white family. At first I had refused, but now I had to be close to Antony and the only way I could be close was to get a job in the white people's area. It was easy to find one—you just went door-to-door and asked them if they wanted a maid. Soon she found me a place, and I worked there, and I could see Antony from time to time.

But now my family started in. "Why is Aman going to work for whites?" Another reason we weren't supposed to mix with whites was that they were considered dirty. It was a religious matter, I think. When we go to the bathroom, we wash ourselves. Whatever you do—you wash yourself. They say white people don't do that. Also what makes them dirty is that they're not circumcised. They're not Muslim, and Muslims are considered very clean. So my father's sons were upset. "What do you think we are?" They gave my mother a hard time: "It's your fault. Why do you make her work? We've got everything. Her daddy is rich, her daddy is this, her daddy is that. Why are you doing this? Why are you spoiling our name? Why are you doing this to our daughter?" My mama had refused at first when I wanted to work for the white family, but I had begged her and she had changed her mind. I was doing this job on my own, because I wanted to see Antony, and also because I wanted to give the money I earned to my mama. But they didn't see all that—all they could see was the name. I didn't care about the name. I wanted something to eat; I couldn't eat the name. I told them it wasn't Mama's idea, it was my idea, and I was going to do it. They said, "No, you have to go back to school, and we're going to support you, and you have to start living in your father's house. You're not going to stay with your mother any more." I told them, "Unh-unh. I'm staying with my mother until the day I die. And I'm going to do what I want, and I'm going to work. If any of you say anything, I'm going to the police. All of you, leave me alone."

But they weren't going to leave me alone, they were going to whip me and give me a hard time. They used to wait for me by the gate, so I had to sneak back home or else stay at work late and go home when it was dark. I was afraid of them. But I was in love with my boyfriend, and he was in love with me. We were talking to each other more—I was talking and saying things to him now too. We would arrange to meet about sundown, when I finished work, in the forest or in the fields or along the river— somewhere we thought there wouldn't be anybody around. He would ride his bicycle to that place. We couldn't ride together, and I didn't have a bicycle, so I had to walk. I had learned how to ride a bicycle well, because he used to teach me sometimes, but I never had one of my own.

When we found each other, we would just ride, or walk, and go somewhere to sit and talk. He talked—he liked to talk, and I liked to listen. That's all we did. We held each other by the hand. We never even kissed. He used to kiss my hand sometimes. And we sat side by side. When it was cold he would hold me, to keep me warm, and I would wear his pullover sweater. His pullover smelled so good, I had never smelled anything so good before. That was about it, that was as close as we got. That was all I ever wanted, that was all we ever knew. I was in love with that boy, like a friend, and he was good for me.

He was going to school, and we saw each other almost every evening—sometimes we would stay together for a long time. When there were other people around, we wouldn't talk—we would just make eye contact. That was enough, just to see each other.

My father's sons made me quit my job—and Hassan and my mama too, they didn't like me working for the white people. I had to quit. Now it was really difficult to see him. They told the policeman at the gate to the white people's compound not to let me in, so Antony started coming into the village. I used to go to the movies at night, and sometimes he would come too and try to talk to me, and people saw us and found out what was going on. Now the whole town started to call me names. They hadn't liked me before, but now it was worse—I was going with a white boy. It was hard for him too. Sometimes I'd seen white people come to our farms and markets, and the children would run after them just to look at them. A lot of children in Mango Village had never seen a white person, so when one came around everyone wanted to see—they were surprised how white a person could be! But some children would also throw stones. Now if they saw us together or if they saw him alone or sometimes if they saw me alone, they always called us names and stoned us. I told him, "Better stay away for a while." But he didn't listen.

His father found out, and he came to see my family to tell them to keep me away from his son. His neck and his face turned red while he talked. Mama told him, "It's your son who's coming into town, so you keep him away from our daughter." My boyfriend was the one who was really having a rough time —he was getting whipped more than I was, children stoned him and called him names and ran after him and hit him and pushed him. Still he used to come, he never stopped coming. But one day they hit him in the head with a big stone. He was bleeding and they had to take him to the hospital and put four stitches in his head. His daddy got frightened and sent him home to Europe, and I was left behind. And at home, everyone was angry with me.

Now I was all alone, and I didn't get along with anybody. I tried to go back to school, I tried it for almost a month, but the children still teased me in the same way. It wasn't good. This time I could have stayed in school—they didn't ask me to leave —I quit. The other children were terrible to me: "Now you're going with a white boy. You don't have any money so you're selling yourself." There were two different religions, two different cultures, two different colours. A Somali girl with a white man was called *sharmuuto*—a prostitute: you're a prostitute—otherwise, how did you meet a white man?

Several times a week you can see girls in a crowd, checking each other's circumcisions. If you weren't circumcised, the other girls wouldn't talk to you or play with you. When a girl your own age or older calls you *sharmuuto*, you compete right there, no matter where you are, by taking off your underpants and spreading your legs and letting everyone see if you are a virgin or not. If you are, you win, and the girl who teases you has to apologize or you fight with her. More madness. So I quit school. I was twelve years old—I was in the third grade, but I was as smart as the kids in the fifth grade.

I heard that jobs were opening up in a new agricultural project and they were hiring a lot of people. So I went back to my relative the District Commissioner and told him I wanted a job. He told me I was too young for that job—it was a fifteen-mile walk outside the village, morning and evening, thirty miles each day. He said it would be too hard for me, but I said, "Never mind. I want it. I can do it." So he talked to somebody who sent word to me to come to work. And I went to work.

The boss lived in Mango Village and gave a ride to me and a couple of other people. Mama would wake me up at about six o'clock—I took a shower and ate a little breakfast or else took something to eat with me. Mama walked with me halfway, until she saw someone she knew who was going my way, so that I could walk with them. I would wait in front of the hotel until they came to pick me up in the Land Rover.

Fatoun lost her job with the white lady—Antony's father talked to that lady and told her how bad black girls were and how he had found out that Fatoun was playing with white boys. She asked me if I could talk to my uncle about a job for her too. I did, and after that we used to ride together. We had to be at work by eight o'clock. The first few weeks were bad. We were farming groundnuts and cotton and papayas and other fruits, and my back got tired from picking cotton and pulling up the groundnut plants. At the end of the day you were nearly dead—you were finished! After two weeks, my back was so sore! But when you're young, you know, you don't care, and besides, we were getting paid well—150 shillings a month—and that was good money, because when we were working for the white families I had been getting 110 shillings.

We got to know everybody, and they were kind to us, so I asked the boss if we could do some other kind of work—maybe clean the office—because the work in the fields was too hard for us; we were both too young, the youngest there. There were two women who sat in the office all day long—they were big women and they could each do more work than both of us together. I asked the boss why he didn't let us do their job and let them work in the fields like the other people. He said, "Maybe that's a good idea. You two are too young. You just sit here in the office —one of you can keep the books, and the other can make tea for us." Fatoun was fourteen by now, and she knew how to read and write Italian better than I did, so she filled out the names— who came in the morning and who didn't, who took a hoe and who didn't—and I checked the hoes in and out and kept the key. It was an easy job. But we didn't just sit there—we used to make tea and roasted corn for everybody else, and people liked us.

There was an Arab grocery shop close to our house, and the 150 shillings I was making each month used to go straight to that Arab man. I would pay our monthly bill. I told Mama to get five shillings of food each day—anything that she could buy with five shillings. He used to give her two shillings in cash for the market and three shillings' worth of sugar, tomatoes, pasta, rice…whatever she wanted!

CHAPTER
7

After about three months I went back to my uncle the District Commissioner and told him I wanted to change jobs. There was another job, as a waitress at the big hotel—the place for government officials to stay when they were in town. The hotel was closer to my house, and it paid the same as my job in the farm project. He said, "Why not? Good idea!"

I worked an eight-hour shift: either six a.m. to two p.m., or two p.m. to ten p.m. The manager and everybody knew me, and all the older people liked me. The manager of the hotel had told me that if I was working the morning shift, I could come to work at seven o'clock, because I had such a long way to come. I had to cross the river from the other side, and early in the morning hippos were grazing along the road sometimes, and it was dangerous. So the manager said, "Take your time. Leave the house at six-thirty and be at work at seven." That was wonderful. I said, "Thank you, Uncle."

I began to earn good tips. Every day I was getting four shillings, five shillings, six shillings, sometimes as much as ten shillings. When the ministers of the government were around, I sometimes got almost thirty shillings, because they tipped better. I was quick and fast; I never said no when they asked me to do something, I never said, "I'm tired." I did everything. I was happy and I was trying to get along with people so I could have some friends.

Antony was still in Europe. He'd been there five months, and I'd heard his mother missed him—he was her youngest child and her only son. I was lonely without him and I really missed him, but I thought I would never see him again. I started talking with other boys, and I liked some of them, but not the way I liked Antony.

One day, when I got home from work at about six o'clock, my mama told me a lady was waiting for me. I recognized her; her husband worked for Antony's father. She said she wanted to ask me about my job at the hotel, because she would like to get a job there too. She said goodbye to my mama, but she wanted me to go outside so she could ask me a question about the job. I went out with her, and she told me, "Aman, I was lying to your mother about the job. What would you like most of all in your life?" I said, "What do you mean? I like a lot of things...." She said, "Are you missing anybody a lot?" I said, "Yes, I'm missing somebody...." She said, "Who? You want to see that person? Come on, tell me." I said, "Probably I won't ever see him again." She said, "Come on, don't say that." Finally I said to her, "What is your problem anyway, what do you want? First you said you wanted to ask me something about my job, now you're shifting to another subject. What is it?" She said, "Somebody you love is over at my house."

I thought: Somebody I love a lot is in her house? I love my mother, and she's right here in my house. I didn't think about Antony, I didn't think he was ever coming back. I said, "My mother's inside my house here, my brothers and my sisters...I don't know who's in your house!" She said, "Come on...see!"

When I walked through their fence into their *daash*, her husband, Khamisi, and the children and Antony were all sitting there. It was him! I couldn't believe it was him. I was dirty, I had just come back from work, I had walked a mile or two and I was tired and sweaty. But when I saw him, Allah! I hugged him and kissed him—I had never kissed him, we had never kissed before that day. We kissed and we kissed and we kissed. His mouth tasted so sweet to me. We held each other, we hugged each other, we kissed each other. We were still outside in the *daash*. After we had kissed for a long, long time, we realized that we weren't alone, and we looked at each other and laughed. Khamisi laughed too, and said for us to go to his room if we wanted privacy—besides, he said, he didn't want anyone else to see us. We weren't doing anything, we just wanted to be together so we could talk. We went to Khamisi's room and we sat on his bed, and we were looking at each other and hugging each other, and I couldn't believe that this was my Antony. He had brought me a ring, and a watch, and a gold necklace, and a scarf, and underwear, and...a pair of shoes, I think. Those were the first gifts I had ever received from a friend, and the first gold. When you are hungry for a lot of things you don't have, and you get all of them at once, it's just too much. I felt I had everything.

We decided to see each other once a week at Khamisi's house —no more meetings outside, anywhere, for our sakes. He went to school in the morning and took a part-time job as a surveyor in the afternoon—helping the men who planned to build houses and streets. He was sixteen—he had a little money, so he could come to where I worked and drink coffee or a soft drink. Sometimes he would come alone, sometimes with his friends. When he came with his friends I liked it better, because I felt more comfortable—I could talk to his friends instead of to him, and that way I thought people wouldn't be as likely to say anything about us. I couldn't go with him, because there was always somebody there who I didn't want to see me with him. It was a nice time for us though—we had each other, and it was lovely.

But they couldn't leave us alone—his father, first of all. He was a real *fascista* and he hated blacks, and imagine—his son going with a black girl? Unh-unh. He was a bad man with a bad mouth. He used to come to our place and get red in the face and scream at Mama and tell her he would shoot me, her, and anybody else if they didn't keep me away from his son. My mama used to shout back at him in Somali, "We'll kill your son if you don't keep him away from our daughter." Every time he heard a new piece of gossip about Antony and me, he would come to our house—bringing Khamisi as his interpreter! Khamisi was the only Somali he knew. But Khamisi never said anything about Antony and me. He always kept our secret. He and his wife were very trustworthy. He must have been afraid, because if Antony's father had ever found out he would have lost his job and his life. Antony's father thought black people were dirty, and he didn't want to get dirty. My mama felt the same way about Europeans. She hated the gossip she heard about us. Everybody was telling her I was a *sharmuuto*. She was embarrassed, and my father's sons were after me...my whole family was embarrassed. Life was a fight all the time...all the time. Unhappy. But Antony and I, we didn't care what they did or what they said, because we loved each other. If I didn't see him, sometimes I couldn't sleep, Rahima. And it was the same for him. I took such a risk, and he did the same thing.

And we were all growing up. I was doing well at work, I gave my salary to Mama, and I was saving a little from my tips to buy my own clothes. I was also getting help through Antony.

He could get all kinds of food—fruits and vegetables, and eggs and bread—through the commissary for free, and he used to send me fifty kilos of fruit through Khamisi every week. I gave it to my mama, and she sold the whole batch at one time to other people who sold it in the market. And she started a new business, taking butter to another town to sell and bringing back raffia to make into baskets and mats to sell in the market. We were doing much better. We were getting our life together. But there was always this problem: Antony and I were growing up well, but the problem grew too—when you grow up, you want to see things your way. For a year and a half we could be together only once or twice a month, because his daddy kept him under control and my family did the same thing with me.

One day it was the big 'Id—our Islamic holiday—and there was a huge party, and dancing everywhere. We had worked out a plan. He and two friends would rent a car, and they would meet Fatoun and me later, around nine-thirty in the evening.

Fatoun, my niece, and I left the house at about two in the afternoon, because there was dancing going on outside the city. It's a big holiday, our 'Id. They sell drinks and food and candies. Everybody puts on new clothes, a lot of the women have henna in their hair, and everybody is clean. Country people come, city people come. The little 'Id is the feast that follows Ramadan— the month of fasting. At the little 'Id we dance for three nights; at the big 'Id, we dance for six days.

At the beginning, people are just looking and walking around. The Italians come to watch and take photographs. Somalis don't like photographs. So sometimes they stone the Italians, but they still come. When the dancing starts, the men are on one side and the women on one side: we face each other. Two or three of the men start dancing, dancing, and as the music gets faster they jump as high as they can, and then each touches the woman he wants. It means it's your turn when he touches you, he prefers you, he wants to see you dance. Then the women do the same thing: go in the centre and dance and dance and dance. When they're about to finish, each touches a man, and the man goes back in to the centre, and does the same thing again. Everybody dances like that until four or five in the morning, when the moon is a big light that shows everything. It's beautiful, beautiful.

So that night we wandered around and had fun until it got dark. Then we went to the place where we had agreed to meet, and waited for Antony. He came at a quarter to nine. I was learning to tell time with the watch he had given me. There were so many people in the narrow street, the cars had to drive slowly. We rode in the car and covered our heads with our scarves so no one would recognize us. But Ahmed, my brother's son, who was a big boy and married—he was the one who used to whip me most of the time and find me all the time, me and Antony—found out where we were, and he was after me. I don't know how he found us. His sister was one of the girls with me; I was in front with the driver and Antony, and Ahmed's sister, Fatoun, and another friend of Antony's were in the back. The car was going very slowly because of all the people. We were just leaving the area where people were dancing, when Ahmed caught up with us.

He opened the door of the car, grabbed me by the hair, and pulled me out. When Antony tried to help me, he slapped Antony in the face. When he slapped Antony, his friend began yelling in Italian, "Let's get out of here before they all kill us... let's get out of here!" and they told the girls to get out. And Antony had to leave. Ahmed dragged me by the hair, kicking and slapping me, all the way home. He told Mama that if she couldn't keep me away from this white boy, he was going to kill me or send me to another part of the country, and they would never see me or hear my name again. Mama got mad and she said, "I'm tired of all of you. Nobody can kill my little daughter. Nobody can touch my daughter. I'll take all of you to the court and put you in jail. If any of you touches my daughter again, you'll see what I'm going to do." And that gave me a little courage.

So what I did was, I went straight to the police station, with my face covered with bruises and blood. I told them who had beaten me. They arrested Ahmed the same night. But his father came to the police station soon afterwards and bailed him out, because he was in the police force too, and he worked with the District Commissioner. The police told him to stay away from me—I had told them he was going to kill me, and they said they would come and arrest him if anything happened to me.

But Antony and I couldn't see each other. Antony's father had seen Antony's face, and Antony had told him what had happened. And people talked, because many people had seen it. His father made him quit his job and stay home in the evening. Now it was really hard for me to see him. I had to go inside the European compound, because he couldn't come out, it was too dangerous for him. I used to wake up in the middle of the night, when my mother had gone to sleep, at about twelve or one o'clock in the morning. I would have a meeting arranged with Fatoun. We would meet at about one o'clock in the morning, which was a bit risky, and crawl through the barbed-wire fence around the European compound. We were skinny, so all we needed was a little hole. One of us held the fence while the other crawled through.

I knew Antony was sleeping—I knocked softly on his window, and he would come to the window. He couldn't come out be-cause there were bars on the window, but to see his face and hear his voice and touch his body was enough. I was happy with that. Fatoun would go off and see her boyfriend when Antony woke up—if Antony didn't wake up, I would go with her to see her boyfriend. Sometimes Antony and I would see each other once a week, sometimes every two weeks, like before, but now it was my turn to take the risk.

I didn't have any friend who knew Antony, except for Khamisi and Fatoun, but I had another girlfriend, Zaytuun, who was almost like a sister to me. We were close neighbours, and our families liked each other.

Zaytuun was older than I. She was small, with big eyes and light skin, sixteen and from Ethiopia. Her father had made her quit school when she was twelve. He had seven girls and three boys, but she was the eldest, and she was needed at home to take care of the house because her mother was sick in bed all the time and couldn't go out. She was like the mother of the house. And she was a real support to me too, because she was the only person who knew everything about me—she even knew about Antony. She always listened to my problems and offered me a shoulder to cry on and gave me good advice, and her mama did too. She was even more than a sister to me. I loved the whole family as if it were my own.

One day I wasn't working and I was over at her house. In those days we were learning to smoke cigarettes, and her place was the only place we could hide and smoke, because her brothers and sisters were in school and her daddy was at work and her mama stayed in bed in one room, so we had the rest of the house to ourselves. Zaytuun cooked spicy, hot food, and I liked it. On that day I went to their house to eat lunch around one and stayed there to smoke. I came back home at about two o'clock, and Khamisi's wife was there waiting for me. When I saw her—whew!—my heart began pounding, because she always brought good news, and I hadn't seen Antony for almost three weeks. She said, "Oh, I've come to ask you…." And I said, "Yes, I was going to come to your house tomorrow to tell you about the job." I had to lie to my mama, because I didn't want her to understand what was going on. I said, "I've got some good news about a job. They're going to have an opening soon…."

When we got outside, she said, "Antony is in my house. He's been there since ten-thirty this morning—where were you? He's a little angry, because he came early this morning…let's go." We went together, but I couldn't wait, I began to run, and I said, "I'll see you later…."

I ran to her house, and then me and Antony, we started kissing again and hugging again. Everything was beautiful that night. The thing I liked most about him was that he wasn't acting as though he was white, he was just a normal person. If you ate, everything you ate, no matter what it was, he would eat it with you. He didn't care; he was just like you. Rahima, you are the second person, the second white person, I've seen like that, who would eat anything—and Antony was like that, no matter what you ate, he would eat with you. Tea was his favourite drink. He used to drink beer too, but I didn't know at that time what it was. But his favourite drink was tea. That night we had a lot of tea, and we played cards, because he knew the way we played. We had dinner there. They cooked dinner, and we ate flat wheat bread and fried meat with them. They were such kind people, people who understood what love was.

When it was time to leave, it was late and it was dark. But I knew all the corners. So I said to him, "Why don't we leave together and sneak home and be together a little longer?" But Khamisi said to us, "You should be careful. Maybe somebody is out there waiting for you. Why don't you go separately and then nobody will say anything. Antony, you stay here a while and let

Aman go on ahead, and then I will take you to your gate, where you will be safe." So we took his advice, and that night we both got home safely.

The next week I went to Mogadishu with Mama to see my cousin Habib because he was seriously ill. We stayed with Habib for ten days and then came home again. I went to Fatoun's to ask her if she had seen Antony while I was gone. She told me she hadn't seen him, but her boyfriend saw him every day and he was fine. I asked her to go with me late that night so I could see him and she said she would, because she wanted to see her boyfriend too. That night, after everyone had fallen asleep, I got up—slowly, because I slept in the same bed as my mother—and went to the bathroom. I waited a few minutes to see if my mother would come after me before I dressed, and left.

At about twelve o'clock, Fatoun was outside waiting for me. We went through our secret place in the fence to Antony's house. Antony didn't wake up when I knocked on his bedroom window, so I went with her to see her boyfriend. She did the same thing —knocked on his window—and he woke up and came out. We all said hello; I waited while they kissed and hugged. We left and on the way back we stopped at Antony's house again. I knocked on his window again, but he still didn't answer. I begged Fatoun to stay with me a little longer, because I was hoping I could wake him up. Finally he did wake up. And he couldn't believe it was me. We didn't stay long. I just let him know I was back and talked to him a little bit, and then we went home.

We continued seeing each other that way. We were never free and we were afraid of both our families. But we didn't care. We took the risk, because we knew we loved each other and wanted to be with each other. People didn't understand that, because we were different colours. But we were colour-blind—especially him, because he never cared what colour I was. We used to wish we were the same colour, so we could be together for the rest of our lives, but that was impossible.

One evening we arranged to see each other at Khamisi's house again. We spent a wonderful evening, and when it was time to go home, we decided to leave together, because it was late and it was raining and we thought there wasn't any danger. But we were wrong. There was somebody waiting for us—Ahmed. He had four others with him, and they were all big boys—sixteen or seventeen. They started to whip us badly, especially Antony. I started to cry for help, and Antony was fighting and shouting. I was bleeding from the mouth, and he was bleeding too. He fell down and was lying on the ground, and they were kicking him in the stomach and in the genitals. I fell down too, when they slapped me, but I got right up again and yelled for help. People came out of their houses, and that's when the boys ran away, because they didn't want to get arrested.

Two men took Antony to the hospital, and I went home. When Mama saw all the blood on me, she took me to the hospital. When we got there, Antony was already there, and so were policemen. The police looked at Antony and me with blood and bruises all over us, and they asked us, "Who did it?" I had to tell the police Ahmed's name and the other boys' names and my name, and the whole story of what happened. And they had to call Antony's father and mother.

Nobody had anything broken, just cuts. My lips were cut on both the top and the bottom, and he had some loose teeth and a cut on his face, and we both had bruises. His father and mother came to the hospital while we were still there. When his father found out that I was still the problem, he wanted to kill me, and if I hadn't had both the doctor and the police with me he would have killed me, but they held him back until he calmed down.

When the doctor finished with us, the police took us to the station. They arrested the two of us, along with Ahmed and his friends, and put all of us in jail for the rest of the night. I'm pretty sure Antony's father asked the police to put us in jail because he thought it would scare us. I couldn't sleep, because I had a fever and I was in pain from the beating and there was no bed to lie down on, not even a blanket or a pillow. My cell was just a small, dark, empty room. But I was glad to be there, because I knew I was safe from Antony's father. Antony's father had said that if Antony didn't promise to stay away from this girl and never go back to her and never speak to her, they should keep him in jail. They told me the same thing. They kept on asking me, "Are you going to stay away from Antony?" I said to the policeman, "No, never, I will never leave Antony. Why should I leave him—just because he's white? I don't care, I don't see it that way, and Antony doesn't see it that way either." The policeman told me I was going to stay in jail until I said I would never see Antony again. And Antony was saying the same thing in a different part of the jail.

We spent the night in the jail—all six of us. Antony and I each had a cell to ourselves, and all the other boys were in another cell together. In the morning they asked us the same question again. Both of us said no, three or four times. At about noon they brought us both out, and my chief came with a police sergeant. The sergeant asked us why we had to go through this. Antony told him he loved me; he loved me as a human being, he loved me as a woman, he loved me as a girlfriend… every way. And he said he didn't see what was wrong with that, because his parents had brought him from Europe when he was three years old and he had grown up here, so he didn't feel different. My relatives were making this matter into a big thing, which he didn't believe in. I told them the same thing. The sergeant shook his head and said he felt sorry for us, and he smiled and said, "You're both smart. Do you know that?" We said yes, we knew that, and we didn't see why people were making such a big deal out of it—we were a boy and girl who liked each other, and we didn't feel any difference. He said, "That's wonderful. But the reality is that you're black and he's white, and God didn't create the two of you to become husband and wife. So the best thing for you to do, for your own sake, is to stay away from each other and listen to what your parents say. Because what they told you is the truth. You are not the same, and you should stay that way." He said he would let us go this time, but next time he would keep us in prison. We were frightened, so we said, "All right," and he let us go.

But the more I didn't see him, the more I loved him. The more I missed him, the more I wanted to go and see him. I didn't see the risk I was running—getting beaten and being arrested by the police and ruining my name. I didn't care, I just wanted him. But I was trying to be strong and stay away, for his sake, and for mine too. It was getting serious, and I was tired of being the bad girl all the time, because that's what everybody called me. I was trying to be the good girl they wanted me to be. I tried to be open and be friends with everybody and talk with everybody and just be nice, but it didn't work, you know, because nobody wanted it to. They wanted to see me as a bad person, so I was always the bad one.

One day, after almost two months, I decided to take the risk again and go inside the European compound. I knew going to his house was no problem when his daddy was at work, because his mother had been good to me when I used to work for the white people. His mother was a lovely woman—she never looked at me the way his daddy looked at me. She let me inside the house; she offered me something to drink and went about her own business. She knew I was talking to her son. Sometimes she would let me in and sometimes not, but she never said anything to offend me. Her face was never mean.

Then one day Antony begged Khamisi and asked if we could meet at his house again, and he said, "No problem." His wife sent a little girl with a message to me. I was really happy, because I knew what it was, and—whoosh!—I went there again.

This time Antony said he had to go back home early. He had told his daddy he was going to have dinner at his friend's house inside the European compound, and he said he didn't want to be late because he was scared his daddy might find out that he wasn't there. We had dinner at about eight, and when he said he wanted to leave it was after nine o'clock. I told him, "Yes, it's time to go, because I have to work in the morning, too." I wanted to stay, if he would stay. But he said he was scared, so I said, "Right, I understand...." But we stayed for a little while longer, kissing…because we had started to really learn how to kiss now. We didn't want to stop! Every time he wanted to leave, I held his hand and kissed him again. And then I left, because Khamisi told me that it was getting late and he had to take Antony to the gate before his daddy found out he wasn't at his friend's house.

When I left, I went straight home. Everybody had already gone to bed. I washed my face and hands and my feet and got into bed; Mama was already asleep. I lay there and tried to sleep, but I couldn't sleep, so I closed my eyes and thought about him. After about half an hour I heard a noise—people shouting and running. I sat up, alert, because every time I heard a noise I always thought it was something to do with Antony. Mama sat up too, and she said, "What's all that noise?" I said to her, "Mama, you can stay in bed. I'll go see what it is."

Before I even got outside I heard people shouting, "A white

boy died." I began to run along with the people. And there was Antony lying on the ground. They had hit him in the head with a tire iron, and they had stabbed Khamisi in the back two times with a knife; they had found out that I had been going over to Khamisi's house to see Antony, and that's why they killed him. They killed him as he was taking Antony to the compound. He left behind his pregnant wife and his three children because of me. The attackers thought they were both dead and they ran away. But Antony got up. He was bleeding everywhere, but he was strong. He made himself walk from where he had fallen to where the streetlight was, and people saw him.

There was blood all over his shirt. The first thing he said to me was "Khamisi is dying. Help Khamisi…." I held him. I kissed him. I cried. Then an ambulance came, and took him to the hospital. They wouldn't even let me ride in the ambulance with him. When they found Khamisi, it was too late. He was already dead.

The next morning Antony's father came to our house looking for me. He had a gun to kill me. But I wasn't there. My mama had taken me, the same night Khamisi died, to a different house. She knew I would be the next to die if Antony's father found me, because my father wasn't there to protect me. She told Antony's father that I had gone to Mogadishu. Antony's father almost attacked Mama, but the two men with him held him back. Mama told him that he would never see me again— that I would stay in the city.

Three days later, my father arrived from the interior. He took me back to his camp, where his two wives and his children and his animals were. I stayed there one month and seventeen days. My father took me there because he was angry with my mother. He told his wives and his children to watch me so I wouldn't leave. I had to stay, but I hated it there because I was too far from Antony and from home. Even though I was afraid of Antony's father, I felt I had to go back. I was looking for a way to escape, but I didn't know how, because there were always people with me.

After a while, my half-sister and I became friends and I told her the whole story, over and over and over. Finally she decided to take me back into town. My father had a lot of grown children at this place, and they took turns each week taking a camel into town all loaded with milk and butter and beans to sell in the market. So my half-sister promised me she would take me with her when her turn came. Remember Abdi, my father's foundling son, the one who gave me the good milk when I was sick? He was still living with my father. Now, when I look back, I think he felt like an outsider, even though we all loved him. He was always very kind to me. My half-sister said she would talk to him, because he went with them on the trips to town, and he wouldn't refuse to let me go. We just had to wait for her turn. It seemed like a whole year to me. Even though I had been born in the interior, I had grown up in Mango Village. Now everything seemed different to me. It was so dark at night, and the house only had a cloth door. You could hear the jackals and hyenas howling. And there were snakes too. I was scared, even though I slept with my sisters at night. I missed my mama and my bed, because out here I was sleeping on the ground.

Finally my sister told me to get ready. We were leaving the next day. I didn't have much with me—only my shoes and two dresses and one piece of cloth—so I got my things together. No one suspected my sister, because she was one of the girls who had been told to watch me to make sure I didn't run away. She said to me, "After you eat breakfast, leave the house just the way we always do." I went with the little children and played with the baby sheep and goats for a while, and then told them I had to go and pee. As soon as I got behind the bushes I ran and ran until I came to the place on the path where my sister had told me to wait. After a while I heard the sound of wooden camel bells—*galug, galug*—and there they were. We kept on going, with Abdi leading the camels and the two of us behind, laughing and happy, talking and jumping.

In the interior, neighbouring families help each other when they don't have a grown man in the family. Abdi had to make three stops to pick up some other families' older boys with their loaded camels. With everyone together, we travelled until nightfall and then stopped. After dinner, the boys hobbled the five camels' legs and made them sit down in a circle with the piles of butter, milk containers, and sacks of corn and beans. This worked like a fence, and we slept inside. I lay down closest to Abdi; my half-sister was next to me, and next to her the children from neighbouring families. We made a fire inside the ring of camels, and with Abdi to guard us, we felt very safe. I wasn't afraid now, and I was glad to be going home. I fell asleep.

The next morning we got up, went to pee, washed our hands and faces, and made tea, and then loaded up the camels and were on our way again. We walked until evening, after sunset, when we came into town. Suddenly I wasn't tired any more. I went straight to the house of my Ethiopian girlfriend, Zaytuun, to ask her about Antony. And she told me everything that had happened.

Antony had stayed five days in the hospital and three days in his house. After that he had been taken to Europe by his mother and father, and his father had left them there and had come back after a month. Antony was gone. That was it. Now I was really lost. Ahmed and my father's sons had killed Khamisi and they had taken Antony away from me. This time, he was far away, where I couldn't go, where I couldn't see him, where I couldn't reach him, where I couldn't even call him. Because I didn't know where Europe was or which way it was.

CHAPTER
8

NOW THE ONLY PERSON WHO understood was my girlfriend Zaytuun. She was there when I needed her. I did the same for her, but she did more for me because she was older. She was a lovely person. I loved her for that. I used to go to her place and cry, and talk about him, and she used to tell me good things: "He's coming back. It's not his fault…." I knew it wasn't his fault. Rahima, I went through hell for a couple of months. People started talking really badly about me. "Oh, her white boy is gone, her uncircumcised infidel lover is gone. She's trying to get another white boy…." Everybody was talking about me, saying bad things—young, old, men, women. Everybody knew me—"That girl." I couldn't sleep. I turned into an animal, because I was jealous too—I was jealous of those girls and of anybody who had more education or more money. I hated them. I knew people talked about me. I used to go and get water from the well. You wait in line with your vase until your turn comes. While you're waiting, you play and you talk. But I was always very sensitive. If somebody said something bad to me, I would fight. And everything I'd touch, I'd damage. I broke their vase, my family had to pay. I broke their necklace, my family had to pay. I hurt their ears...always something to pay! So even my family didn't like me because I was a trouble-maker. I was the bad one in the whole village, I was the bad girl.

I thought about becoming truly bad; if they're calling you bad anyway, you might as well do it. I talked to Zaytuun and told her, "If I don't fight, I don't think I will ever have peace. The only way I have is to fight and show them who I am." She said, "It's not a bad idea." She started to help me. She would talk with the girls and spy on them to see what they were saying about me. She would hear a girl say this and this, and she would come back and say, "So-and-so said, 'This, this, and this.'" I would go straight to the girl and say, "Why are you saying this about me? Is it true you said that?" If she said yes, I didn't wait for anything else. I would slap her and beat her. I carried a little knife with me, to scare people, and sometimes I would cut them. I didn't care. It was a good thing I was strong. Even though I was skinny, I was strong. I never fell down. I was angry and I had this spirit, and that was what made me very strong.

I started with the girls, and then I fought with everybody. Anybody who looked at me, anybody who said something bad about me, pow! A fight. I didn't care who it was—man, woman, I didn't care. Fighting: that was my revenge.

Now everybody, especially the girls and the young women, were scared of me. I even took money from the girls. Movie money, and Coca-Cola and candy they used to sell inside the movie—Rahima, every girl would send me something. I got everything for free. After a while, when I went to the movies, I would have three or four tickets waiting for me. "Fatima left this. Khadija left that. So-and-so left that." Respect.

During those days, I went to the movies as often as I could. One night I snuck out of our house while Mama was sleeping, jumping over the fence. Mama wanted to whip me when I came back. So I jumped the fence again, and I went to my brother's house and slept there. Early in the morning, I came back home and started to make some bread, to bring to Mama to sell in the market. I was sitting on the four-legged stool, and I felt something hot between my legs...something pushing me...something not quite right. I tried to get up, but it was like I was glued to the stool. I pushed the stool down, and I looked around me. It was...I couldn't believe it...blood, a big circle of blood.

There was a lady who lived in one of our round houses. I knocked at her door. I called "Halima! Sister Halima!" And she said, "Come in, come in, what is it?" I told her, "Look at what happened to me, look at what's happening!" I lay down on the floor, opened my legs, and let her look at me. When she saw the blood, she said, "Ohhh! I saw you running last night—when you jumped over the fence, look at what happened. You split your circumcision, and now you have to be sewn again!" I said, "No-o-o-o! I don't believe this!" I ran. At home, I took a mirror, I went to the bathroom, I looked at myself. There was a lot of blood. I couldn't believe all that blood could come through this little hole. I thought maybe I was dying. I just *hated* the blood! I looked again in the mirror and I saw I was sewn. "I'm still sewn!"

I went back to Halima. I said, "You're a liar! I'm still sewn! Where is this blood coming from?" And then she told me, she said, now you're a woman. I said, "What do you mean? I was a woman before." "Now," she said, "you're a woman, you have your first period." Then I became a little happy. I considered myself mature, you know. And I ran to the market to tell Mama. Mama was happy. She smiled at me. "Now you're a young lady!"

I kept going to the movies. One night I saw a film about a pilot, and that was what I wanted to be. Ah, I'd think, I can fly, fly, fly! Ever since I was a little girl and I saw my first airplane flying, I wanted to be a pilot. My dream was to have what we didn't have then. I used to say to my mama, did you see the judge's home, the government official's home? Those are big houses where the Italian bosses live. The judge's house was white, and it was next to my aunt's farm. Her farm was close to the river, so it grew every fruit…every fruit. There was so much I liked about that place: you could watch the river running, you could climb up in the tree and get the cacao fruit. When you opened the fruit, it was white like cotton, with big, black seeds. I thought it would be beautiful to have the judge's house and my auntie's farm as one home. That was what I dreamed about: being a pilot, and having a house and a green, rich farm full of every fruit, lots of cattle, and all my family around me.

I was still being bad when my grandmama died. First Antony died for me—because it was like death when he left—and now my grandmama. Why did everyone go that I loved? Now I changed—became another person—cool, no talking, no fighting, no argument. I wanted to stay home and not see people, because people made me angry. My grandmama was like a mama to me, because my mama—she was like a father: she went out and did the family's business, bringing in the money, the food, and everything. Inside the house was Grandmama. And Grandmama was a small, gentle woman. When Mama talked you could hear her in every room, but when Grandmama spoke, I remember, her voice was always gentle and soft. Sometimes I loved Grandmama even more than my mama. And now I had lost her too. Rahima, half of my life was gone. I was there, but I wasn't there. At one time my mind was on Antony, and the rest of the time on my grandmama. I would lie down on the bed and think about them. If somebody came to me and wanted to talk, I didn't want to talk to them, because they would break my concentration, so I would say, "Shhhhhh," and keep right on lying there.

I stayed like that for a couple of months, until I couldn't take it any more. I couldn't breathe any more. Now I started to go out and breathe again. The first thing I did was go back to see about my job in the hotel. I got my job back. My sister Hawa had married again after Grandmama died, and I started going to her house to visit. So there was work, and my girlfriend's house, and my sister's house. I was very cool—totally different from the way I had been before Grandmama died. Then I was like an animal—wild, out there fighting every second, every minute, all the time. But now I wanted peace. Thanks to Allah and Zaytuun, I went back to being Aman.

I was still working at the hotel, but Mama's business was going downhill, because when Grandmama died she had to spend a lot of money for the funeral. We had seven days of reading the Qur'an, and people came to eat and to give sympathy to Mama—seven days, day and night, twenty-four hours. We had food ready all the time for all the people, some of them came from a long way away in the country. After that, Mama was short of money and couldn't afford to go on a long trip to get butter and the other things she sold. When you're really poor and you're angry, you see things the wrong way. Mama was down when Grandmama died, like me. That's why I went back to work, so the money could go to Mama—the 150 shillings I made I brought home, plus all the tips I got. Now I was growing, and I began to buy all my own clothes. Before, Mama bought them for me. (Daddy used to buy clothes for me for special holidays too, when he was around.) I began to buy things I liked: shoes, a scarf, a belt. But I was sad because of

Mama's situation. All I could think of was how to make more money—that was my one idea. After Antony went and Grand-mama went, there were so many changes, and so much pain. The more I grew, the more the problems grew, and I got tired thinking about how to make money to help Mama and everyone else I loved, and myself.

After a while, I started going out. I met some other boys—especially one, an Arab boy—he was like me, a very sad boy. His girlfriend—the girl he loved—had married another man, because her daddy had given her to another man. He had asked to be transferred to Mango Village so he wouldn't have the pain of seeing her all the time. We offered each other a shoulder to cry on. We talked about our problems. I told mine and he understood, and he told his and I understood.

By this time I was grown. I was born in 1952 and now it was 1965. I was thirteen. I had had my menstruation two times. I remember I was thirteen years and seven months old when I was married.

An uncle on my mother's side—his wife had just had a baby, so he called me one Friday to help her. He took me in his Land Rover to the market to buy the food. He gave me money and told me what they needed, and he waited for me in the Land Rover while I went to buy the things, and when I was finished we went to their house. That's when I first met him—my future husband. He was a friend of my uncle's from Mogadishu. My uncle had a maid who was a big woman, but she had Fridays off. So I cooked for them and washed the dishes, because when women have a new baby they don't cook unless they have to. They have to rest and stay in the house for forty days and play with the baby.

After this man saw me at their house helping out two or three times, he started to talk to me. I knew something was going on, but I didn't know what it was. They talked about me, and looked at me when I took things to the table and when I brought them something and when I dumped the ashtrays. He looked at me in a different way.

He began to come over to their house almost every Friday, and it went on for about two months like that. My uncle told me, "This man is my best friend." He told me about the man's important job. He told me the man's brother was a government minister. He told me they were a high-level family. He told me the man liked me and the main reason he came to the house was me. I said, "Oh, that's why you all talk about me and look at me so funny." And he said, "Yes, you're a clever girl, you understand. Think about what I've said." And then he used words I hated: he said, "Think about your mother. All of you need help and this man can help." I hated that. I really did. The first thing in my life was my mama, because of all she had been through and all she had done for me, and I didn't need someone else reminding me, but that's what he did. I felt hurt. I got angry and told him, "I'll think about it," and I left.

I walked and walked for miles and miles, just thinking about what he had said and what I felt, and tears were running down my clothes. I was talking out loud to myself—repeating what he had said and thinking why he had said that—because of money? I walked until I couldn't walk any more. I sat down and got angry and cried again, and I prayed to Allah to help us. I sat and I thought and thought and thought. And I decided to go for it—to get married to him. I didn't have money. I didn't have Antony. I would get married, at least to get money and be somebody. I thought: Maybe you can even see him—your boyfriend—one day. Because you'll have money, you can go back to school and finish your education—because Antony was from an educated family. I thought maybe I could get away from Mango Village.

In Somalia, in those days, if you don't marry you're nothing. You have to marry, and young, too. Otherwise you'll disgrace your family! It's a disgrace if you don't marry at fourteen, fifteen, sixteen. By the time a girl's eighteen she's too old and it's considered that nobody wants her. At twenty you are superold. I couldn't wait, myself, to get married. Hawa was already married when she was my age. I felt like nobody would want me. They were saying I was bad, so I thought I might never get a chance. I wanted to show them I could make it. And I knew that once I married, I could divorce and they wouldn't say I was a girl, they'd say I was a woman, a *divorced* woman. I'd have a little freedom. I could do what I wanted.

So I decided to marry this man.

I went home. I was dirty, and I had tears all over my face, and my feet were filthy, because I had been running and walking fast. I took a shower. I was tired, and I fell asleep. The next day, after work, I stopped at my uncle's house and told him I had been thinking about what he had said and I agreed to marry his friend if he would accept what I wanted. My uncle said, "What do you want?" I told him I didn't want him to tell my father's side or anybody; we would just go get married, he and I, and after we came back we could tell my father. But before the marriage, I didn't want him to ask my father or wait for my father to give me away or ask my brothers. Because usually your family negotiates. The man has to come and ask your family, and if your family says no, and you really love him, you run away together and get married. From where you live, it has to be a hundred miles away. The Muslim religion doesn't allow you to marry close to your family if they don't approve. But if the men in the family say yes, they negotiate how the husband will make your life, how he'll pay and what he'll give the family. They're not selling their daughters, it's about respect. "I raised this beautiful daughter"—and they expect something in return. And it's not buying either. When your daughter gets married and she leaves, there's an empty, empty space. A gift makes you not so sad about that. Also, a father values his daughter, and he needs to know the man won't divorce her or mistreat her. The more money the husband pays, the more the father knows he loves his daughter. And he knows the husband won't want to divorce her if he's given a lot for her. If he hasn't—easy come, easy go. So a large gift lets the father know she'll have some security. That's how our culture is.

But I didn't want to do it that way—unh-unh—because that way they would get the money. I wanted to get the money from him first, without letting my family know. I told him if he agreed to that, fine, but I didn't want anybody to know until afterwards.

My uncle said, "Why are you being that way? Most of the girls like people to ask their father so they don't get a bad name. The way you want it, it's as though you ran away with him, as though you were nothing." He was right. The girls I knew all waited until somebody came along and asked their family for them and paid a lot of money and camels and guns and horses and gold and clothes. He said, "You should be proud. You've got a man with a name and money, and he's ready to do whatever you want—pay whatever you want—because he likes you, and you don't want to do that. Why?" But I didn't want to tell him; even though he was from my mother's lineage, I still didn't want to tell him what my plan was. So I said, "I feel shy, because he's old and from another lineage." He said, "I understand," and he said he was going to tell his friend that I had said yes, and that the marriage would be in a week or two. I also told my uncle to let him know I wanted money—a lot of money. I said I wanted gold and clothes, and I wanted cash in advance. He said, "Don't worry about it!"

I went to Zaytuun's house. I didn't tell her, because I didn't want her to give me good advice, like a sister, even though I knew I was doing things wrong. I wanted to get money so I could help my mama. But even if Zaytuun had known that, she would have told me to stop, or she would have told my mama to stop me, and I didn't want her to do that. My mouth wanted to tell her, but I kept it to myself. She knew I was keeping something from her and kept on asking me, with a nice face, smiling; she tried to make me happy so I would tell her. When I didn't, she got angry and said she wasn't going to speak to me any more. But I still wouldn't tell her.

That man came on Friday again, and my uncle invited me over to help them. But this time I wanted to watch him, to see how he looked. I told them, "I'll just come. I don't feel well today. I don't want to do anything. I'll just come and keep your wife company." I didn't want to work and have him watch me. I wanted to watch him and see what he looked like, because I hadn't looked at his face that much. Because when you're a girl, you don't look big people right straight in the face that much. You look down. I had never looked at him completely. This time, I wanted to see him. I wanted to make sure of what I was getting into.

I felt shy, and my heart was pumping, and I was thinking, "What am I going to say to him if he starts to talk to me?" I had never talked to a big man. I had never dated a big man. I had dated big boys, but I had never dated an old man. That's what he was—an old man.

When I got to my uncle's house, I went into his wife's room, but I left the door open so I could see him. But the only time I could see him was when I went out to the bathroom or the kitchen. Every time I went by, I stole a glance at him. Sometimes he would catch me looking at him, sometimes not. The first eye contact is kind of a little shame. He was a clean old man, nice skin, a lot of soft hair…a very nice man. But he was like my grandfather! He was an old man. He was fat, short, light-skinned, with a wide face. He was fifty-five—something like that—fifty-six…close to sixty, with a big stomach, a clean body, and clean clothes. You could tell he was from a good family.

The men ate, and I ate a little bit with my uncle's wife. Of course she knew about everything, because her husband had told her his friend wanted me. After we had all eaten separately, the men called me to have tea with them—with just the two of them in the living room. She told me, "Go see them. Don't be shy. Be clever. Be smart." She was young and cute too, and she was married to this man I called "Uncle", who was older than her, but he had a good job, which brought her good money, and she said, "Did you think I married *him* for love? I married him for money. Go!"

I went out into the living room and sat and drank tea with them. The man asked me a lot of questions about my family, especially about my father. I answered all his questions—I guess he was checking whether or not I was stupid, and he could tell I wasn't. He started liking me…the way I talked.

That day, after we finished drinking tea and talking, he gave me two hundred shillings. That was a lot of money in those days; it was more than I earned in a month. Our family was living on five shillings a day. So I took it. All I wanted, anyway, was money. From that day on he brought me things every week —clothes and a watch and gold chains and rings and soaps. He used to bring me everything. I really liked it. The more he gave me, the more I liked him; it was like that. Now I couldn't wait to get married.

After three weeks we decided to get married. He spent a night in our town with my uncle so he could pick me up in the morning. I stopped by the night before to make the arrangements. I told him I wanted to leave town early so people wouldn't see me riding with him. He said, "All right." I went straight to see my niece, who was like a sister to me. I told her I would need her the next morning. It took me about two hours to explain to her what was going on, but finally she understood and she agreed to go with me. I went home and had dinner with Mama. I had a nice talk with her and made her happy and told her a couple of funny stories to make her laugh, and cooked tea for her. We had a great, great dinner, and then I asked her if I could spend the night over at my niece's because it was Ramadan and there would be feasting and reading of the Qur'an over there. She said, "All right." I took the dress I wanted to wear with me and went back to my niece's house.

In the morning we woke up at six-thirty. I had told my mama that I was going to work from there that day and I would see her the following evening when I came home. But I wasn't really going to work, you know, I was going to get married.

We left town in the morning—him, me, and his driver, and my niece. We went to another town—because, as I said, when you run away and you're young you have to go a hundred miles from the town you live in if your daddy or your brother doesn't give you in marriage. We were going to another district quite far away.

You can marry at any age if your father approves; but if you're on your own, you have to be over fifteen. I was so young; I was tall and skinny, and you could tell I was young, even though I was smart-talking. My husband said he was going to pick up one of his friends to be a witness in case the magistrate suspected I was too young. This man could say he knew me, he was my uncle, and I was sixteen, eighteen, twenty—whatever. So we picked him up, and he went with us. When we came before the magistrate, I lied—I told him I was seventeen. The magistrate looked at me. The other man told him yes—I was seventeen.

That was how we got married. After, my husband paid the magistrate, and we took his friend back to his house and my husband gave him some money. My husband wanted us to spend the night at his house, but I told him, "No, I want to go home." I was afraid that if I spent the night at his house something might happen, and I didn't want that. I didn't want him to touch me at all. So I told him, "No…unh-unh, take me home." He said, "What if we stop at my niece's house so they can meet you? I told them about you." "All right," I agreed, "but not to your house." We went to his niece's house, and they offered us tea and cakes and soft drinks, and everybody was saying, "Oh, she's young and cute. She's pretty," and asking me what my name was. I was shy and embarrassed. When we said our goodbyes, they all said they would see me soon.

In the car, about halfway back, I told him he had to give me some money. I wanted to go to Mogadishu; half my family was there—my father's side and my mother's side, cousins, aunts and uncles. I said I needed to go there to buy myself some gold and some clothes. He said, "Sure, don't worry. I'll give you some." He asked me how much I wanted, and I told him I wanted two hundred shillings. He said, "Sure, no problem." Rahima, I was happy, I was very happy. I said, "All right!" He had a little suitcase, and he opened it right there. He gave me two hundred shillings and said, "If you need some more, let me know." Rahima, I had never had money so easily. I couldn't believe my heart inside me.

He took me to my father's house, because I was scared to go to my mother because of what I had done. I thought Daddy wouldn't be there. But when he took me to my father's house, Rahima, he *was* there. He had just come in from the bush that evening. I wasn't usually that scared of my father, but now I had made a big mistake.

Before we went to my father's house we had stopped at my uncle's house—the uncle at whose house I had met my husband —and my uncle had come with us to talk to all the men on my father's side. But my father wasn't doing his duties as chief that night. He was at home. So what we did was, when we got inside my father's house, we separated—my niece and I went to one of the round houses, and the men went to another.

You know, Rahima, as soon as I got back to Mango Village and saw my father's family, I realized the mistake I had made. I changed my mind. I decided I wanted to be divorced and give him back his money, because I was scared. They took a long, long time to discuss it—almost three hours. We sent the little boys to listen to what they were talking about, and the boys would come back and tell us. Every time they came back they would say my daddy didn't want it. He was saying to my husband, "An old man like you—how did you get married to my daughter? Who gave you permission to run away with my daughter? Aren't you ashamed?" My uncle on my mother's side was trying to calm him down. But my father was saying, "Go get your chief! I want to talk to your chief, not to a half-person, a half-man like you." He was really angry. They couldn't finish the matter that night, so my husband had to leave. Daddy called me and my brother, and they started yelling at me: "Why did you do this?" I was really scared, and I told him I wanted a divorce. "Give me a divorce. You're saying I'm too young to be married to him anyway, so I'm not married to him. I want a divorce."

They yelled at my niece too: "Why didn't you tell anybody? You know she's thirteen—you should have stopped her!" My brother took me to my mama's house and told her what had happened. She couldn't believe it either—she yelled, and asked my brother, "Where did she meet this old man?" He said it wasn't his family's fault. It was her side. I told her he was right —it was her cousin who had introduced us.

The next morning my niece told me my husband had come, with his chief and two or three other old men from different lineages, to talk to my father. They came over to our house around one in the afternoon and said that an agreement had been reached and that they had performed the ceremony again, with my father there, to make the marriage valid. They explained to my mother what had happened, and she had to accept it—there was nothing she could do, but she was so angry!

And I was angry too, because things weren't going the way I had asked Daddy to do them. I had asked him to get me a divorce. I had told him, "I don't want him. I made a mistake. I won't do it again…." But it didn't help. My father said, "You chose him," and he had married me to him. He told me that since nobody knew I had run away with this man, we should only tell people about the second marriage, because otherwise it would be too embarrassing for the family. So that's what I did—and though I put the whole blame on my father, it really was my fault.

I went to talk to Zaytuun, to tell her how I had changed my mind and how I didn't want to be married now, and how it had all happened. She asked me why I had done it. Why had I taken his money? I told her, "Well, I knew Mama would stop it if she knew, but I needed the money for myself and for her. Don't you see how down my mother is? Don't you see that she doesn't go out and do her business any more? She doesn't have any money." I told her I was also doing it for Khamisi's family, because I never forgot him, and I gave his wife some money, but I wanted to give her more. "But now I want out." She said, "Aman, it's too late. Your father agreed, and your whole family has accepted it. Now if you do stupid things"—because I said I was going to run away with the money—"if you do that your family will have to pay all the money back, and then you'll get cursed by your mother and father and by all the people. Don't do that. Wait until you go to his house, and then do what you want. But until you go to his house, don't run away. Your mother will have a terrible shock because she won't know where you have gone, and your father the same, and everybody else who loves you. Stay, and go to the big city with him, and then tell him you don't want him."

I had thought it was easy to be married, but it wasn't… marriage was something else altogether. But I couldn't forget Antony. No matter what I did, no matter who I went with, he was always on my mind. He was always there, no matter how much pain I had, no matter how sick I was, no matter how angry I was, whether I was at work or at home. I saw him in my dreams most of the time, and I said one day I would see him. I decided to go with this man I was married to, and get as much money as I could so I could go to Europe and see Antony. I thought it was that easy; that was my dream.

CHAPTER
9

So I STAYED AT HOME FOR TWO
months. My husband and my father made me quit my job because I was married. Once a girl is legally married, she stays at
home until her husband has made all the preparations for the
final wedding ceremony. Also, it's the culture to stay a little bit
with your family before you leave them. I stayed home and
helped my mama. Mama and I were the only two at home now.

My mama felt as though she had lost everything when Grandmama died, because her mama was like a part of her being —
ever since my granddaddy had died, long before, they had been
together through everything. She stayed at home and was full of
anger and nervousness. She didn't care whether I was there or
not, because some people still gossiped about me because of my
white boyfriend, and she was tired of hearing about it every time
she went out of the house. She was angry at me, and I understood. I loved my mama—my sister was gone, my brother was
never there, and my grandmama was dead, so I had to be there
for her. She yelled at me a lot—everything I touched or did or

cooked was wrong. I was learning to cook a little better now because I had more time, and I was trying to please Mama by making good meals for her. I still had money my husband had given me, so I bought good food and little gifts for her, but she didn't care.

Mama didn't get better—every day everything was the same. She began to hit and slap me, with her hand and with a stick, and call me names she had never used before. I used to go to a friend's house or to the movies, just to get away. She started following me and whipping me and cursing me in front of whoever was there. When we would get home, she would whip me again and then tell me to take off my underwear and open my legs, and she would take the kerosene lantern and look at me to see if I was still a virgin. She started to do that every time I went out, day or night, even if I just went to the market. I didn't like it. It was her duty to do all that, she wasn't the only one to do that to her daughter. Everybody was doing it: when a girl did something wrong, she got whipped. Still, every time she whipped me, I felt ashamed and I felt hurt.

After a month and a half, I couldn't take it any longer. I went into the interior to spend the rest of the months with my father before my final wedding. This time I was going to the countryside of my own free will, to get away from my mama, so I enjoyed it more than I had the last time. Though I was in pain thinking about Mama, I was glad to get away. Before I left, I gave her most of the money I had, and only took a little bit with me.

Three days after I arrived in the bush, Daddy had to go back to town. When you're a chief, you are like a policeman—you go wherever the problem is...by foot, by car, any way, and you solve the problem. Sometimes it's a problem between two tribes, sometimes someone is in trouble. Any problem, my father has to take care of it. This time he was going to town. I asked him if we could send Mama some food, and he said, "Sure. I'm worried about her. Get Abdi to help you get some of our maize and beans and some sesame oil, and some butter and milk, and I'll take it to her when I go."

When my daddy left, his wife started to ask me all about what happened to my mama. She was jealous because my mama was independent and my father loved her and she knew that.

I liked being with my brothers and sisters, and went to work in the fields with them. My daddy's farm grew beans, corn, peas, and watermelons. It was what I always liked—all the colours, the smell of all the fruit…. After the work, all the children played and ran around. There were dances in the evenings, with a big one every Friday. The boys would start the dance by clapping and singing and beating two iron hoes together so the other young people all around would hear and would come and dance. It was really fun, with a big bonfire, and dancing all night long—different dances, with different songs.

After twelve days, my daddy came back. I asked him how my mama was, and he told me she had gone to the *zar* people and they had told her she was possessed by a spirit that we call *zar*, and that the spirit was making her sick and she needed to have a *zar* ceremony, and that it cost money. They had set the date for the ceremony for a week from the next Friday. I told Daddy I wanted to go back home so I could see Mama and go to the *zar*, and he said he would take me back to town when he went.

Two days later, we went back. Daddy left to go to his house, and my mama started to ask me questions about what it was like in the bush and what I had done, and she asked me about my daddy's wife, and I told her everything. My mama was jealous of her too.

She told me a little bit about the *zar*, but not all the details. She seemed calmer with me than when I had left, and I could tell she had missed me. We began to talk more every day, and I told her everything—that I hadn't done anything wrong, that I had never made love to anybody, and that by getting married I was just trying to help us all. She understood, and cried, and forgave me.

Ever since they had set the date for the big *zar* ceremony, the man who did the *zar* had sent three men each morning to check on Mama to see how she was doing. Because she was possessed by a *zar*, the men came every morning to give incense to the *zar* so she would feel better. When they came, Mama would give them breakfast and burn incense while they were eating. After breakfast I cleaned away everything, and they told Mama to sit down on the floor. They gave her three small cups of coffee to drink and told me to bring a big bowl full of dirt in case she wanted to vomit. One of the men sat in front of her on a four-legged stool. Mama had her head covered with a white cloth and the man took the incense burner and put it under the cloth right near her face so she could breathe in the smoke from the incense. She would cough a lot, and he would say, "Good, good, that's the sign of the *zar*," and he would ask her to open her mouth and breathe the smoke in deeply. The man pounded her on the back and on the head, hard, with his hand, and shouted at the *zar* to come out and tell its name—he said he knew it was in her, and why did it want to make her sick? She coughed and vomited in the bowl, and then they would do the whole thing again. When she was sweaty all over and couldn't stand it any longer, they stopped. They put special perfume on her before they left. Every morning they came to do that, until the day of the big *zar* ceremony.

The day of the ceremony—Friday morning—came. My aunts and some of my mama's friends and relatives had come to spend Thursday night with us. In the morning everyone was eager to see the ceremony, because most of them had never seen one before. We all got up early in the morning to get the house ready for the people who were coming to do the *zar*. The leader of the *zar* came in the middle of the morning with six of his followers. We already had the big room clean and full of cushions and grass mats, and we had filled the incense burner full of glowing charcoal and put the incense nearby, and we had breakfast ready for them. They all went into the room and sat down. They told Mama to go get ready, to take a shower and put on clean clothes, and to come back into the room when she was finished. While she was doing that, the rest of us served them breakfast.

When Mama came back into the room, she was dressed in her best clothes, and she had some of her jewellery on. She asked us for something cold to drink, because she said she was afraid. I gave her a glass of water. When she had finished it, it was time to go into the other room, where the man who was leading the *zar* was sitting with his followers. The *zar* leader told Mama that she was the only one who was to come in, and she went in and closed the curtain behind her. After that, I couldn't see anything.

But I heard it. They were saying something out loud that sounded like the Qur'an. Then some of the *zar* leader's people came, because they had to cook their own food. With them they brought a live sheep and a live goat—big ones—and a lot of other food to cook. There were four men and about eight or nine women, and some young boys and girls who came with their mothers. They told the children to play, and we all went outside so they could have the space in the *daash* for their cooking. The men killed the goat for the women to cook, and they tied the sheep to a tree to wait until the leader gave the order for it to be killed.

After a while, we heard the sound of drums and dancing. We ran back in to see what was going on. The leader was sitting, since he was older. The rest were standing. Mama was sitting in front of the leader in the middle of the circle of people. She was covered with a big white sheet, and I could see her shaking underneath it. It was as if the spirit was moving her. The leader's assistant was beating the drum. They were all singing and dancing, and the smoke from the incense filled the air. Afterwards, they went to kill the sheep. They brought the sheep into the *daash*, and placed it in front of the leader, and they let Mama sit on one of the small stools. The leader had a bowl in his hand, and he said something, talking to the *zar*, something like "This sheep is for you, and you are going to drink its blood, and I want you to leave her alone." And they cut the throat of the sheep in front of Mama and put a bowl under its neck to catch the blood. All the blood went into the bowl, hot and bubbling, and he gave it to Mama to drink. She said she couldn't drink it, but he told her she had to drink it, and she forced herself—I could see her face, and she didn't look the way she used to look. She drank a little bit, I think, and then I heard her say, "No, no, I can't take any more," and that's when they all started drinking —passing the bowl and drinking, all of them, and acting as though they were crazy. They were sweating, and you could see they had something in their bodies like a devil. They didn't even have human faces—their faces were different, especially when they were drinking the blood and sucking the blood from their lips. It was terrible. We couldn't take it, we ran away. We went outside, and I threw up.

After that, they started beating the drum and dancing. When the dancing stopped, everyone came out and got some fresh air, and some went to the bathroom to wash themselves because they had been sweating a lot. Mama was the first one to eat.

Then the *zar* people started eating. Nobody else could eat until after they had tasted the food and given permission, because this was their service and they had to feed the devil and themselves first and then the rest of the people, so we had to wait. Besides, they had had to cook the sheep meat for themselves, which was why they danced so long—so the food would be ready. It was late afternoon when they ate, and that's when they allowed every one else to eat, and we ate too.

Before they left they gave Mama three long connected necklaces of beads and two others that were separate, and they gave her a silver ring and perfume that they had bought with the money she had given them for the ceremony. They told her she could do this for herself: every morning she had to burn incense and pray and talk to herself. They gave her all the equipment she needed. And she was supposed to wear the necklace whenever she did that, and the veil that she had been wearing during the ceremony. They told her everything she needed to do, and said she could also come any day to the *zar* leader's house, because every week they had drum-beating there. Mama said, "All right." And that was it—everybody started to go home, and when they had left we began to clean up the house.

Mama began going to this man's house—where they had the ceremony every week—and she became calmer, very calm. She wasn't well, not that well, but she wasn't nervous the way she had been before. I was glad she was better, but I was scared also, because of the fresh blood she had drunk. I thought she was becoming a different person, because I had never seen a live person drink blood, and my mama was the kind of person who didn't like that kind of thing. She was a religious woman. I believed she had a devil in her, because Mama hated blood and she had drunk it. If she didn't have a devil, I don't think they could have forced her to drink it. It was a little scary. But—she was better.

Now it was getting close to the time for my marriage—when I would have to go live with my husband. The time for me was short; I was afraid to leave my mama and I was afraid to go and live with this man. I was wishing that the time I had was longer. I was unhappy, knowing that I had to leave, but I was happy for my mama.

Mama now started going out and coming home late; it was the first time she had ever done that. She told me she had never gone dancing—because the boys and girls go dancing in the evening. She never went to the movies, she never went anywhere except outside to do her business. And there she was, over forty, and she was going to the *zar* leader's house every night and coming home late. They would go to other small villages, to other *zar* ceremonies, and Mama started going with them. When this had been going on for about three weeks, Mama met a man in another village. He had a wife and children and Mama knew that, but he was healthy and had a name. The *zar* leader married them. All of us were angry and surprised. We couldn't believe it. Hassan came. Hawa came. My mama's sister came. How come? A big surprise: a woman was sick, and she was looking for a cure, and there she came with a husband. Everyone wanted to know how it happened, especially me and my sister and my brother. We didn't think Mama would marry again, because we were all grown up and from different fathers, and Mama was getting old, so we were very upset. Hassan told Mama she had to get divorced or he would never come back, and he left. But I stayed and my sister and my aunt stayed.

We talked to Mama. She was feeling guilty and shy. We asked her why she did it; we talked to her woman to woman. Hawa had had three marriages, back to back, all of them to old men—she never loved one of them. I was thirteen years old and married to an old man over fifty, and I didn't love him. My aunt had

had only one marriage, but to a man who was much older than her. My mama had married another old man, who had two wives and a lot of children, and she didn't love him. Why did we do that? Mama said she had done it because she was scared. We were all scared, all of us, for different reasons. We were just looking for some security, I guess. That's the truth. We all ended up like that, Mama and the rest of us. And we understood exactly what she meant. She said to my sister, "You are gone;" to me, "You are going;" she said, "My mama's gone, I don't have anybody, I need somebody in the house. I was scared. That's why I got married." We all cried. We all understood each other. "We can bear it," we said. "Let's just go on and see what happens—go on with our lives, and wish the best for each other, and stick by each other—look for the best and go ahead."

The man used to come every two or three days, and whenever he came he was welcome in our house, because there was only me and Mama there. He helped us—he gave Mama a little money and clothes, and he started bringing containers and sacks of food, and really showed that he was a man in the house. I didn't like him and I was jealous, but I never showed him that. Mama was relaxed and calm—so maybe marriage was good for her. The time was very short for me, but we enjoyed it. We talked and understood each other and made peace.

One night I was in the kitchen cooking dinner, when somebody knocked on the door. It was Habib and one of his friends. When Mama finished praying, she came out and said hello. They told her they needed her at their home, and if she didn't mind could she get dressed and go with them. I said, "I'm going too!" They said, "You can go!" Mama said, "What happened? Did you all have a fight?" They always called her when they had a problem, and she would come and solve it, because she was the aunt and the head of the family. But they said, "No, no, no, it's something very good. We just want you there so you can identify a person." She asked, "Who is this person?" "You'll see. Let's go," they said.

The whole time we were driving to Mogadishu, she was asking Habib, "What is it? What's happened?" He started to ask her questions: "Would you remember what your brother looked like, even if he were a grown man, after twenty-five years?" She said, "Yes! I will always remember my brother!" He said, "How, Auntie, would you recognize your brother?" And she said, "Oh, he had a couple of birthmarks on his back, and he had three burn marks on his stomach, and he had another scar on his shoulder. What happened? Is he at home?" And he said, "No, Auntie, there's a man at home saying he is my uncle, and we want to make sure he's the one, because many people get cheated by this kind of person. Don't act too excited until we look at him and see if he has all the scars and birthmarks." She said, "I would know my brother even if he were a hundred years old. I knew he was coming back. My heart is telling me he is the one at home waiting for me." And she began to thank Allah, and cry.

When we got there Mama said, "Where is he? Where is my brother?" So a couple of people took hold of her and took her into another room and told her, "Wait until the boys look at him." In less than ten minutes they came out, holding him up, carrying him, shouting, crying, "Uncle! Uncle! Uncle! Brother! Brother!" Allah! He and my mama remembered each other, even though he was eight years old when he got lost. They couldn't let go of each other, they were holding each other, looking at each other, and crying.

We stayed there for a few days. Mama asked him to come live with us, but he had a wife and she was pregnant. She was from Ethiopia and didn't speak our language. They had come on foot and had been travelling and hiding for one month, because they had run away. Both of them needed rest. He said he would come to my wedding, because it was going to be soon, and Mama agreed, "All right, we'll go, but I'm coming back." And she did; she started going back there almost every day.

When Mama found her brother, she forgot she was married! Her new husband got jealous and began to ask her why she was always going to Mogadishu—what was up there that was better than him? And she said, "My brother." I asked Mama what about her husband and she said, "I married him because I was afraid to be alone, and not for love, and now that I have my brother I'm not alone any more and I don't need him." She didn't care now if she got divorced or not. So we travelled back and forth to Mogadishu to see her brother as often as we could. We had a good time, but I was afraid, because I had to leave all this happiness to go with my husband.

CHAPTER
10

AFTER TWO MONTHS WERE OVER, it came time for my wedding day—the day when you go to live with your husband. I had to have a big goodbye party because I was going to live in Mogadishu. You have dancing for three days, if you can afford it—people who come to dance want to eat and drink, and you have to pay for all that. That's what we did, because my father and my husband were both rich men, both with power. You dance and have a good time for three days and three nights. The two first nights are for the young people, but the big day, when everybody has to be there, is the last day, when the bride has to leave with her husband.

So on the last day we had a big party at each house, both my mother's and my father's house. The women and children were at my mother's house, and my friends—all ages, from thirteen to twenty-five—were at my father's house. The old people—my father and his friends, all the chiefs, all the government officials —they were at the hotel where I used to work. They had a party there with drinks—no alcohol, because they don't drink alcohol

—only tea and soft drinks. We had dancing at our party till twelve o'clock. The Arab boy whose girlfriend had been married off to someone else was there too. He was like Zaytuun—they were the only two who knew my problems, especially Zaytuun, but he knew some of my problems and he was always my friend. It all felt as though it was happening to someone else.

Finally it was time to leave for my husband's house in Mogadishu. My mama and the older women came and took me to another room and told me that it was time to get ready, and that I should go to the bathroom with this old servant woman and she would give me a shower and dress me in my new clothes. This woman can be middle-aged or old; she goes with you to be your nurse because you are a virgin, and once your husband disvirgins you, you can't pee and you can't walk, so you need her to nurse you and help you. She is just for you—she feeds you, she bathes you, she dresses you—she does everything for you until you feel better, no matter how long it takes.

I went and took a shower and she put my new clothes on me. My cousin had gone with me before the wedding to a store with cloth and a tailor. We picked out the material and the tailor made the dresses the same day. One had many flowers, the other was white with long blue stripes. She put a lot of gold and perfume on me—jasmine—and my feet were dyed red with henna and black with *qaddaab*. She put a new shawl on me, with gold threads shining in it and fringe on the edges, and covered my face with it, and then the woman carried me from the house and put me in the car. Besides my woman companion, my niece went with me, and Zaytuun.

When you're going to another city after the wedding, everybody rents cars and goes along with you. They ride along behind one another until you get to the halfway point, when you all stop, and dance and sing and stay there in the middle of the road for another hour or two, just dancing. Then you kiss each other and say goodbye—you may never see each other again.

After we left the halfway point and had been driving for ten or fifteen minutes, I fell asleep. When I woke up, I was in front of his house. It was a big house built out of stone that had been painted white, with beautiful tall trees in the yard, surrounded by a stone wall. In Mango Village, only the white people's houses, the police station, the hospital, the school, and the cinema— only those buildings were made of stone or cement.

In the yard there was a tent, where his daughter was giving a party for us. Everyone was out there waiting for us to arrive. But we were tired, so we went straight into the house without joining the party. My woman companion carried me in and laid me on the bed in the bedroom. My whole body was covered with the big silk shawl with gold threads in it. She told me not to show my face to my husband until he gave me some gifts that are called *wejifur*—"open the face". Then my husband came in and put gifts around me on the bed, and said, "I brought you this, darling, I hope you like it. I want you to open your face and look at this, please, my sweetheart," and then he left. I looked, and there were gold bracelets and earrings and everything—nice gifts—clothes—a lot of clothes, and several pairs of sandals and shoes, and handbags.

Now my woman companion came in to see what I had been given, and she liked it, she was proud of me. There were gifts for her too, and for my niece and Zaytuun. My companion told me I could open my face, so I lifted my veil. All the guests came in and looked at me and shook my hand. They saw how I looked and what I had on, and looked at my gifts that my husband had given me.

After everyone had left, I was tired and wanted to sleep. My companion took me to the bathroom. She asked me if I wanted to take a shower. I told her no, that I was cold, I wanted to go to sleep because I was tired. So she took me back into the bedroom and put me in the bed and said good-night, and left me. I covered myself completely with my shawl, with the sheet on top of that, because I was afraid he might try something, even though it was late and the first night you are supposed to be like a guest.

And he did try it.

He came to me, but I told him, without opening my face, "Please leave me alone. I'm really tired." I called him "Uncle" too, because he was old. So he backed off. That night I slept well. But I was worried when I woke up. I knew tonight he would ask something from me for sure, because he had tried it the night before, and tonight I wouldn't have any excuse for refusing him. I wanted to run away. I made a plan with Zaytuun and my niece. After we took a shower and had our breakfast I told them to go outside and find out where we were. We didn't know where we were, because I only knew the part of Mogadishu where Mama and I had lived; I didn't know the whole city, and we had arrived at about three in the morning.

Zaytuun and my niece came back, and they told me where we were. We knew we were close to the section of the city where my family lived. It was Ramadan and everybody was fasting, except I wasn't fasting because I was newly married, and neither were Zaytuun and my niece, since they were travelling with me. My husband had two people working for him inside the house, and an old man who worked as a night guard who came every evening. I was looking around to see when we could run away. I had the money he had given me for my wedding. I had enough money to run, and I had decided to run. Every time he looked at me he made me sick, he made me angry, the way he looked at me as though he was in love, when he came close to me and touched me. I made a mistake, and I'm sorry I cheated him, but whenever he touched me his hand was like fire. And the time— it seemed as though I had been in his house for years, even though it had been less than twenty-four hours. I couldn't stand to look at his face, I couldn't stand him.

I told the other two girls, "I have to leave now." They said, "At least wait until it's dark and they start eating their meal. Wait until they all get busy eating, and then you can run, and we'll come after you as if we're trying to catch you, but we'll just follow you so we don't lose each other." I told them, "In case we get separated from each other, let's agree to meet in a place we know. When you come into the city, there is the Fiat store and across the street from it there is a bar, and next to the bar is a big, old Catholic church with many steps in front. I'm going to run until I've lost them and I'm sure nobody's following me, and then I'll stop and ask somebody where the church is. Both of you do the same thing. We'll meet there, no matter what time it is…whoever comes first, wait there for the others…until morning."

Because we didn't know where we were going to be that night, we ate a big meal. We had to eat before the others because we weren't fasting like they were from dawn to dusk. My husband was in the bathroom, and that's when I went to get ready. The gold he had given me the night before for my *wejifur*—I put that on. I tied some of it in a headscarf around my waist, under my slip, and some I wore. I was ready. The time was so long. We had to wait until dark, around seven. We were all nervous, especially me. Husband is there talking, and his family is coming and going to see me. I wanted to smoke, and I couldn't—I hadn't smoked since I left Mango Village—and I felt nervous. Finally the time came. It was six-thirty, and they started to get ready to eat. First they prayed the sundown prayers and then everybody was busy with the food, and there was only one old man outside, the night guard, and he was eating too. My husband was eating. What was I waiting for? I had a good chance. The door was open. Rahima—I ran, and I was skinny. Whoosh! I put my shoes under my arm so nobody could see them, and I made it in two steps from the door to the gate. The night guard, who was sitting eating outside the gate, said later he thought I was a cat. Rahima, I ran and ran, and all these people were running after me and shouting, "Catch her! Hold her! Somebody help!" And I was just running, zig, zig, zig, zig.... Everybody was running after me. They couldn't catch me, but they were still yelling, "Catch her! Hold her!" Somebody was yelling, "She's my daughter! Somebody help catch my daughter!"

I was running in the right direction—Allah must have been guiding me that way. I came to a place with big houses and hotels. I knew the place. I said thanks to Allah for pointing me the right way. I went to the front of the church—there were more than thirty steps up to the church, because it was built on a little hill. People slept on the steps—there were a couple of old men sleeping there. Everybody sleeps outside—even at your own house, when it's hot you sleep outside—because our country was always safe. I lay down there. I was worn out and breathing hard, but smiling inside: At last, I'm free! I was so happy. I waited and waited. When I had cooled off, I looked around. It was beautiful: so many lights—red, blue, green, all mixed—I had never seen so many lights, in so many different colours. I loved the lights. In Mango Village only the main street had light, so at night everything else was dark—unless we had a moon, a full moon. In Mogadishu, day and night, there was light! Aah, I loved the light! And the buildings...everything was different...very nice and clean, with cement streets. There were a lot of taxis in the streets, a lot of cars. And now I had time to sit and look. I was busy with the lights, when Zaytuun and my niece showed up. They were tired. I laughed at them, and they laughed at me, and we held each other. We laughed and we cried, and I said, "Wow!" It was like a joke—it was scary but like a joke. We were just kids. We sat down and started looking at the lights and the cars passing.

We sat there for almost an hour, watching the cars and the people. We had a great time. After a while we said, "Hey, where are we going to go?" I said, "Don't worry. We're not going to get lost, we can ask somebody. We know the name of the section of the city that we want to go to, so all we have to do is ask." Two more old men came up who wanted to sleep there, and we asked them where to go—they asked us where we came from, and which tribe we were, and we told them. Then they told us that the area we wanted was behind the church, about ten minutes' walk. I was trying to get to my girlfriend's house. When she married someone in the city, her sister and I had come with her and stayed one night. My plan was to go to her place to hide, because I was afraid to go to any of my relatives' houses.

It was about nine o'clock at night when we got to her place. We knocked on the door and her husband opened it and let us in. They were surprised when they saw me, because they had heard I was married. So I told them I had run away. We had another dinner there, and we had a great talk. We sat and played cards and talked until one a.m., when we helped her cook the last meal of the night, eaten about three a.m. during Ramadan.

Zaytuun had to go back home. Even if I had stayed with my husband, she had planned to go home on the third day anyway. She left the next morning. I told my niece to go back with her, because anyone looking for us could find two people more easily than one—one person would have a better chance to hide. I told them to tell my family that they didn't know where I was, but that I was fine and I could take care of myself. They left, and I was in Mogadishu by myself. I stayed at my girlfriend's house for three days, thinking about what I was going to do. I had money, but I didn't know what to do or where to go. I knew I wanted to go as far away as I could, but I didn't know where to begin. I was scared, because I didn't really know where I was—I didn't know the city that well—and my family knew all the places I might go. I didn't know very many people in the city—only my relatives and friends, and I wasn't with my family, so I had to be with friends. So they found out where I was, and they came and got me.

It was morning when they came. I hadn't eaten breakfast because now I was fasting too. When they told me they were going to take me back to my husband's house, I was scared and angry, because I didn't want to see the man again—I hated him, I just hated him. I knew what he was going to do to me, that's why I hated him; I didn't like it, and I was scared. But they took me back.

In the evening my brothers had to leave, after they ate the first meal of the evening to break the fast. After they left, my husband began to ask me questions: "What happened? Why did you run away?" He asked me if I wanted something to drink or eat, and I said no. I didn't want the conversation to go beyond "no", so every time he asked me something I said no. He stopped asking me so many things, just kept on looking at me and trying to be nice, and watching me so that I couldn't run away again—the door was double-locked, and there were watchmen everywhere. It was as though I was in jail. I was thinking what to do—what could I do? I knew they were watching me closely now.

Night came, and after we ate dinner he wanted to go to bed. I was scared to death of what he was going to do to me. I went to bed and lay down on my stomach and told him I had a pain in my stomach. I started saying, "Unh-unh...my stomach," so he wouldn't touch me. It didn't help. He locked the door. The light was on. He had on a *hoosgunti*—the loose wrap-around piece of cloth that Somali men wear. He dropped it and came to me naked. That was scary...scary...scary. Rahima, I jumped and sat up. I said to him, "Hey, Uncle, aren't you ashamed of yourself? You could be my father and you're naked—put your clothes on!" I was scared, I was trying to make him embarrassed —I was talking loud so the neighbours could hear, so he would be embarrassed and leave me alone. But he said, "Don't worry about it..." and he started coming to me, and he was so big, with a big stomach, and I was a skinny little girl. I tried to get away, but I couldn't. Thank God, his stuff wasn't that strong. But he was trying to stiffen his penis with his hand and his fingernail was scratching me. I was jumping up and down, trying to get away, and I was crying and asking for help, but nobody would come, because that's the system—once you're married, even if you cry as much as you want, nobody will come and help you, because that's your husband and he has to disvirgin you, and they know it's painful, but that's the custom. So I cried and I shouted, but nobody came.

It was a good thing he couldn't do anything. He couldn't disvirgin me, so he came between my legs. It was so filthy, it was so stinky. I told him, "I'm not going to touch it. Clean that dirt off." He wiped it off, and I went to the bathroom and washed myself off and went back into the bedroom. I put powder between my legs and perfume and changed my clothes. Then we both went to sleep.

The next morning we woke up late—about ten. I felt a little more relaxed because I knew now he couldn't disvirgin me. I was still looking for a way to escape, but he left four people watching me. His niece and her friend came over to visit. We began to play cards—that's all people do during the day when they're fasting, play cards or sleep. My husband came back late in the afternoon with something wrapped in newspaper in his hand and set it on top of the sideboard in the dining room. After he and his niece had talked a little bit, she and her friend got ready to leave. He and his daughter walked them outside to say good-bye. When he went out, I unwrapped the newspaper and looked inside, because I thought he had brought something for me. When I got the bundle unwrapped, I saw two padlocks with keys and two chains and a pair of scissors and a razor. I wasn't stupid. I knew he was going to chain me to the bed and use the scissors and razor to open me up. And I knew I could die that way, if he cut me the wrong way. Allah! But I couldn't get away, because they were all watching me. When he came back, I couldn't get away.

He tried to use those things that night. After we ate dinner, he told me to go lie down—he wanted to go to bed early. He was ready, he said, "Let's go." Because I knew what he was planning to do, I talked to him and told him I was afraid and I didn't want any pain. I asked him instead to take me to the doctor in the morning, so the doctor could give me an injection so I wouldn't feel the pain and the doctor could cut me open. I said I wouldn't tell anyone—I knew he would be embarrassed if people heard he was afraid to be tough with me, or didn't have a strong enough erection to open me up—I told him, "I know what you've brought, and I know what you're going to do, and I'm scared because I might die. If you want me dead, do it. Otherwise, take me to the doctor in the morning." The old man understood, and he said, "You know, you're smart. Why didn't I think of that?" I just wanted to put it off for one more day.

Whew. And he said, "All right, let's do it like that." That night I gave myself to him, because I knew he couldn't go inside me. I knew what he had done the first night, and I knew there was no pain with that. But he was still using his fingernail and that was painful. He did his thing—he wiped it off—I went to wash it off—we slept peacefully.

In the morning, he took me to the doctor. I wanted to change my mind, but I was afraid to because I knew he would do it himself if I refused. Besides, I wanted to go out of the house so I might have a chance to run away. He took me to a private doctor, an Italian doctor. I said to the doctor, in Italian, "My father is a chief. If you touch me, they will take you and put you in jail or kill you, so you better leave me alone. Tell this old man some lie—that you can't cut me or something." The doctor said, "You terrible girl…!" But he told my husband that it was illegal for him to disvirgin me, he didn't have permission to do that and he didn't want to get in trouble. My husband had to take me to another doctor. But this time I changed my mind when we got close to the doctor's office. I told my husband, "I don't want the doctor to do it. I'll tell you what—take me to my mama's house back in my home town and let the lady who circumcised me do it." He said, "No! She doesn't have injections or painkillers. She's not a doctor. She doesn't have any education. No, a doctor is better." I said, "No, I don't want any doctor. One has refused, the other one is going to refuse too. I don't want it…." He got angry and took me home to his house.

Now he said he had decided to take me to my mother's the next day and let the lady who had circumcised me do it, the way I had suggested. But he was angry, because he didn't want anyone to know he couldn't disvirgin me on his own. When he got me home, he went straight to bed and went to sleep, then woke up and went out.

I was no longer afraid of him. I had to figure out how to get away. I started to talk nicely to the two house servants: "Bring me some coffee," "I've got a headache; I want some aspirin," because they didn't keep aspirin in the house. One of them went to the store to get aspirin, and the other one was cooking. Now I only had to deal with his daughter and my companion—my nurse—and my nurse was my servant and didn't have the right to hold me or touch my body unless I let her. I was praying to Allah that my husband's daughter would go to the bathroom, and she did! Rahima, the door was open for me again, and it was in the daytime. I ran again, and I ran…. I got away. I had my money with me. I sat down. Freedom…another night of freedom! I was so happy, I was so tired, I was so scared. I didn't know where to go. Now I had to sit and think of who I knew, one by one, and who they knew, and who I could go to, and how I could find them.

My brother had some cousins, and some of them lived in this part of Mogadishu. I thought of one of them—a woman—and I decided hers was the only place I could go to that night. I went around asking, "Who knows family So-and-so…?" I asked and asked, and found her house. She knew I had run away again. Everybody in the household knew. They said, "Hey, you ran away again! We have to take you back." I begged her. I said, "You're a woman too, you have feelings. You're married to a man you don't love, that they made you marry, and you know how you suffer, how can you make me go back? Let me stay, please, my sister—my brother's sister." I begged her. And she understood. She said, "You stay tonight and leave in the morning, because I don't want to have trouble with the family." I said, "All right, thank you—just tonight." She gave me dinner, and a place to sleep, but after she had fed me breakfast in the morning she told me to go, and I went.

I went downtown. I walked, you know, looking around, looking at the people, looking at the buildings, looking at the shops.

I bought something to drink in the street, even though it was shameful in those days for a woman to eat and drink in the street, though it was less shameful than going inside a restaurant, because there were only men in there. At that time women didn't go into a restaurant unless they were on a long journey, and even then they would carry their food outside and eat it in the car or truck. (A few women might go into a restaurant back then, but they would eat in the restaurant's back yard.) Anyway, I bought myself cookies.

Six o'clock in the evening came. I went to a movie, I still loved movies. There were a lot of girls and women and men. In the intermission, they turned the lights on so people could get drinks and candy and roasted groundnuts, and go to the bathroom. So I bought something to eat and drink. When the second intermission came, I saw some girls my age sitting on the chairs over on the other side. I was looking for some girls to meet. I got up and went over to that side. I wanted to talk to them, but I was shy, so I just sat in a chair close to them. After I had sat there a little while, one of them called to me, "Hey, little girl, why are you sitting by yourself? Come over here, you look lonely. What are you doing, and where do you come from?"

I was glad to make new friends. It was like a door opening for me. I was so happy to meet them! I started to talk to them, and to tell them who I was. I told them my tribe, because we use tribes; especially when you are from a good tribe, you are proud of yourself, and the first thing you use is your name and your tribe. "Oh, you're the daughter of a chief!" I was shy to tell them I was married—I told them I was new and had just come from my home town. They said, "Oh, you're from Mango Village. We like that place!" Rahima—I had made new friends. I talked and talked—I asked them where they came from, and where they lived, and what their names were, and what tribe they were, and once you know someone's tribe it's as though you have known them for a long time—you go on from there.

That night I didn't have anywhere to go except to my family. I had money, but I didn't know how to go to a hotel, and I was too shy to ask these girls if I could spend the night with one of them. I stayed in the movie until they left and I left with them. I had decided to go to my cousin's house. I didn't know how to take a taxi, but I knew that taxis existed. So I told them I wanted a taxi, and they took me to where the taxi stand was. They put me in the taxi and said, "Let's meet tomorrow."

Behind the movie house there was a big shop with the latest-fashion European clothes—Alta Moda. I had heard that all the girls liked to go there to look at the clothes, so we said we would meet there the next day. We didn't set a time—that means after you wake up, that's our tomorrow: no fixed time, nothing.

I went to my cousin's house and knocked on the door. I was sure she would open the door to me, because it was late. I told her through the closed door that it was me and she let me in. She fed me. I was filthy dirty and she told me to take a shower. I had a good night's sleep in peace, even though I was scared of what was going to happen in the morning.

In the morning, I woke up and tied the sarong she had given me around my left shoulder and wrapped it around the waist. I left before she woke up because I knew what she was going to say: "Why did you this? Why did you that? Why did you run away? You have to go back...." And she might tell my family I was there. I left about six-thirty. I washed my face, and whoosh! I was gone.

Walk...walk...walk...walk, stop, look at the buildings. It was an old city, but many of the buildings were new and tall, and the older ones were painted so they looked new. I had never seen all this. There were a few trees around, so when I got tired

I'd sit under the trees and look at the people and the cars and what was going on, because all the traffic and commotion was something else I had never watched before. I liked it, even though I was scared. I was like a tourist.

After a while, I went to buy something to eat and walked some more and looked at the shops until I went to Alta Moda. The girls weren't there yet, but the shop was fantastic. There were some women—white women—standing inside, and beautiful clothes everywhere. I sat down on the sidewalk beside the shop until the girls showed up. They came after noon, after school let out.

When I first went to these new shops downtown, I'll never forget: I saw one shop with a big glass window, and I thought it was open space! When we went inside Alta Moda, there were women standing there half-naked and without moving. This woman, I thought she was alive, but she didn't move. I asked my friends, "Why do white women do that?" I couldn't stop looking at her. She stayed in the same position. The girls told me they weren't real women—they were made of plaster. I looked one of the women right in the eye, and she didn't blink. My friends said to me, "Touch it—don't be scared." I realized that what they were saying was true—she was made of plaster.

We began to look around the shop. Everything was expensive, because it was a high-fashion European shop—the only one in the whole city. The odour was different from the stores at home, because there was no odour, no smell of the road, or the animals. That was the first time I ever saw a bra, and I bought one—the kind that makes your breasts look bigger.

Then we took a taxi to the beach—to the sea. I had never been to the ocean. But I knew how to swim, because I had grown up by the river. The beach had a bar—Bar Lido. This bar was only for prostitutes and people who drink alcohol—no young boys and girls went there, because it was shameful—only white people and prostitutes and pimps and people who drank. So what we did was, we just sat there and watched who was going in and coming out of the bar—women with short dresses, and a white man and a black woman together kissing each other, walking to the sea and having a good time.

One of the girls was my grandmama's lineage. She treated me like family after I told her that. She asked me what was wrong with me, because even though I was smiling and laughing, you could tell there was something wrong by how scared I was acting, how I was always looking around because I was afraid somebody might recognize me. She asked me why I was doing that, why was I scared? I told her, "I ran away." I lied, you know. I told her, "My mama beat me so much that I couldn't take it any more." I was shy to tell her I was married, because I was younger than her. She said, "Ohhh...so you don't have...where did you sleep last night?" I said, "My cousin's house, but she told me not to come back." She said, "You can stay with me. I'll tell my mama, and if she refuses I have a friend. She's a big woman and has her own room. She stays with her mother, but she has her own room. She's from the same lineage as you and you can stay with her." I said, "Thank you a lot." I was feeling relief again, and I was glad I had met her.

But her mother didn't really make me welcome. She was lukewarm. We left again and met the other two girls to go to a movie, and after the movie they met their boyfriends—all of them. The boyfriend of the one who had taken me to her place came to pick us up. He took us around, around, around. No disco. There was one, but we didn't go in that night. Very few girls went to clubs at that time, because any girl who went to a club they called a *sharmuuto*, a prostitute, even if she wasn't. Before, if you went to the movies they called you a *sharmuuto*, but everyone was beginning to get used to girls going to the movies—now it was clubs. At that time, a few people would go to a club once a week—the women hiding and covering their faces. Anyway, we just drove around and around; bought food—sandwiches and drinks—and ate inside the car. My girlfriend said to me, "Aman, we better check my friend's house, because I didn't like the looks of my mother's face today." I told her I didn't like it either…because you can tell when somebody doesn't like you. We went to find her friend. Her friend was old—about twenty-five or something like that—and she was living with her mama because she was divorced, and her father had another wife that he was living with. She let me stay and I stayed there for two nights.

The girls told me we would go to a disco the next night. I had left my dress at my cousin's house because it was dirty. I couldn't go to a disco in a sarong, so I had to go back to my cousin's to get my dress. But when I got there my brother, my aunt, my aunt's husband—half the family was there. They had caught me again. I told them that my husband had been going to cut me and maybe kill me, and that I hadn't wanted to die, so I had run away. They took me back to Mango Village, to Mama. I spent the night there with my mama, and my husband came there the next morning and they asked him if what I was saying was true, and he said, "Yes." My family all got angry and asked him who had given him the authority to do such a thing. Especially my mama was angry, and she asked him why he hadn't brought me home and talked to her. He apologized and asked her to help us. And he gave her some money to have a little party and to pay the woman who had circumcised me to come and cut me open. Then all the men left, because this was women's business now.

Mama sent word to her friends and relatives to come that afternoon. They greeted me, and Mama began to speak and tell them what the party was for, because she hadn't told them when she invited them. She reminded them how people used to talk bad about me. Now I was married, she said, but my husband couldn't disvirgin me, and that was why she had called the lady who had done my circumcision to cut me open. She said that before the woman cut me open she wanted everyone to look and see if I was a virgin or not. She told me to take off my underwear and show the people. So I did, and the people were surprised, and some of them had to eat their words. After that everyone sang "Lulululululu!" and we had a good time eating and dancing.

The next morning the circumcising lady came and cut me open. So the sides of my wound wouldn't stick together, they put a piece of cotton soaked in oil into my vagina, but I took it out. They took me home again to my husband's house. I knew what was going to happen that night. After dinner...I couldn't even eat dinner, because I had a fever, and I was angry and afraid, and I was in pain and tired from the long trip. And I had been cut open.

After he ate, he took a shower and relaxed a little bit, before he came to bed. He didn't care if I was sick or not, he wanted to do it. He did it. I cried, there was pain...because he was using his finger to make my hole bigger. I hadn't let the circumcision lady cut a big hole—as soon as she had cut me open a little bit, I had jumped and told her it hurt and that was enough, and I refused to let her do any more. So he found out the hole wasn't big enough. He didn't have enough strength to go ahead and finish the job, so he used his finger and that hurt...the fingernail cuts you.... I started crying and fighting back, and he slapped me a couple of times because I was kicking too, and biting and scratching. He came during the fighting—while we were fighting, he just did his thing. This time, he didn't wipe it off; I ran to the bathroom and took a shower and washed it off. While I took a shower, he stood outside the door, waiting for me.

Now I was like a slave. When I finished my shower, he brought me in and put me in the bed, and he double-locked the door. If he wanted to go outside to the bathroom, he locked me in the house first, by locking the front door from the outside. In the morning he went to work and his daughter went to school. He locked me in and took the key with him, and told the servants to give me my food through the window. My niece and my friend Zaytuun had left me long ago, and the lady who had served as my companion and nurse for my wedding night had gone too. Now I was really alone and I was locked in as if I was in jail, and there was no way I could get out.

When my husband was at home, he let the front door stay open, but he always put his chair close to the door. I saw I would have to cheat him. I said, "Why don't we go over and see your niece?" He said, "All right, we can go later on, after I eat and relax and sleep a little bit; around four or five we can go and see them." I said, "Great!" We ate, we slept. I didn't act up with him this time because I wanted him to take me out. I went to bed. I let him do it again. But he couldn't go way inside me, he was just barely inside. He wanted to make my hole bigger, but he didn't stay that long. He just made a little bit of pain and then he came, and after that it was calm. I didn't want that. I hated that. He slept, he snored, but I wasn't sleeping—I was thinking furiously…how to get away…where….

When I came back from the shower, I went straight to the bedroom. My husband was in the bedroom. He had a towel over his shoulder and his daughter was sitting beside him, and they were mouth to mouth, and she was holding him around the neck. When I came in, they both jumped. I had never heard of daughter and father kissing mouth to mouth, even though they were pretending they were European because of their money and their education. But still…your daughter…mouth to mouth? When she left, she didn't say a word. I asked him, "What were you doing with your daughter?" He said, "I was kissing my daughter. I always kiss my daughter because I love her. There's nothing wrong with that. You don't know what love and kissing are, because you're from the countryside." I said, "Ohhhh." I knew it was wrong, but I couldn't tell him why. And he knew I felt there was something wrong with him.

When we were on the way to his niece's, he told me, "Don't tell anybody what happened, because there's nothing wrong with it. It's only your mind, because you're from the bush and a little village, and you think the wrong way." I said to him, "Don't worry. I know what's wrong and what's right. Don't worry." And then I ran again. He was old and fat and couldn't run. He yelled after me, but I was gone. I ran and ran and ran. It was evening and this time a lot of people ran after me. My husband was shouting after me, "Help, help, help! She's my wife, she got away!" I ran to a house—because back home they leave their doors open. I ran into this house, and I locked their door behind me and cried, "I need help…I need help." The lady told me, "Go to the bathroom and jump over the wall to the other side." She waited until I had jumped over the wall, and then she opened the door to my husband. But I had got away.

CHAPTER

11

THIS TIME I FOUND JOWARA, A GIRL I had known when Mama and I lived in Mogadishu. I was so happy when I saw her, because I hadn't seen her in a long time. Her father and mother had died when she was young. An old man had asked her relatives if he could marry her, and they just gave her to him, and I knew she didn't like it. She was happy to see me too. We held each other. We had to talk quickly before her husband came out to meet me—I whispered to her, "Why don't we leave together—run away together, and leave these old men!" She said, "All right—we'll leave tomorrow." I spent the night with her, and then she and I ran away the next morning.

We took a small bus that went to a town on the river a little ways from the city. We stayed in a motel there. The next morning we crossed the river and caught a ride in a truck to a big town, Baidoa, that is halfway to the Kenyan border. In my mind, I had started to make a plan to go to Kenya.

My father's cousin, who I called "Uncle", was a judge in Baidoa, but I didn't want to go to his house because I knew he would send me back. In the evening we went to walk around and see the town. Baidoa was beautiful—a lovely town; I liked the people. But I wanted to go on to another town, to find a friend of mine—remember the Arab boy at my wedding in Mango Village, the one who had offered me a shoulder to cry on before I got married? They were building a big hospital in this place, and my friend was the electrician for the project. In the morning, we paid ten shillings for a ride there in a government Land Rover. Everybody knew my friend, and a few young boys took us to his house. The lady who owned it had four rooms besides the one she lived in; he rented one of those rooms for himself. I told the lady I was his cousin, because if you are cousins it's all right to sleep together in the same room. The place was very beautiful and clean—a nice village, with just a few houses. When you got up in the morning, you could see clearly for miles and miles.

The first night we spent there, my friend came back from work with two other men who worked with him and also lived in this house. We all ate dinner together, and talked and talked, and listened to Somali music on the radio, and we went for a walk. It was night, but the moon was so bright you could still see for miles and miles. One of the other boys began to talk to Jowara, so my friend could talk to me. We separated; she went one way with them and I went a different way with him. He and I had kissed before and he tried to kiss me again, but I wasn't ready for it. I pushed him, and he insisted and gave me a kiss, but it wasn't a nice kiss—no feeling. So I pushed him away. I said, "No, I don't feel like it." He got a little upset. When we got back, he wasn't talking to me the way he used to talk. My girlfriend did the same thing—she refused the other man. Thank God the woman who owned the house offered to let us sleep with her that night.

The next day my friend came home from work in the middle of the morning. He told me there was a car coming from Baidoa to bring some things for the hospital, and it would be returning to Baidoa that same night. He said we should get ready so we could go back with the driver in the car. And that was it. I said, "All right, fine." We decided to go back to Baidoa and find another car that was going to Kenya. We thought Kenya was very close. Later on I found out that it wasn't.

Before we left, my friend called me aside and took me into his room. He said he didn't want me to be angry with him. He said, "I don't want to lose your friendship. We're good friends and I love you as a friend, but I'm a man, and I need a woman, and seeing you every night would be too hard for me, because I can't force myself on you." And he gave us twenty shillings to spend on our journey.

In Baidoa we went to the same motel we had stayed in before. We were having a good time through all this. We were just free birds, me and my friend! I was glad I was very far from that man—my husband—far from everyone who knew me. There was a beautiful waterfall in that town. We went to the market and bought some bananas and mangoes and then went to the waterfall, where we sat and ate and looked at the waterfall. We sat there until evening, when it was time to go to a movie.

We wanted to see a movie every night, especially me. At that time you always found boys at the movies, whether you liked it or not. When you went to the movies, if you were a big girl and you were alone or with a girlfriend, boys would always come close. They look around while the lights are still on and see who is sitting there. When the lights go out they just get up and sit behind you and start a conversation—start talking to you. If you refuse to talk to them, they move somewhere else. When the movie is finished and you go out, boys come after you and follow you; wherever you go they are after you. If you want, you start talking and let them take you where you are going, but if you don't want, you just say no, and they go back. They can't force you.

So while we were in the movie, there were the boys. Not boys, men, big men. They started talking to us: "Do you want some…?" "Where do you come from?" and so on. When the movie was over, they came after us and we talked to them for a minute, but we didn't like it, so we left and went to our motel and ordered dinner inside the room.

Every day we tried to get a ride to Kenya. We stayed five days in Baidoa, and we got to know a lot of people there, men and women and families, and made friends. And so my uncle found out I was there. The next night my friend and I were at the motel, and the police came. We opened the door, and there was my uncle with two policemen. They came into our room. I knew my uncle by sight. He said, "You have two choices. Either you can come with me, or go to the police station. Which one do you prefer?" I begged him: "I'll go with you, Uncle. Don't send me to the police station. Please don't send me back. Send me to Kenya, where they can never find me again." He said, "We'll see. Let's go."

The next day he sent us back to Mogadishu in a police car. The police took me to the house of my chief and that same night my uncle sent some people to find my father and tell him to come.

Everyone was watching me, and I couldn't sleep all night—I just lay there thinking about what to do. When my daddy came, he got mad. I told him I was going to kill myself, that I didn't want to go back to that old man, that I didn't want to see him, that I didn't want to go. My daddy, the chief, and my uncle talked. They decided to give my husband his money back, so he could divorce me. They called for him and he came there, but he refused to take his money back. He said, "I don't want it, I don't want it even if you double it. Even if you make it four or five times as much, I don't want it. I want her." My daddy said there was no way he could give me to him: "She doesn't want you, and that's it. I don't want to lose my daughter because of you. She said she is going to kill herself if I make her go back to you." My husband said, "I don't care. If she runs away, either you go get her or let someone else in the family get her. We know where she can hide, and now she doesn't have anywhere to go." So my father asked, "What do you want me to do? She runs away all the time, and I run after her. I have a lot of business to do, and I'm not taking care of my business any more. From now on, if she runs away, it's up to you to catch her." So my husband said, "Give her to me now. I'll take her with me." My daddy said, "You know, you're not taking her. She'll go with you if she wants to." My daddy was angry at him now, because he had been trying to be nice to him and give him all his money back. To me he leaned down and said, "Go, daughter, wherever you want. From now on, you're free. Go wherever you want. Nobody is going to force you." I said, "Really?" But I couldn't leave in the middle of a fight between my daddy and my husband. My husband was saying, "No. I'm not leaving here without her…" and my father was very angry and said to me, "Go! Didn't I tell you to leave? Leave! Go wherever you want. Go straight to your mother's house!" He grabbed me by the hand and put me out and said, "Go, and take your little friend with you too. Go home. Go wherever you want. I want to see if he would dare to come after you and touch you."

So I left! I still couldn't believe it, Rahima! We both left. We ran and ran, even though nobody was after us. I went to my cousin's house and told her, "Believe it or not, I'm a free woman!"

She said, "No, I don't believe it…. Uncle was just angry. I don't believe he would do that." So I said, "Well, believe it or not, that's what my daddy said."

The next morning my cousin went to the chief's house, to see what had happened. He told her my husband and my daddy had had a big argument and my daddy had said, "I'm not going to give you any more money, because I offered you your money back and you refused when I treated you nicely, and now you don't get anything—no money and no daughter either, because you already cut up my daughter, you ruined her virginity, and you don't get anything more. We're even." And then he said he had separated my daddy and my husband and after a while my daddy had left, and he had talked to my husband and told him, "She's just like your daughter—younger than your daughter. You have to understand, if a little girl doesn't want you, she doesn't want you. They're just children. Just take your money—there are plenty of other girls around—plenty of other people who have a name and everything, from a good tribe—you can find one, divorce her." My husband said, "I'll think about it…." But I had started running and I never went back.

That's not quite true. One time, I went back on my own. I met a girl who said she knew an old man who knew how to do magic to make divorces. I asked her to take me to him. She said he charged fifty shillings—fifty shillings at that time was a lot of money, to me it was like a hundred dollars—but I said, "No problem. I have the money." I had plenty of money anyway—all that I had taken from my husband, and I had saved some from what he had given me. I always carried the money around my waist.

His place was in Afgoi—about half an hour by small bus. From the bus stop, we walked past old houses and woods. Afgoi is where they have the stick fights every year. The men hit each other with big sticks—there's blood everywhere! They do this once a year because they believe that to make the crops grow, blood should fall to the ground. The clubs have thorns. They hit each other hard—especially in the head because that makes the most blood. Many people come to watch this. Even tourists come to take pictures. It's scary, weird.

His house was way back in the woods. The women invited us to come in. They gave us four-legged stools to sit on. They offered us water, because we had walked quite a way. The girl who had brought us there told the women that we wanted their husband. A woman went inside one of the rooms, and came out. She said we could go in.

The room was so dark you couldn't see anything. It was divided in the middle by a big hanging sheet—on one side we were sitting and on the other side he was sitting, and all we did was talk. We never did see his face.

He asked what the problem was. I told him, "I'm married to this old man and I want a divorce. Can you help me?" He said, "Sure. All I need is your name and your mother's name and your husband's name." He asked me if I knew my husband's mother's name, and I said, "No!" He said, "All right, it will cost you fifty shillings." I gave him the fifty shillings. He said we would have to wait a couple of hours because he had to go into the jungle to get some leaves.

When he came back, he gave me a little square piece of folded paper with some writing on it, tied with black thread, to wear around my neck as an amulet. He also gave me some leaves, telling me I should get off the bus before I arrived in the city and chew these leaves until they became soft and put them on my face and my arms and my feet—everywhere my husband could see me, everywhere my body wasn't covered.

He told me to do this: Go straight to my husband's house and tell him I love him and want to come back and to stay with him, and he would say, "No! I don't want you! Leave my house! Don't come back!" and he'd put me out, and the next morning he would divorce me. I said, "Are you sure?" and the man said, "Yes, I'm sure! You'll get a divorce!" I couldn't believe it, but I had to try it.

I did what he said. When we got off the bus, I started chewing those terrible leaves, and after they were soft I put them all over my face and arms, with my saliva, and I waited until it dried. It was a long way to my husband's house at the other end of the city. When we got there it was already around dinner-time. I knocked at the door. The watchman couldn't believe it was me.

He opened the door, and my friend and I went in to see my husband. Everyone was surprised to see me—it was supper-time, so everyone was there. My husband stared at me. I was here by myself, nobody had forced me. I had come on my own. He got up and asked, "Who brought you back?" I said, "Nobody. Me and my friend came." He went outside to see if somebody else was there, but he couldn't find anybody. He came back inside and said, "Tell me the truth, wasn't there a car that dropped you off?" I answered, "No, we walked. Don't you see the dust on us and how sweaty we are?—how dirty-looking I am? We walked miles and miles." And he said, "This is a surprise. What happened? Did somebody talk to you? Tell me what happened—what brought you back?" I said, "I'm just tired of running around. I just gave up. I came home, I realize that the best thing for me is to be at home with my husband, so I came back. And my friend helped me too, you know. She talked to me about marriage. That's why I came back." He said, "That's something. That's really something. Thank you, Allah! Thank you, Allah!" And inside me I was saying, Liar! That old Afgoi liar, why did I believe him! I was angry and scared, because I was in trouble now. But I said, "Just believe me." He was surprised, and he was very happy, and everyone else in the house too. But his daughter was looking at me strangely, and I was scared.

Again he said, "Thank you, Allah! Thank you, Allah," and he began to hug me. He asked me if we wanted to eat and take a shower first—me and my friend. My clothes were filthy. I said, "No, no, no. We're going to eat, but we're not going to take showers because we're not going to stay." He said, "Why? If you came back, why aren't you going to stay? First you said you were going to stay, and now you say you're not going to stay!" I said, "No, I didn't mean that. I'm coming back in the morning. I just came here to ask you if I could come back. I didn't bring my things with me, and I am not ready to spend the night here until I bring my stuff with me." So he said, "When are you going to bring your stuff with you? And what stuff do you have? Everything you have is right here. What else do you have? A couple more dresses? Give them to your friend! Tell her to take them!" I said, "No, I wasn't at her place—I was at another place. Don't force me. I'm coming back tomorrow morning—if you don't believe me, don't go to work in the morning. Wait for me here at ten o'clock."

Since I had come back on my own, he had to trust me, and I insisted, saying, "Trust me...who forced me to come back? I want my house and my husband. I'm tired of running around. But don't force me all the time. Give me a little time." He said, "You're a smart little girl...all right. But you have to eat." I was very relieved. My heart...my whole chest was thumping.

I ate fast, and I was the first one to wash my hands after I was finished, saying to him, "Thank you for the dinner. We're leaving now." He said, "No, wait a minute, no, I'll take you." I said, "No, really, I ate too much and I want to walk. Thank you very much, but I'd like to walk." He insisted, but I said, "No, thank you. Don't force me—there you go again, forcing me. Don't force me!" He said, "All right, all right!"

So we were out! Out of that house again, and on our own! We walked fast, fast, fast to the corner, and as soon as we got around the corner we *ran!* When we finally got tired, we sat down. My friend said, "Girl, you are smart, very smart—you cheated the old man!" I said, "But I had to do it, because that other man cheated me, and took my money, and put me in danger! I had to lie." She said, "I was scared too—I'm glad you lied."

It wasn't too late for us to walk, because back home you can walk at any time of night. Twenty-four hours a day people walk. And they aren't frightened—you can sleep in the street. I loved the whole system. When you don't have to go back home, when your mama won't be able to ask, "Where were you?" When you won't get whipped or smacked, when you won't have anybody yelling at you, when you don't have to make tea. We could do whatever we wanted. Just have fun. Yes, it was nice. We felt we were free!

CHAPTER
12

I LIKED WHAT I SAW. IN THE CITY, the girls went with their boyfriends, or they could go to movies, in front of their parents. The big city was a little wild; people did whatever they wanted to do, and it's normal. In the village, there was a whole lot of shame, everything was shame. Don't talk to men: shame. Don't go to movies: shame. If you did anything except stay home and cook, you were a *sharmuuto*. Back home, every time I went past, the girls and boys or older men and women would say something about me behind my back and I would think to myself, I know what you all are saying about me: "Look at that *sharmuuto*!" I know it and I feel it, and I feel angry every time you say it. And I became a fighter: fight, fight, fight—an angry girl. I hated everybody, I guess—except myself—the way they hated me. But in the city, nobody knows who I am, nobody hates me, everybody likes me, and I say, Why should I have to go back? I was relieved, and I was looking with a new look. If I couldn't find the one I loved…I had to find a way to find him—him, or another one like him. So I left my way open…all my doors open.

Every day I used to meet with at least three or four friends—
men and women, and girls. And they had cars. Every night I
rode with my friends, meeting new people. We usually went to a
party in someone's house, but sometimes we would all go to the
disco. The girls were very elegant and the way they spoke was
very different from the girls in Mango Village. I used to think
these things didn't matter much, but they did. The way I talked
was different; the way I combed my hair was different; the way
my clothes were sewn was different; my actions were different—
everything about me was different, because I was born in the
bush and raised in a small village. There were a lot of white
people in the city, and there were a lot of other people too. And
the rest of the people were not just from one tribe or two tribes;
there were a thousand tribes living together. That was beautiful,
and the city was so big! I walked all day long, as soon as I woke
up, sometimes just by myself, if all the girls were gone.

I used to love it downtown. In my country in the morning
everybody goes downtown, especially the women. They shop for
food, and for clothes, and they shop for gold…for everything.
Between twelve and one o'clock, they close the shops and everybody goes to eat. The people who don't want to go home go
under a tree and rest, or else they go to somebody's house and
ask if they can stay half an hour, maybe two or three hours, and
people let them in and give them something to drink and eat.
The shops open up again around three-thirty or four o'clock in
the afternoon and stay open until nine in the evening. The city
is always crowded—people walking, shopping here, buying
there. And they have a bar where you can sit out in front and
have a coffee or tea and just listen to some nice music and look
at the people walking by. There's always somewhere to go.

One night one of my friends took me to a party. There were
a lot of handsome men there. There were a couple of whites

there too, even though the party was mainly for Somalis—all of them were well educated, and the majority worked in banks or in big offices for the government. Some were businessmen, some worked in the Ministry of Agriculture—they had nice positions, all of them. I was embarrassed at the way I looked—my clothes, my hair—my dress and the way I acted weren't like the other girls. I was natural, and flat like a boy. All the other girls were really sophisticated, and I wasn't. And I was upset…why couldn't I be like them? I had left all my new clothes with my husband. The girls here didn't wear sarongs like we did in Mango Village. Their dresses were sewn together, shorter, prettier. They even had better shoes—European shoes I had never seen before.

I didn't enjoy the party, even though I was trying to. I didn't know how to dance the way they did. I couldn't dance because I felt embarrassed. I was afraid people would laugh at me if I tried. So I was saying no, because I had danced before, but not the way they danced. This was during the sixties, so they were doing the twist and other rock-and-roll dances. I just sat and looked around. All the boys and girls were drinking. I remember the names: Heineken, Amstel, Becks, Tuborg. In the big city, they consider themselves *elbah* for drinking—it means you're civilized and educated. I had heard that if you drink you lose you head and become crazy and kill people, and it gives you a bad name. But I liked the way they held their glasses. And the way they smoked…I smoked, but the way I smoked was different—just puff on it and blow all the smoke out at one time. These girls could smoke and hold their breath and talk, and you didn't see any smoke coming out of their mouth or nose. I was saying to myself, I wish I could do that! One day I will!

A couple of boys tried to talk to me at the party—they asked me where I came from, and I gave them different names and

different tribes and different cities so they wouldn't tell somebody that they had met Mrs. So-and-so. I knew now that people
talk, and I didn't want my family to hear that I was at a party in
the city. The first one who asked me my tribe, I told him I was
Ethiopian. Everybody was saying, "Oh, you're beautiful!"

The next day I was angry because I felt so unsophisticated. So
I told my friend, "Take me to the hairdresser." And besides, with
all the running around I had done, I had head lice—that little
insect that gets in your hair if you don't comb your hair properly
or wash your hair properly. I saw all the other girls had smooth,
soft hair—in the country the girls' hair was usually long and
curly, or braided in rows. When I asked how they did their hair,
they said they went to the hairdresser. So I decided to go too, and
make my hair beautiful like theirs. Slowly, slowly, I would look
like them, and then all I had to do was walk and talk like them.

When I got to the hairdresser's, the man there showed me a
book full of white women's pictures, showing their hair in different styles, and I chose one. He asked me whether I wanted
only a shampoo, or did I want my hair straightened? I asked him
what straightening was, and he said that it made your hair soft,
like a white woman's, and you could comb it easily and style it
easily; it was almost like having a wig. I said, "I want that!" Another reason I chose to have my hair straightened was that he
said he was going to put strong chemicals on my hair to make it
soft, and I thought the chemicals would kill the head lice. He
put this strong, smelly cream on my hair. I sat there with it on
my hair for a while—it stung and burned—and then he washed
it out, and told me to touch my hair. When I touched it I couldn't
believe it—it was like silk! I had long hair, so he put big rollers
on it and put me under the dryer. This hot thing was blowing
my hair and my ears, and he put a wet towel around my forehead

and a lot of cotton. I stayed in there and I stayed in there, and I thought, Good. This heat will kill all the lice. Finally he combed my hair in the style I had chosen. Beautiful—the bottom flipped up! And the lice and eggs were gone! It was so beautiful that we went straight to the movies, because it was evening. Everybody was looking at me—everybody.

My family was still searching for me, but they couldn't find me, because now I knew the city—I could go one day on one side of it and the next day on the other. And I didn't go to visit my relatives' houses any more, although everyone knew my father had said I was free.

In the big city, the girls could go to a man's house—like I said, they went where they wanted. In the middle of the night, they would go back to their own houses. Sometimes they would sleep with the boys without doing anything, and they would go home the next morning, lying to their parents, saying, "I was at my girlfriend's," or "I was at my auntie's." I'm sure the families knew, because they did it often. But in Mango Village, a girl couldn't even speak to a boy in the middle of the street, where people could see. You could hide it at night, but in the daytime you couldn't just stop in the street and talk—it was shameful. But these girls went to boys' houses, and I went with them.

I met new friends—new girlfriends—and boys. I was really looking for a white boy...if I couldn't have Antony. White boys were the ones I liked, and they had to be at least five years older than me. I was tall, but I was skinny, and I liked a big handsome man—he had to be tall, and nice. I hadn't found one yet. But I found out something. Men in Mogadishu liked me. In Mango Village nobody liked me, except my family. If you had TB, nobody even wanted to speak to you. The few who did speak to me were close friends who liked and respected my family. But the others...I never had a date when I was back home, when I was a little girl. I never had a Somali boyfriend really like me. I had friends—I used to play that I was one of the boys—but I never had one who said, "I like you," or "I love you."

Another night, at another party, I met another friend. This time it was a small party at a house where two men lived. There were about six or eight men, and some of them were married. We were all young girls. The men at this party were handsome, really handsome. They were older than we were—in their late twenties and thirties. The one I liked was about twenty-eight, tall, very light-skinned—because he was an Arab—and he had straight hair. I was shy. The other girls knew the men. They used to go there once or twice a week. When girls didn't have anywhere else to go, they used to go to a man's house and relax and have a drink and talk, and kiss too, if they wanted—it was up to them. Sometimes they would go to four, five, or six different men's houses in the same night. If nothing's happening at one house, you just go to another.

And there was this beautiful man—a man I liked. But I was so shy. Every time I looked at him, my heart would start bumping and I would get a shiver all over my body. He came close to me, and he told me his name, Umar, and I told him mine. Someone asked us what we wanted to drink and I said, "Fanta." He said, "No! Fanta? Where do you come from?" Of course I was lying to people, but I really wanted to tell Umar where I came from. So I said, "Why do you want to know where I come from?" He said, "If you were from here, you wouldn't be acting like this." Some of the girls were saying to me, "Go ahead and drink." But I said, "Unh-unh. I don't like it." I had never drunk alcohol before. One of the other guys said, "Give her time—she's new, you can tell, poor girl—leave her alone," and he got me a Fanta.

There was Somali music playing—just three-string guitar and one person singing. The men were drinking whisky, drinking heavily. They started kissing some of the girls. Sometimes these situations scared me, and I wanted to run, but I knew nobody could force me to do these things—I felt very strong, like a lion, because of the tribe I was and who I was and what I had been through. Everyone else's tribe seemed lower to me than my tribe. That's why I didn't worry—about rape and all that. Nobody knew about rape in those days in our country. It existed, but it was very rare. I wanted to do the same things my friends were doing, so I said to myself, One day I will! Everything I saw, if I liked it, I said to myself, One day I will!

And Umar and I, we talked and talked, and every time I wanted something to drink or eat he brought it to me.

When it was two o'clock, all those who were drinking were drunk. Time to go! My cousin's house wasn't too far from where the party was, so another girl and I went there and knocked on the door. She knew who it was—if someone knocked on the door late at night, it had to be me! She opened the door and I stayed there again.

Every time I came there I had a new girlfriend, and every time she would say, "Where did you meet this one?" and I had to explain it all to her. Anyway, we talked that morning, and she said, "Why don't you want to go back home? Why do you want to make your family suffer…?" Talk, talk, talk, but my mind was somewhere else. I said, "Oh…I'll go back…it's not time yet…I have to get divorced first…." She said, "You can get divorced if you go home. Stay with your mama until your daddy comes and gives that man his money…but what you're doing now is not good for the family and not good for you. You're beautiful and you're young, and you've got a big name. It's not good running around, one night here, one night there, with girlfriends, in the street, in the movies, in the club…soon you're going to be a prostitute. Really. Don't do it, go home."

I cried, and said, "Oh, sister, I'll go back home. I'll go get my stuff, and then I'll come back and you can take me home....." She said, "What stuff?" I said, "I bought some clothes and they're at my friend's house. I'll go get them, and you can take me home." She said, "All right, are you sure?" I said, "Yes, I'll go and get my things and come back and then you take me home." She said, "All right, I will." So my friend and I left, and I said to myself, I'll never come back to your house!

I didn't care what she said. I thought, You're going to call me names anyway, so call me whatever you want. I knew what I was —I knew I was good inside. Besides, no one would find me, because one night I was here, the next night I was there, the next night over there, the next night back there, the next night somewhere else.

I wanted to buy myself some new clothes. I went to several different shops, and finally I found what I wanted. I bought enough cloth for two dresses for myself and one for my friend. Inside the shop they also have a place where they make the cloth into dresses—you just pay a little extra money. I asked how long it would take and the man said we should come back around five o'clock, because he had other customers ahead of us. So we went walking. We didn't have anywhere to go—we were just walking in the street, pretending we were shopping for something. We would go into a shop and ask how much something was and feel the cloth it was made from. We would go into a jewellery store and do the same thing—put a necklace on and look at ourselves in the mirror. We did that until five o'clock, when we picked up our dresses.

We had walked all day long. It was hot and we were sweaty and our feet were covered with dust. It doesn't matter how often you wash your feet or take a shower, you always have dust on your feet, because most of our roads aren't paved. We took a shower at a friend's before going for a drive with the boys we had met, because I just wanted to see everything, everything I hadn't seen before.

We decided to go to Merka, a town by the sea. Everyone said it was a lovely town and I had never seen it before. We didn't know anybody, so we went to a hotel. They sold food and alcohol there. The owner was Italian, and men came there to drink and eat in the evening, and women too. I don't know if they were prostitutes or friends or wives, but they were Somali women with white men. We went to the bar downstairs. It was an open place, with small umbrellas over the tables, and there were different-coloured lights—red, green, and yellow—and I loved those lights, so I suggested we eat outside. But the others said they would be too embarrassed, because none of us knew how to hold a knife and fork. I said, "No—let's be like them and enjoy ourselves outside. Let's try it—nobody knows us here, we're in a different town and the people are different. Let's enjoy ourselves and pretend we're civilized, like them." I insisted and insisted and besides, I was the one who was paying, so I guess they agreed with me! We were all shaking and shy, but I was pretending that I knew everything—Miss Know-it-all. And I was the one who didn't know anything!

We sat at a table way over in the corner, where we could hide behind some plants. The waiter came and brought the menu. I didn't know how to read, but one of the other girls did. Still, she couldn't understand the menu—steak, cutlets, and so on. So we just told him what we wanted to eat, without looking at the menu.

I was used to eating either with a spoon or with my hand. I had tried forks and I didn't like them—they don't pick up much food—hand is better, or a spoon. So I grabbed a spoon and squeezed a lime on top of my food and cut a banana onto the same plate, and ate it! But nobody saw us, because a nice distance separated us from the other people, and the plants were between us. You could see the ocean, and smell the ocean—it was beautiful outside by the sea. When we got upstairs, we talked until we finally fell asleep.

As the sun was coming up, we took a bus back home. It wasn't really home for me—everywhere was home for me, I just went with my friends. If this friend didn't want to go somewhere with me, I had another friend who would, so I was always in a different place. My mama was looking for me though, and I worried that my husband might come after me and say, "Why did you lie to me?" and take me back with him for good, or kill me. I was still scared, but I was enjoying myself. I was just running around.

CHAPTER
13

Two NIGHTS AFTER WE GOT BACK
to Mogadishu, I saw someone I knew. Do you remember Umar,
the man I met at a party, the one who was nice to me? I saw
him at the movies. And he saw me too. If you're a girl and you
want the man, you can't go up to him, because you're shy; he has
to come up to you. But you have to make sure he sees you. I always had a big shawl over my head. But when I saw him there in
the movie, I realized that if I wrapped myself up in my big
shawl he could not see me. I said to myself, I want him to see
me! When it was dark, I got up, pretending I was going to the
bathroom, without my shawl over my head. When you don't
have your shawl over your head, all the men look at you—a
pretty girl. So he came after me, pretending he was going to the
bathroom too.

Where you go to the bathroom outside the cinema, it's a little bit dark, and that's where we stood. He greeted me—my
heart was going boom, boom, which told me I wanted him, because I hadn't felt this way about other boys I had met, except
for my boyfriend Antony. I showed him I was happy to see him,

because my big mouth was open—I had a wide smile on my face—you can tell when you're really happy to see a person. And he was happy too! So we made arrangements to meet after the movie.

That night I had only one friend with me—the others had gone back to their families. They were all little runaways, like me, for one night or two nights, but after that some of them went back. When you do that—spend the night outside your home—people call you *sharmuuto*, bad girl, but we weren't, and we knew it, and that's what counts. We had run away to be free and I didn't see anything wrong with it. But they wanted us to stay in the house and work for the family until we got married. The girls I was with had had it with that.

There were a lot of wild girls. There were several different types of women. The real *sharmuuto*s were the girls who sold their bodies in a bar. They would go there and bargain with the white man and ask him "How much?" There were other girls who went door-to-door, knocking, selling their bodies. There were other girls in the street—young, thirteen, fourteen, or even younger—and men used to pick them up. It was usually old men who picked those girls up. But we weren't big *sharmuuto*s, we were just runaway girls—out there. We were just a bunch of kids who wanted to see what was out there, nothing more. Most of us were virgins—good kids.

When you come out of the movie, you can't go straightaway with a man. You have to tell him to meet you over in a corner so nobody will see. Umar came and stopped the car and we both got in. He told me to come sit in the front, but I was too shy. I told him, "No." He said, "No, no, you sit in the front." If you sit in front, that means you are his girlfriend—you are with him—that was what we used to think anyway, and I didn't want that…. But he kept on begging me, so I said, "O.K." I sat in front. He said, "Let's go for a ride. Are you hungry?" We said, "No!" Even if you are hungry back home, if somebody asks you if you are hungry, especially a man, girls usually say no, because they're shy. So we said, "No, we're not hungry." We went for a ride—a long ride. He was talking, talking, talking, and we were talking, singing, talking, singing. He was a handsome man, very handsome, and I wanted to kiss him. But I wanted him to kiss me first—to make the first move. I felt my heart and my whole body—just going.

We went way, way, way outside the city. Finally we stopped at the side of the road and climbed on top of the car and just sat there. A soft breeze was blowing, and the moon was out. We talked and sang. He held my hand. My hand was all sweaty. I wanted him to hold me tight and squeeze me, but he was shy and thought I might refuse. If a man does that the first night, or the second night, or the first week, before he knows the girl really well—if he does that, it's very shameful. And if the girl tells other girls, it's hard for the man to find a date, because they say, "You're bad—you force the girls." So everybody is careful —the boys are careful, and the girls are the same way.

We went to eat at The Jungle Club. It was on the main road, but way out in the bush, a restaurant so beautiful I couldn't believe it when I first saw it. The trees are very big there, and the branches are like a great thick canopy around each tree, sweeping down to the ground and making a large space inside where they lay mats and pillows so the ground is covered, it's like a room. They cut an opening in the branches, and hang a cloth down over it to make a door. When you drive up in your car, boys are waiting to run ahead of your car and bring it to a tree room that's empty. There is a big pot of warm water waiting for you in the room so you can wash your hands and clean yourself. We ordered our food in our room under the tree. It was cool inside.

You had to take off your shoes and sit down or lie down on the
mats. We lay down, because we had been riding around in the
car for almost three hours and we were tired. That was where he
first kissed me. It was beautiful-lovely-beautiful, he had warm
lips. I was a good kisser, because my European boyfriend had
taught me how to kiss. We kissed and we kissed. We didn't stop
kissing. My friend said, "Stop! You two cut it out!" We turned
the hurricane lantern down so there wasn't much light, but we
kissed until they brought the food. We ate the food—goat meat,
camel milk, and rice. A delicious meal. You can stay all night in
your room under the tree if you wish—once you have the room
for your meal it is yours for the night. But we went back to my
friend's house in the city and Umar made an appointment for us
to meet the next night at the movie.

This time he didn't have to beg me to sit in front with him. I
sat there on my own, because that was my place! This time we
drove around inside the city. Finally I had found someone I really liked. I was very choosy, but now I was happy. Umar took
me to the house where we met—the house where everybody was
always singing. In those days, we used to sing a lot; singing was
in fashion and everybody had a lovely voice. This house became
our "meeting house", whenever we wanted to see each other.
After seven or eight days, we had seen each other every night. I
always had a friend with me, I was never alone, so he didn't have
to ask me to do more than a kiss. I remembered my husband—
how he had done things—and every man is like him. So I always
brought a friend with me.

One night Umar told me he had to leave in two days—he
was going to move to another city on the coast, where there is a
fish processing plant, because he worked for a fishing company.
He didn't know how long he was going to stay there, but he
knew it would be more than one month. I said to myself, Allah,

why me? Everyone I love, why do you take them away? First Antony, and now this one that I just met and I'm beginning to love…. Why? I was scared and shocked. I told him not to leave, but he said that if he didn't leave he would lose his job and he didn't want to lose it, because working with the tuna fish processing was a good job. I said, "O.K." I didn't love him the way I loved Antony, but he was sweet—a very sweet man, very gentle, very understanding. I hadn't yet told him my real name and my real tribe and that I was married—I hadn't told him all that. He knew me as another person, someone I was not—someone totally different. But he liked me for who I was, and I wasn't bad, I was just hiding my past. Besides, I was growing and I wanted to learn these things between men and women. I knew my heart was looking for love—that was all I was looking for, love and a good life.

Two more days. I didn't want to leave his side. I told him, "Every minute I want to spend with you." He was staying with his family. He couldn't take me to his house. So we met outside, and we spent a lot of time riding around in his car, going somewhere, just the two of us. We spent all the time we could together. I would lie down on his chest, and we talked and talked: "When are you going to come back…? I wish I could go…. I wish I could stay…."

The two days passed as though they were two hours. Then it was time for him to leave. He had to fly, so we went to the airport. It was the first time I had ever seen the airport. I hated it, because I knew Antony had flown from the airport and now I was taking this person I liked to the airport to leave too. Six of us rode in a car to the airport together and stayed there for about half an hour, until it was time for him to get on the plane. We kissed until he left, and I cried, and he waved goodbye to me. Then he was gone.

He had the address of one of my girlfriends, and he wrote me a letter before a week was up, saying that I should wait for him and not go out with anybody else, and that he was going to send me some money and I shouldn't do anything wrong—I shouldn't date anyone else because he loved me and wanted to marry me. All that! All the things he couldn't say to me when he was with me, he said in a letter. I didn't know whether he meant it or whether he was lying, but I think he meant it. I wish I had waited for him.

And then one day, the fifth day after Umar left, I was inside the cinema, and the next thing I knew there was somebody behind me, holding me by my neck and turning my head around by force, twisting it so he could see my face and make sure it was me. He made me stand up by pulling me up by my neck—I was so little and skinny that I just got up, because it was painful the way he was holding my neck. Some people nearby asked what was the matter and told him to let go of me. I said, "Let me go! Let me go! You're hurting my neck, at least hold me by the hand!" and he let go of my neck and grabbed me by the hand. Oh, Rahima, it was my husband! We were still inside the cinema and everybody was looking at me and at him. He held my hand tight and dragged me outside. People came out too, to see what would happen. I told my friend who was with me to go call the police. I told her that I didn't know him and he wanted to kill me. My friend knew who he was though, because I had told her what my husband looked like. I began to cry and fight back and scratch him. He was dragging me by the arm. Someone called out, "Why are you dragging her? Where are you taking her? Who are you?" Everyone thought he was my father, and I was yelling, "No! He's not my father! He's not my brother! He's no relation to me! I don't know him, and he wants to take me." The people asked, "Who is she? Who are you?"

The police arrived. He had dragged me a little way from the cinema, but I was still fighting, and people were trying to stop him and trying to talk to him and find out who he was. He said he was my husband. I said, "No! He's lying! I'm not his wife!"

When the police took us to the station, I had to tell them he was my husband. He told them I had run away. I said yes, I was his wife, but the reason I had run away was that he had cut me and he wanted to cut me again, because there was nothing he could do with his penis, and I hadn't wanted that and that's why I had run away. But the police arrested me when I refused to go with him, and made me spend the night in jail, until the next morning, when they could take us all before the judge. I told my girlfriend the name of my chief and where he lived and asked her to go quickly and tell him to come and see me.

In the morning, my chief came and talked to the police. He asked them to give me one more day before I had to appear before the judge, so he would have time to tell my family. They said, "O.K.," and he sent someone to Mango Village to tell my mama and my family. But they kept me in jail so I wouldn't run away again, and because my husband was a powerful man—he was a big old man with money. Mama, Hawa, and Hassan came that evening to see me in the jail.

The next morning the police took me before the judge. When I got there, both my family and my husband were already there. My husband talked first. He said, "I paid this, I paid that. Her mama did this, her daddy did this. They cheated me. I don't have a wife. I haven't had her for three nights straight—they brought her and the next day she ran. Now I'm tired of all this and I want either my wife back or my money back!" He was saying, "I want my wife back," because I was still a virgin, really, and he wanted to disvirgin me at least. I couldn't even look at his face. He made me sick and he made me scared every time I saw him. Every time I even saw somebody who looked like him in the street, it killed me. How scared I was, how mad I was, how everything I was.

Then the judge asked me, "Little girl, what have you got to say? Tell me your side of the story." I didn't have much to tell, because really it was my fault—I *had* married him, nobody had forced me. So I told him I just didn't want him—I had made a mistake, I had thought he was a good man, but he wasn't a good man, because as soon as they had taken me to his home, he had started cutting me with knives and razors and scissors and had tied me down and frightened me, and now I was scared of him—I was afraid he might kill me. I didn't say he was impotent, because when you said that the judge needed proof—he would have made the two of us go into a special room and make love so that he and another witness could watch through a hole in the wall. If your husband was impotent, you could get a divorce immediately. But I didn't want anyone to see me naked or watch me make love, so I didn't say anything about all that. I just said I didn't want him.

With the Muslim law, if your husband leaves you, it's one matter. But if you leave and say in front of a judge that you don't want this husband, and there's no reason—just that you don't love him or don't want him—you can't get away with it. But if you insist you don't want your husband, even though your husband doesn't want to divorce you, they have some kind of system where you won't be divorced and you won't be married— you can't marry any other man—and it's bad, according to the Qur'an, very bad, very bad. You're not a wife, you're not a divorced woman, so you're *nashuusha*. Everything you touch is forbidden to others. Everyone is afraid of you, as though you are a devil, exactly as though you are a devil—they treat you like a devil. They say that a bird that flies over your head won't find anything to eat that day. That's how bad you are—something like a witch, a bad, bad person.

So the judge said, "Do you want to be *nashuusha*, or do you want to go with your husband?" I cried, "No, I don't want to go with him, I don't want to go with him." Everybody stared at me —my family—because they had heard of girls becoming *nashuusha*, but they had never seen it happen, and now it was happening to their daughter. I looked at all their faces, and I listened to my heart and my head, and I looked at his face, and I said, "Unh-unh, I'm not going with him. Do whatever you want, but I'm not going with him, ever again. I don't want to see him. I don't want anything to do with him."

The judge said again, "Little girl—do you really prefer to be that way—*nashuusha*, bad?" I said, "Call me whatever you want…." My mama cried, "No! No! Let me talk to her!" I said, "No, Mama, I don't want him. Do you want me to die? Because that's what I'm going to do—I'm going to kill myself if you let me go with this man." Rahima, he was ugly, ugly, ugly! To me he was ugly—he wasn't really ugly, but that's how much I hated him—that was how I felt. I couldn't even look at his face, I was so angry. So the judge decreed that my husband was not to touch me—that if he even talked to me, I would get a divorce; that if he tried to attack me, I would get a divorce; that I couldn't get anything from him unless I told him I was going to be his wife; that we didn't have anything between us—we were like two strangers to each other; and that he couldn't talk to me and I couldn't talk to him. So I said to myself, If he can't talk to me and touch me, I'll take that!… Forget the divorce! I don't care about the divorce!

The judge gave me that bad status—not divorced and not exactly married—and he read verses of the Qur'an and said, "You all can go now."

I said to myself, "Thank you, Allah! I'm free at last!" but everybody was sad…nobody was talking to anybody…everybody was looking down at the ground. They said, "You've embarrassed us." Mama was crying when she told me, "You've given us a bad name. We have never seen anyone do this…. We've only heard about nashuusha…and now it had to happen to us…. How am I going to face the world…how can I face anybody…how can I go out and talk to somebody when you have disgraced me?"

Rahima, we went home to Mango Village. I tried to talk to Mama all that evening, but she was the same. The next morning, I ran away again. I knew that from now on, whenever I wanted to come home to Mango Village, I would have to come in the night so the neighbours wouldn't see me. And I would have to leave the same night. I was thinking, I wasn't doing anything wrong, but everything I did they said was wrong. And now I'm the one who is nashuusha. So I ran away, back to Mogadishu, where all my friends were. I went to look for my friends.

CHAPTER
14

Back in the city, I found a friend and I said to her, "Let's go over to the meeting house and see if they have any news from Umar." We went there and I asked if they had any news, and they said, "He's fine, he's coming, he's coming. Don't worry…. You can't wait to see him, right? You love him, don't you?" They were teasing me a little bit. They didn't really have any news about him.

My old friend Jowara found me again. She had run away from her husband and she wasn't going to go back this time. She had a relative whose husband was in the military. The husband had been transferred to another town, but the wife still lived in a military compound. Jowara said that would be a good place for us to hide, because it would be hard to find anyone who was staying there. Jowara's family was looking for her too. So we went to the military compound and went door-to-door asking, "Who knows Mrs. So-and-so?" until finally we found her. We told her who we were and she welcomed us, with a nice, warm, open face and open arms and an open house. We told her we had run away from our husbands, and she said we could stay as long as we wanted. We told her we didn't want to cause her any problem, but we had nowhere else to go. I didn't tell her that I was *nashuusha*…a devil woman…a witch…. I just told her I had run away. She said that all she could do for us was give us a place to sleep and food to eat, for as long as we wanted. We said, "Thank you."

In the mornings we worked for her. We washed the clothes and dishes, cleaned the house, cooked, and helped her. She had four children, and we bathed them and played with them. We were like her daughters. In the evenings we were free to go where we wanted. So now we had a schedule—not like before, when you go all day and all night—now we had to work, which was good for us. And it was good for her too—she needed the help. We ate and slept regularly—it was like being at home. We even wore her clothes—where else could you find that? The neighbours thought we were her sisters from somewhere else. She had a nice stone house with three bedrooms. She was a beautiful person, and she gave us everything she had.

One night, at a party, I met a man named Nuur. "Nuur" means "light", and there was light, because he was very light-skinned. I danced with him that night—the first time I danced since I had started going to parties. I had been watching people, how they moved, and I was a fast learner—I picked everything up fast. I danced a slow, close dance with him. He had very pretty teeth, a nice mouth. I like a clean mouth. I don't care how pretty you are, if your mouth doesn't smell good and it's not clean, I don't like it. Nuur was very clean. He was a driver for the Italian embassy. He spoke Italian and many different languages.

I met him again after two nights, at another party. This time I was dressed right, like the other girls; my hair was right, my nails were right. We were making our own dresses—pleated dresses—short but not like a miniskirt, they were down to our knees. Now there was very little difference you could tell between me and these other girls. I was talking with a much better accent. And I was pretty—very pretty. All of us were pretty. And Nuur liked me. I liked him a little—he was better than nothing, that was the way I felt—better than nothing…you have got to at least try….

He invited me and my friend the next night, and the next night, and the next night. He was a heavy, heavy drinker. But the more he dated me, the more I liked him. Just like—no love. I only loved one person, Antony. Every time Nuur took us out he brought a nice gift—small things, to make you happy, little things that a girl needs. I had never used Kotex before, and he brought me some the day after I had my period and got blood on the seat of his car. I had never had ice-cream before, so he bought me some, and I liked it. And there is another sweet thing we call *halwa* that people like to eat in the evening, and he would bring me some of it every night. Always, when he dropped us off, he would give me a little money to ride in a taxi or go to the movies the next day, until we saw each other again. It was very nice—I didn't have anybody else who was giving me that. See, I didn't have anything. No education, no money, even in my family my mama had become poor. I still thought, if I could get a good man, I could really help myself and my family.

I showed Nuur where we were staying because he picked us up and dropped us off every night when we went out. And by a friend-to-friend link, Jowara met one of his friends, and so we became a group. And Nuur was friends with the people who lived in the house where I used to meet Umar. The men who lived there were surprised when they saw me so quickly with Nuur, after I'd been asking for news of another man. Nuur and

I dated for about a month, I think, and it was very nice, very nice for me, and we didn't do anything more than kiss.

Then I began to sip beer too. This is how I started: first, I tasted it. Nuur wanted me to taste it because he was a heavy drinker, and he insisted and insisted. So I tasted it, and it was terrible…a terrible taste! Ugh! He said, "What does it taste like?" I said, "It tastes horrible!" It was burning my mouth and my tongue and the gas bubbles went *s-s-s-s* all inside my mouth and my nose. I said, "It's not even sweet! How can you all drink it? Why don't you put sugar in it?" So he said, "Do you want some sugar? Try it with sugar." He brought me the sugar and brought me a spoon and a glass, and we put some beer and some sugar in it and mixed it. I tasted it and it was better. He said, "Drink it, now it's good." I drank it, and then I went to the bathroom and made myself throw up by putting my finger down my throat, came back, stayed a little bit, finished the other half of what he had given me, stayed a little bit longer, went back to the bathroom, threw up again, and cleaned my mouth. And I was a "good girl"—everybody clapped and said, "Good! Good! See? It's nothing…everybody drinks…it's normal—good girl!" They wanted everyone to be drunk like they were. They didn't know I had thrown up.

But little by little—not heavily, but every night, little by little —I learned to drink…never more than a glass. I didn't know much about Nuur except for his name and his tribe. He didn't know anything about me either, but he was with me every day. Except when he was at work, every night he was there with me.

One night we all went out—six of us—three girls and three men. These other girls, they were always older than me, but they weren't married. Girls in the city, they can stay without marriage till eighteen or twenty. When I was first with them, I thought, what is wrong with them? I thought *I* had waited a long time to get married. Now I would have been ashamed to tell any of them I was married. Everybody called me a little girl. Still, I liked to be around them. I felt free.

We went to another town to have dinner. When we were halfway back to Mogadishu, we stopped by a hospital that had just been built in the countryside. And around the hospital were farms and empty land—a place where young kids would go in those days and park their cars and drink and kiss each other. It was a big open field, it was dark, and nobody bothered you. We went there this night, as we often did, to listen to the radio and talk. We sat outside, the ground was nice…it was cool, the moon was shining on us. The men had had a lot to drink…but they always drank. When men stop the car, you know they want to talk to the girl or pee, or something.

So when Nuur slowed down and turned off the main road onto a dirt road that led into the bush, I asked him, "Why are you going in the bushes?" He said he had to go to the bathroom, so I said, "All right." I wasn't worried, because I had known him for more than a month and he hadn't done anything wrong—he hadn't tried anything—or even asked me…. So we all got out and peed. But he and I were the only ones who came back. The others all stayed in the bushes. We waited outside the car—I sat down on the front of the car. He got up there too, and lay down on me and began hugging and kissing me. But I didn't like it, because drinking makes your mouth stink…smell…. His breath smelled awful. So I pushed him away, and told him I had had enough kissing. He was drunk. Rahima, when I pushed him, he got mad, and he grabbed me by the hair. He was big—tall and heavy. In less than a second, he put me down on the ground beside the car and raped me. Raped me and disvirgined me. I fought, but he was strong and drunk, and he began to slap me. I yelled for help, but he put his hand over my mouth. None of the others came. I will never forget the pain. I remember hearing my circumcision rip open with a sound like the tearing of a piece of cloth and feeling at the same time the most awful pain. Then I became unconscious.

When I opened my eyes, the five of them were fanning me with the other girls' shawls. There was blood…pee…and dirt… everywhere, because I had been struggling even before he put me on the ground. I was in so much pain that I couldn't move my legs. It was as though I was paralysed. And the blood wouldn't stop flowing. There was nothing we could do but take me back to the compound. I was hemorrhaging, but I couldn't go to the hospital, there was too much shame. They took the scarf from around my head and used it to stop the bleeding.

I had an infection…everything. Jowara helped me. She used to wash me with warm water and salt. My genitals were swollen, hot and throbbing from the infection, so she used a raffia fan to make it cool down and feel better.

He didn't come to see me at all. And even after I was well I was ashamed to come out, because of how I had lost everything I had, so easily. And because of whom I had lost it to—I didn't even love him. So I was very, very ashamed. I can't find words to describe it, but I know I felt all the pain—so ashamed and full of disgust. I was ashamed to go out with my friends that I knew, because I wasn't a virgin any more. I didn't have anything any more, really—nothing. It was as though I was dead.

CHAPTER
15

So I stayed home at the house of the lady in the military compound. I ate and slept, and thought about what had happened to me. Once you lose your virginity, that is the end of you. It can break your heart. Especially the way I lost mine. It was horrible and dreadful and shameful, and if anybody knew and told my family, or told any other people, for that matter...it was shameful—very, very shameful. I had killed my name. I wished I was dead so my family wouldn't see my face any more.

I stayed in the military compound for two weeks. Every night I thought, Why did he do that? And why hasn't he come back? And why doesn't he at least say something? Why did he do that? I was sure that just pushing him away when we were kissing wouldn't have made him get angry like that, and grab me by the hair and put me on the ground and start to beat me. I began to think it was something he had planned, because when I yelled... nobody came. I began to think the men had planned the whole thing. When I asked my girlfriends why didn't they come when I yelled—when I needed them—they said the men were holding them back and there was nothing they could do. The men told them, never mind, they're just playing and probably Nuur's kissing Aman and she doesn't want to be kissed. So I think it was something he had planned. But still I couldn't believe it. Why? Why did he wait that long to do this disgusting thing that he did?

In those days, it was shameful even to ask a lady—especially a young girl—to make love. Boys wouldn't try to force you because they were scared of your parents; they were afraid your brothers would come to kill them. But then, I think, many of the men realized that if the girl does tell her family, they will just say it's her fault: "Why were you there in the first place?" "Why did you go with him?" Girls couldn't tell their families because they were too ashamed and scared they would get whipped. So a lot of girls kept it to themselves. I kept it to myself.

I thought maybe since he was *shaanshi*, an outsider group, not Somali, he knew he could never marry me; they hardly ever marry outside their own tribe. He wanted this pretty girl, and maybe he only wanted me for sex. But since I was little and a virgin, maybe at first he just wanted my companionship. Or maybe he drank a lot and wanted to get it over with and be done with me. Or he found another girl, bigger than me, or prettier than me, and he just wanted to see what he could get before he left me.

I was full of anger at him, so I had to see him one more time —to see his face and find out what he had to say. I said to my girlfriend one evening, "Let's go find him." I had been too shy to go out, because I thought everybody knew what had happened to me.

She came with me and we went to the meeting house where I had first met Umar. The people there looked at me differently from the way they had before—at least, that's what I felt—

perhaps it was my imagination. And they acted cold towards me too—at least, that's what I thought. But they invited us to sit down and offered us something to drink. I asked for a Fanta that night, and without any question they gave it to me—that's what made me suspicious. They said they hadn't seen Nuur for two nights, but that he might show up and I could wait if I wanted to. I said, "I will." I was different too—there was a lot of anger in my face. They were acting as though they wanted to ask me questions but were too scared. There wasn't a lot of talk, and no singing. If they said anything, it was just a few questions, like "Did you go home?" or "How've you been?" but it wasn't friendly the way it had been before.

I was careful, as if everybody knew what had happened to me. I wasn't talking "Ba-ba, ba-ba" like I used to. I was watching the people, to see if they were talking about me. But nobody was talking about what happened to me, although they did know about it, because they later let me know they knew.

I became sick because I didn't eat; all I did was cry and cry and ask myself, Why did it happen to me? Why didn't I wait for Umar? Why? Why? Because when I lost my virginity, I thought it was the end of me. Because they tell you that's all you've got, when you're a girl. And I lost it so easily, and I lost it in a way that I never thought I would.

Jowara told me she saw Nuur with another girl at a party, and she took him outside. She asked him why he had done this and, since he had done it, why hadn't he come to see me? Because I could have called my brothers and they could have killed him, because his tribe was a small tribe of people from Mogadishu—they are all white, with straight hair and green eyes. They are called "the tribe of the city". They are afraid of the rest of us, especially of my tribe, because it's so big and powerful. Even Mogadishu was originally our tribe's land. It is my land.

People from all different tribes live there now, but originally it was our tribe's land.

He knew who my tribe was and for that reason we couldn't think why he had done it. She said, "You know we can kill you. They can do anything to you they want. You know they can make you marry her by force, even though you are *shaanshi*, because you disvirgined her. You know you will have to pay a lot of money because you caused her damage. You know all this. If she takes you to court, you will have to pay a big amount of money. If she becomes pregnant, the child will be a bastard, and that bastard is yours. You will have to give her a lot of money. You will have to marry her. You know all this, and all this you have ignored for over two weeks now. You didn't come and apologize, you didn't even know whether she had died or not. You know how she was bleeding when you disvirgined her—the dirt she was lying on was covered with blood—the ground was wet with blood as though they had killed a cow there. She could have died of hemorrhage any time. Who do you think you are?" He said, "I was afraid. I was scared. I made a mistake." She said, "All right—you made a mistake—you were scared. Now there are two things you can do—either you can repair the damage or our family is going to repair the damage. Which do you want?" He said, "I'll fix it." She said, "O.K., fix it then. Let's go."

She brought him to our house. He waited outside in the car. She told me he was here. When I got close to the car, my heart started beating loud. But I was angry, and acting as though I were big and strong so that he would be frightened. I was breathing hard. I went up to the car and stood beside it. Jowara said, "Get inside the car, so nobody can see you." So I opened the door and got into the back seat. I didn't say a word. Jowara got in too, next to me, and closed the door behind her. We drove a little way away. He said, "I'm sorry. I know what I did was wrong.

I'm sorry. I'm sorry." I said, "It's too late, 'sorry' won't fix it. Now I'm disvirgined." But actually I was closed up again—I had stayed in bed for two weeks and my circumcision had almost closed again. I had lost the one inside, but the outside one—its flesh had been torn, and when you put the torn edges together again, they heal together. And we had put on the black paste that we use like glue on a girl's circumcision when she is circumcised, so that it would heal closed. But it wasn't the way it used to be.

I said, "You disvirgined me, and your being sorry doesn't help me. You have to do something. And I think I'm pregnant too, because I'm throwing up. Now you have to marry me." I was trying to scare him. I wasn't pregnant—and if I had been, I couldn't have known it yet because it hadn't even been a month. And I was already married anyway. He said, "No—you're not pregnant—you're not—we have to make sure first before we decide anything—we have to make sure." I said, "I am sure. I'm pregnant. I've been throwing up from the day you raped me until now, and what does that mean?" His skin was light, and he turned red. He was sweating. He got out of the car and wiped his face and said, "No! It can't be! It can't be!"

He said he would talk to his parents and his parents had to go talk to their chief and their chief would have to talk to my chief and then, after the two chiefs had talked, whatever they decided, his family and my family would have to do. I thought, "No, no, no, I don't want my parents to know about this." I said, "No, let me tell my family first. Don't say anything to your family. Do you want to marry me—yes or no?" He kept on saying, "Yes, but we have to make sure you're pregnant first!" He kept on saying that: "We have to make sure...."

When we went back to the house in the military compound, Jowara's relative told me that Mama had come looking for me. She said she had told my mama that I had been gone for a long time—she didn't know where I was. She said that Mama was very worried and cried, so she told me to go and see her. But I was scared to go home, even though I wanted so badly to see Mama. I said I would, but not yet, not while I was in this condition—because my mama might say to me, "Come, show me! Are you still a virgin?" and I didn't have anything to show her.

Nuur would come one night to visit, then for two or three nights he wouldn't come. He was making excuses—I think he knew that I wasn't really pregnant, that I was trying to trick him, that it was my revenge.

So I began to look for him. He was hard to find. But I got his last name, his father's name, and that's enough to find out the area where someone lives. So I went to the part of the city where his tribe lived. He lived in an old part of Mogadishu, a part where his tribe kept their boats when they first came to Somalia, and then they built homes there, very strong, white homes. They used to say his tribe built those homes by mixing clay with milk instead of water. Even the sea couldn't damage those buildings. They looked like castles or fortresses; some of them had small turrets on the top level so people could watch over their boats in the port.

I started going down the narrow alleyways, knocking door-to-door on the first floor, saying, "Who knows Nuur Haaji?"

Finally I found him. We were three of us girls together that day, going door-to-door in the old city, and we found a man who knew him. He said, "Come on over to my house first and have something to drink, and then I'll take you over there." It was one of the buildings that looked like a castle, winding and tall with four or five levels. He asked us what we were doing in this area and why we were looking for Nuur Haaji. They protect each other. Nuur's grandmother was one of our people, so I told him I was from his grandmama's family. He said, "Ah, so you want to see one of your people? You've never been to his home before?" I said, "No." "So you don't know his children?" I said to myself, "Children?" But I caught myself in time and said, "No, I haven't seen his children…or his wife…this will be the first time, and I'm so excited about meeting them." "Do you want to go now?" he asked. "I'll show you his door." He showed us where the door was and told us to go through the door and up the stairs.

We started up the stairs. We didn't go all the way up though —we stopped and talked quietly. We were surprised. "Wife and children?" "Wife? And children?" We looked at each other and we laughed. I was so shocked—there was nothing you could do but laugh.

But I was really angry too, because he had destroyed me. I told my friends, "He broke my heart, he broke my virginity. I want to break his life." I whispered to them, "Listen, I'm going to tell a lie, and you just be quiet and pretend like it's true." They said, "No, Aman! The guy is married. Are you crazy… going into his house and talking to his wife? Please, let's go!" I said, "No! I want to make sure he never cheats another girl."

We knocked on the door. My heart was beating fast and I was sweating. A girl opened the door and I asked if this was Nuur Haaji's house. "Yes," she said, "who are you?" "A friend," I answered, "can we come in?" She said, "Wait!" and went back and I could hear her talking to a woman. She came back. "Yes, come on in." A woman came and greeted us and asked me what my name was and what we wanted. I told her we were looking for Nuur Haaji—that I was a friend of his wife's. She said, "Which wife?" I said I was a friend of his wife Zenab, and that she was in the hospital. I said, "Last night, after he left, her labour began and we took her to the hospital and she had a baby and the baby died, and we're here to tell you so you can tell him that they need him in the hospital as soon as possible." Her mouth was wide open. She called another, older, woman over, saying, "Tell this person what you just told me." Slowly—I was shocked when I saw this older lady and she told me she was Nuur's mother, and I was scared—I repeated the story slowly—that the baby had died, that they wanted him in the hospital as soon as possible. The older lady asked me what Nuur looked like, and I told her, and she said it *must* be him, so I knew I was at the right place. She told us, "Thank you," and said we should leave now. We ran and ran down all those winding stairs. I said, "Thank God! I did it! I did it!" Rahima, I felt relieved—as if I had been born again.

We went to the house of one of my friends. I had already had to leave the house in the military compound, because Mama knew I was staying there, and Jowara was missing—I never saw her again. I think her family took her back to her husband. One of my friends kept me for two nights, but then the next day I had to leave. I went back to the house in the military compound, because I had some clothes there and I was hoping for news of Jowara. Her relative told me Nuur was coming there every day to look for me.

After four days, I was at a friend's house—it was evening—when Nuur came with the police and dragged me by the hand to the police station. He told the police I had destroyed his house. He said his wife had left him—she had broken all the furniture in the house and had left and taken the children with her. I messed him up, he said. Of course he didn't tell the police about the damage he did to me, and I couldn't tell them. So they arrested me. But this chief of police was my tribe, and when they brought me to him he asked me my name. He noticed that the way I spoke and the way he spoke were the same. He asked, "Who are you?" I told him my name, and he asked me if I was the daughter of the chief of Mango Village. I said,

"Yes, that's my father." He said, "I know your father. I don't believe it—what are you doing here, in jail, and away from home?" I said, "I was at my friend's house, and this man told lies to the police so I would be arrested." He asked, "Why?" I said, "He loves me. He lied to the police and told them I destroyed his life and his home, but I didn't, Uncle, I didn't…."

"Go home," he said to me. "Be careful and don't mess around with these city people—they're different from where you come from." He gave me his name and told me to tell my daddy what he had done for me.

CHAPTER
16

WHAT I THOUGHT WAS BEST FOR me, and for everybody now, was not to go back home but to face the world alone, no matter how things were going to happen. So I decided not to go home. Anyway, I couldn't go home because of the shame it would be for Mama. There was no reason to go home either—once you're married you're a grown woman, even if you're only twelve years old. It would have been painful too. I didn't want another humiliation. In that small village, they would say, "See. We were right. She couldn't keep her husband. She doesn't want him. She's this. She's that. She's a *sharmuuto*." I didn't want to hear that.

And I was trying to build a new life, no matter how badly I did it. I had started with a low group—sleeping in the street, no friends, nobody knows me—and then I started learning. When I first came to Mogadishu—when I first ran away from my husband—I thought I was from a better tribe and the city was mine, because even though I wasn't born there, the land had belonged to my tribe. I didn't know who owned things now, or how they owned them, or what the system was. It took a while to learn.

In Mango Village, your name is more important than anything. If you are from a good family and a good tribe no one can take that away from you. That's what I believed. Even when my mama became poor and I was sick, even when I was a kid and the others teased me because I had had TB, I was still from a good tribe and my daddy was a chief. I thought my daddy was rich, to me he was rich, so rich. Everybody would say, "Oooo! Your daddy!" But after I moved to Mogadishu, I realized my father was poor—because all he had were his animals and his land. It was nothing like the wealth that people had in the big city. If my daddy wanted money, he'd have to sell some of his cattle or crops, and Mama's money from her business was yo-yo, come and go. These city people, *they* had money…buying this and selling this, they had cars and lots that we didn't have. That was what I saw: in Mogadishu your tribe or name didn't matter, it only mattered if you were rich and could buy what you wanted. I had considered myself high-family when I was back home, and it was hard for me to be low. I came from the country, so the city people considered me *reer-baadiyo*—uncivilized. I was trying to go higher, higher. I was hoping I could move up, up, up.

But I faced a very dangerous situation, like the one all runaway kids face. You really get tired when you run around and spend one night here, one night there, and the next night with no sleep because you're in the street. You need a place to go that you can call home, and I was lucky, because after I lost Jowara, I found a friend—Maryan. Maryan understood me. Her man was European, so she knew what it was like to be in trouble, to be called *sharmuuto*. Her home was like an escape. Maryan said if I was really in trouble and had nowhere else to go, she would feed me, and wash my clothes. But she was afraid of my family, so I couldn't stay there all the time. I could only go for a night and leave the next morning. I thank Allah for her.

It was dangerous—very dangerous. No money—one day you have some and the next day you don't. One day you eat, the next day you don't—you're hungry. Sometimes you sleep in the street. I faced it—all that danger. Sometimes men left you way out in the bushes; when you refused to make love to them, they just left you out there in danger from hyenas—you name it—snakes. Nobody killed you, but animals could kill you. You could get beaten or raped. You went out with a man because he could buy you food. You might have your friend with you, so he spends more money. Girls would always go together in twos or threes, unless you knew the man well—enough to know what he was like—because a man thought if only the two of you went out together, you automatically made love. So you always took someone else along, to show you wouldn't do anything. But the boys know the girl will always bring a girlfriend along, so they bring a boyfriend along too…he brings his boyfriend and you bring your girlfriend…. There are so many games they play: this way is shameful, so you do it that way—and then they have another way to get around it.

The older men were better because they had money, and I needed money for my family and myself. They take you to dinner, and even if you don't do anything, they give you some money. But it was all on a day-to-day basis—you never know about tomorrow.

I was good company because around me you never got tired. I sang, I talked, I talked sense, and I knew how to kill time. People told each other about me: they said I was witty, a storyteller, a comic. The only thing I didn't like was to make love, because nobody gave me time to learn or decide—everything was a rush and I didn't like it because it was painful and I thought it was always like that. Otherwise, I was a good companion.

One day I was at Maryan's. She was cooking lunch, when there was a knock on the door. She opened the door and there he was —my husband. Only Allah knows how my stomach twisted and twisted with fear. I looked at him and I thought, Why did you bring him?

I got up and washed my hands. I knew everybody was watching me, because they knew I was going to run. I pretended that everything was fine. I greeted him and invited him to sit down and asked him what he wanted to drink. Men would never get even a glass of water for themselves. The man brings home the money, the clothes, the food, the woman does everything for him—carry water to him, and bring him soap and a towel. My heart and all my body were shaking; even though I knew he couldn't take me, I was still scared. But I was pretending to be strong, and laughing and asking him whether he wanted tea or water or orange juice or milk—whatever he wanted to drink, as though nothing had happened between me and him. He said, "Water!" So I went and came back fast with the water and gave it to him. I pretended I had to get water for myself, and as I was walking back, I threw the glassful of water one way and slipped out the back door the other way—I was out of the house and the whole area in less than five minutes. I ran until I saw a small three-wheeled taxi and stopped it and got in and told the man to go fast, fast, anywhere he wanted, because someone was after me who was trying to kill me.

I didn't have any money. He rode around and rode around, because I told him I would pay him whatever it cost and he believed it. All the time I was riding, I was thinking, What to do? Where to go? When you get scared and your heart is beating hard, you can't think—disaster is close and you don't know what to do. After a while, the driver stopped and said, "Listen, little girl, where do you want to go? Now you're out of danger—nobody's running after you now. And you're not rich so you can't ride around all day and pay me. So where do you want to go?" I told him I didn't know—that I didn't have anywhere to go. I told him the truth. "I was married to an old man, and I don't want him and I ran away from him. He is still after me, and I'm not from here and I don't know where to go. I don't have any money, so do what you want to do." And I cried. He held me and told me, "Don't cry." And he took me to his house. He had two children and a wife. And he told his wife to let me stay there as long as I wanted.

They were a lovely family. I told them the whole story, and they were sad, very sad. They were a very low tribe—as a matter of fact, they are called Addon—a slave tribe. Originally they were from somewhere else—another part of Africa. They don't look like us, they're different. They say they used to be slaves, but nobody owns them now, they're free—they speak the same language and have the same religion and everything. They just have a different look—they have a big nose and we have a small nose, they have kinky hair and we have soft hair, they have rough skin and we have soft skin. Nobody marries them—they marry each other. But they live everywhere, especially along the rivers and near the coast. They work hard on the farms or they work in the cities—the girls and the men—as maids. You can tell that they used be slaves, because they still act as though they were slaves—they do all the menial work, and they do it for very little money, sometimes no money, in exchange for food or a home. In Mango Village, there are a lot of them—they stay under the rule of my tribe. They're kind people, very kind people, but they're considered low-caste.

He told me to come and go as I pleased. I was like his family, like his own daughter or sister. So I stayed—I was very tired, and I stayed for a little while that day.

It was soon after this that I heard Umar was back from his work with the fish company, but I couldn't face him. His friends told him I wasn't a virgin any more. They told him who disvirgined me, because Nuur told everybody. They told him I was going with a different man every night. They told him a lot of lies, with some truth. Anyway, Umar didn't look for me. I wanted to see him, so badly, because he was a peaceful man. I had known him for quite a while and he never ever even tried to make love to me, he didn't even mention it.

I went to the house of a girl who knew him. She told me he didn't want to see me because of what I had done—I hadn't waited for him. He loved me, but he didn't trust me. I begged her until she said she would invite him to lunch at her house. I went to her house the day she had said she was going to cook lunch for a small group. He was there. When I saw him, oh, it was beautiful, just to see his face—he had an angel-face, an innocent face, and he was a comic—he talked a lot, you couldn't keep him quiet. And when I was face to face with him and made eye contact, he was smiling. I was smiling too, so he got up and put his arms out, and we held each other tight. He pulled back and looked at me and changed his face to an angry one and sat back down again. I held him tightly around the neck and said, "How are you? How are you doing?" His friends looked at him and said, "Hey! Talk to your friend! What's wrong with you? She's holding your neck and you're trying to push her back! Say hello to the girl. Where will you get a lovely, funny girl like this?" Then we kissed each other on the cheek. He looked at me and said, "Are you O.K.?" And I said, "Yes, how are you doing?" We sat there, and talked and talked. He never asked me what I was doing; I asked him about his trip and his work and the fish—you know, the new place and all that.

After we ate the others left, one by one. I kissed him again—modest, on the cheek—but he told me, "No," and he pushed me away and said he didn't need that. I said, "I need that. It's been so long since we have held each other. Everything was good when you left—what is it?" He answered, "You know what's wrong. You know what happened." I said, "O.K., it's my fault, everything is my fault." He said, "Yes, it's your fault. If you did it for money, why didn't you write me a letter? I know you ran away. But if you didn't want to go back home, the least you could do was stay with this friend and she would have sent me a telegram or a letter, and I would have sent you money every month. You didn't want to go with me. Me and you, we're through."

I begged him, but finally I said, "All right, I accept it. I was wrong, very wrong. I didn't know what was going to happen. How could I know something like that was going to happen? At least let's be friends." And he said, "We are, and I'm still going to help you as a friend, but not as a boyfriend. I love you, but I can't take it. All my friends know what you are. Where can I take you? A new city with new people? I can't—this is my country, this is my city, and these are my friends. And this is you. You did it, I can't forget it. But anything you need…anything you want…if you want to talk to me, anything…you know how to find me." He even told me where he lived. And we really were friends; I used to see him about once a week. I would rather be friends with him than be zero.

Now I really became a wild girl. I learned a lot. I knew what men wanted, and I could even tell by their looks who was dangerous and who wasn't, who was more dangerous and who was less dangerous.

I didn't like the old ones much, but at least they weren't violent like the young ones. So I liked the old ones. Not as men—by now I wasn't looking for love. I was looking for security, and the old men helped by giving you money, and I wanted the money first for Mama and then for me. I wanted to be on my own—I wanted to have a house and decent clothes and look like the other people. Some of these old men loved me like a daughter when they met me and I told them that I wasn't doing anything—that I wasn't what they thought. But then…if you go three or four nights with them and see that they like you and respect you and they kiss you, the next thing you know they want to take off your dress. You say no and say no, and then you get tired of saying no. In those kinds of situations, girls would allow men to "paint" them by "brushing". You didn't allow them to go in—just held your legs together and they put themselves between your legs. "Kiss and brush" if you wanted to stay a virgin. They did their thing between your legs—like that uncle did to me when I was a little girl. It's filthy, and your clothes would smell—horrible. But many of the girls were doing it.

Very few girls could work in those days—married women sometimes—but if the young single ones took a job, they were *sharmuuto*. So men were the only way, and letting them paint you—it was like a giveaway. For some of them, I was doing it as a favour; they had done me a favour, and at least this I could do for them. I thought that was just the way it happened. What I could get from them I would get, and what they got from me they got. But doing that is hard, very hard. All you see is pain, pain, pain. No more love either.

One time I didn't have any money, and it was the end of Ramadan—the 'Id was the next day. I had looked for money all Ramadan, but still I had no money. There was an old man who liked me, and he had offered me money, but I had always said no, no. But tomorrow was the 'Id, and I couldn't *stand* it, knowing my family would have no gifts coming from me. Because my family was counting on me. I brought gifts all the time. It was almost ten o'clock and they close the shops at twelve the night before the 'Id. So I went to that man, and I let him paint me, and I got money. I made it to the shop. I bought everything I wanted for my family.

In the morning I took the first bus going to Mango Village —an hour and a half drive. I was there by eight o'clock. I gave them their clothes. Everybody took a shower and put on their new clothes. I was there. I was very proud. Very proud.

CHAPTER

17

I WAS TIRED OF BEING IN THE street and having no home to go to. I had destroyed my family name and my name, and I didn't have anything. The other women they called *sharmuuto*—most of them had houses and money and gold and everything they wanted. And there I was, just fourteen years old, and I had a bad name and nothing. No more hope.

One day, after I had been disvirgined for about three months, I went with a friend for a walk downtown. It was Friday and all the shops were closed, and there were very few people in the town. We were looking at the dresses in the windows of Alta Moda. There was an old white man with a white car who passed by slowly on the street, and when we looked at him, he winked at us. He stopped the car and told us to get in. We told him, "No! No, no, no!" We began to walk down the street, but he followed us in the car and kept on telling us to get in. We said, "No! Here everybody can see us. If you go somewhere where nobody can see us, we might get in." We walked all the way to the beach, which was quite a distance, where the fish market is, and nobody goes on that street because it stinks. He came, and we covered our faces and got in, all three of us, in the back. He drove out of the city. We weren't scared because there were three of us and he was alone.

He took us to a restaurant. All of us spoke Italian, but not well. So we said, "You sit alone and eat alone, and the three of us will eat by ourselves together. And we'll see you in the car. Or else drop us before the restaurant and let us go in alone." So he dropped us off first, and we walked to the restaurant and sat at a table far away from him. He had sent the waiter to our table and told him to give us whatever we wanted to eat. This restaurant was out of the city, in another town, so we could smoke. We all ordered different brands of cigarettes, so we could have three full packs, to have some for tomorrow. We stayed more than three hours.

When we got tired of that, we got up and began to walk out of the restaurant and down the road. He got his car and drove behind us. When there were people in the street, neither of us stopped, but finally we came to a clear space in the road and he stopped. We got in fast, and he drove away fast too—if anyone had seen us, they would have stoned us, because we were Somali women with a white man. It was evening, and he took us for a ride in the country to see another town on the beach. When we came back to Mogadishu, I told him how to get to a place near Maryan's house, and said, "You can drop us off here. Thank you very much for everything." He asked me if he could see me again, so I said, "Yes, why not?" He asked if it would be all right if he saw me the next night, and I said yes. He said, "How about if you go to a movie, and I'll meet you where I met you this morning?" That place would be dark at night. And that was the cinema I liked to go to all the time—the one near Alta Moda. I agreed and he gave me money to go the movies the next night. I was very happy, because I was broke. I couldn't wait until he left, so I could look at the money and see how much it was. Rahima, it was twenty shillings! It was a lot of money for me then.

The next night, I went to the movies with one of my friends. At nine o'clock he was there. The place he took us this time was a European restaurant—there were very few Somalis there. We sat together at the same table and he ordered champagne. We said, "What is champagne?" He said, "It's a sweet drink." The old man kept on insisting we taste it. I was the first to taste it, and it was sweet. So I convinced my friend to taste it. She liked it too. This was nice! The champagne made us talk too much. I think we were drunk because I remember my tongue was heavy, my head was heavy, my feet were heavy. When I got up—my feet felt like elephant feet—I could barely pick them up. He helped us, and we were laughing—"ki-ki-ki-ki"—me and her. He was in the middle and we were on both sides, and he was holding us by the shoulders to steady us so we wouldn't fall. He put us in the car, and we spent the night at his house, because we were drunk. He had a beautiful home, with a big bed. All three of us slept in the bed, but he didn't touch us.

In the morning, he got up. He had a man who worked for him, for cleaning, who ate outside. He told the man to cook us breakfast. He woke me up and gave me a kiss and told me he was coming back later. We could stay home and the man would fix food for us. In case we couldn't wait or wanted to go out to eat, or whatever, he left one hundred shillings with me. Whew!

Who would want to go out, with a bed like that, so comfortable? Rahima, I slept until almost one o'clock, it was so nice and clean and soft. We took a shower—a nice, clean shower. Even in the big city, at most of my friends' houses they just used a bucket and cup and poured the water over. So we stayed under this shower for a long time! When he came back, we talked. He came and put his arm around my shoulder, trying to hold me close. He smelled good, a very clean smell, but I was shy, and besides, he was old—not very old, but he must have been over forty, close to fifty. He was a sporty man—he always wore white pants, white socks, black shoes, and a white sportshirt. The colonizer's dress. His name was Carlo.

He said he had to go back, but why didn't we wait for him until he closed the shop. We said, "What shop?" He said, "The shop I own." He said he was going to take me to see the shop one day, but why didn't we wait for him to come back and then we would go out for dinner. He kissed me again and left. Around nine o'clock, he came back and we went to a different place—a restaurant that served Somali food—and there were a lot of our people there, so we had to cover our faces and eat at separate tables. After that, Carlo asked us if we were going to go back to his house to sleep. My friend said no, and then I couldn't say yes. I was scared, after all I had been through. So I went with my friend to her house. I still had the one hundred shillings he had given me in the morning, but he gave me another one hundred shillings, and said, "Go—both of you—to a shop tomorrow, and get some nice clothes." We took the money and said, "Thank you." He told me to meet him in the same place I had first met him on Friday morning. My friend and I were happy. We had a lot of money: two hundred shillings, plus a couple of shillings left over from the twenty he had given me that night!

In the morning we went to get some clothes, shoes, scarves, underwear—everything I needed and everything she needed. We bought some perfume and powder. After we took a shower, we just put on a little powder and perfume. (We didn't wear any makeup or lipstick.) When we went back to my friend's house, we took a taxi! We put on our new clothes and went downtown to the movies. We came out about nine o'clock, and there Carlo was, waiting for us.

So it was like that every day. Perfect. Money was everywhere. That night, my friend said she had to go home. He begged me to stay. I said to myself, Anyway, you're not a virgin any more. What are you afraid of? This man is kind and he's an old man, maybe he can't manage much. So after we took my friend home, I came back with the man to his house. He left in the morning after he kissed me and gave me money. Now I started sleeping in his house. I was glad I had found somebody who really wanted me, but I said I couldn't stay—I couldn't live with him —because if my family found out, this was the worst thing of all the things I had done, to live with a white man. If they found out, either I would die or he would die. They would kill me. But by this time I had a lot of money—well, enough: I had something in my pocket all the time.

CHAPTER
18

I HAD CHANGED—I WAS DRESSING
nicely, I had little high-heeled shoes and everything. I went to
the hairdresser once a week, and every week I bought a new
dress. I became more relaxed and started to enjoy my life. I knew
I was destroyed—that I had destroyed my family's name—but I
felt a bit better about myself since I had found this man.

Now my old man wanted to make love to me. This time I
wanted it, because he was kind to me. It was right for me to pay
him back. A little, a lot, no matter what he had, he would give it
to me, even without my asking. He made love differently from
the others. First he kissed me, and then he kissed my breasts
and my nipples and then my stomach, and then he wanted to
kiss farther down. I pulled him up, but he still wanted to go
down. I was laughing, because his tongue was tickling me. He
held my hands quiet and went all the way down and kissed me
on my genitals. I was laughing so hard that I peed on him! He
stopped and we got up and changed the bed and washed ourselves off. I was still laughing when we finished cleaning up.
Then we made love the usual way.

The next morning, he told me to take some money and go shopping for myself, and he kissed me and asked me when he would see me again. He knew he wouldn't see me for a couple of days, till I spent all the money, and then I would come back. He was giving things to me—and I took them and I had to give him what he wanted, which was my body and myself. He was getting what he wanted, I was getting what I wanted. It was what I had to do to survive. Otherwise I'd be in the street again. I was not happy to do it. But there was no other way. So I did it….

But he got tired of that. He said, "Why don't we get married, and if you're afraid to stay here, I'll take you to Europe and we can stay there, or you can stay there and I'll come back here and you can come and see me every year, or I can go there and see you every year. Then maybe after we have a baby, your family will forget all this, and if you're gone a long time they'll miss you a lot. You know they love you, so they will forgive us—they will forgive you." And I said, "No! I'm married!" He said, "What? Married? Married to who?" I told him, "Another old man!" Rahima, he turned red, and blue, and he got mad: "Why didn't you tell me?" My Italian wasn't very good—I would mean one thing and say another—but everything people said to me, I could understand almost completely. I tried to explain myself, slowly. I said, "You didn't ask me. You know when you met me and used to pick me up—I was running from my husband. I don't want that old man. I'm going to get a divorce, and then I'll marry you. Just don't rush, wait." He said, "But how long…? I love you…." I said, "I love you too." I lied. But I liked him—he was a good man, the way he respected me. I had respect for him too. He never forced me; if I said no, it was no. No madness, no rape, nothing. That was very good.

One day he said, "Listen, why don't you go and talk to your husband and see if he wants to take some money to divorce you?" I said, "No, that man…he refused money from my family…how can he take it from someone else?" He asked, "How much did he refuse?" I said, "I don't know, but my daddy offered him money and he said he didn't want money." He asked, "How long ago?" I said, "A long time ago. He refused many times." He said, "Do you mind asking him again?" I said, "No! I don't ever want to see that man. I'm scared of him and I don't like him, and I don't want to see him." And Carlo said, "O.K., O.K., I'm sorry. Forget it."

But soon he asked me again whether I would go and talk to my husband. He told me to tell him he would give him anything he asked for if he would just divorce me. I was worried, but I couldn't stay the way I was, because I was lying to people, very few people besides my family knew I was married. And I didn't want to stay *nashuusha*—it was like being a witch, in over ten thousand women you might find only one considered *nashuusha*. So I wanted a divorce, really, before anybody found out what I was. If Carlo offered to pay my husband more than my daddy had, maybe he would take it.

The more I thought about it, the more it seemed like a good idea. After all, my family, the people in Mango Village, my husband and his family, they all thought of me as a *sharmuuto*, since I wasn't with my family and I wasn't with my husband. (They used to call me a *sharmuuto* when I was with my family—imagine now, I was a big, big *sharmuuto*.) I said to myself, Maybe your husband won't want you back—just go and tell him, "I became a *sharmuuto*, and I go with whites." Because if you go with whites, nobody wants you back. They think you've got a disease. No one from our culture would want you back. You might make peace with your family, but you wouldn't find any man who would marry you. You would carry that bad name for the rest of your life, and they would call your children bastards.

Even if you were married to the white man and he became Muslim, still your children were bastards.

So one day I decided to go and face my husband. I went, but my heart—Allah, my heart! This time, Maryan went with me, because I told her about my plan. She said, "Where are you going to get the money? Are you selling your body?" And I said, "I've got an old man who loves me and wants to marry me, and I want to marry him." So the two of us went together. I felt safer, because she was big, tall, and healthy. I was afraid he might grab me and keep me in, but he couldn't do that with her. Of course we went in the evening when nobody could see us.

His face seemed to say, "What is she doing here?" He let us sit down and offered us something to drink. Maryan started. She said, "Since you went to the judge she's not at home and nobody knows where she is—she's in the street all the time and she's spoiled her name…." (She was trying to say I had become very bad, so he would divorce me.) "And she's going to stay in the street as long as the two of you are married. So why don't you do her a favour and take whatever you ask, even more than the money you paid, and divorce her? She's little, she's only fourteen years old, and she's already in the street. You have a daughter too—do you want your daughter to be like her?" She cried, and I cried. I said, "Please, Uncle, please. Just leave me alone, divorce me and take your money. Leave me alone. I don't want to be a witch, I don't want to carry a bad name. I want to go home and stay with my family. Please, I want to marry who I want." I was praying to Allah that he would say yes. He said, "I know what you want to be, which you already are and already were before I met you—in the street, with the whites…." But he said he would think about it. He said he would have to remember and write down all the money he had spent—every penny he had spent.

I went back to Carlo and told him what had happened, and he said, "Whatever he asks, I'll give it." And I said, "Thank you."

After ten days, my husband came to Maryan's house. He said he wanted three thousand shillings total—one thousand for each *dalqad*, each "I divorce thee"—because when you divorce in Islam, the man has to say it three times, with the woman's name. And I would have to give up the right to my *mahr*. *Mahr* is a gift you are given when you marry—what you agree you will be given if you are divorced. It might be a Qur'an, it might be a camel, it might be money.

He said he didn't want anyone to know he was taking money. He was playing the role of a big man who didn't need money. He said for us not to tell people—he just wanted to do it quietly, in silence—and he would bring his witness and we should bring the money to his house on Friday night.

Maryan told me the good news. I said, "Great, I'll go bring the money now." But she said she wanted to go with me. "I want to see this white man you're talking about and see if it's true or not, and see what he wants from you." She wanted to make sure I wasn't in trouble—selling my body to more than one man.

I knew where Carlo's shop was—I used to go to the shop if I was downtown, just to see him. I went to the shop a little afraid to tell him that Maryan wanted to see him. But he noticed—every time I had a little problem and went to him, he could tell, because I was always turning my head down and not speaking properly. So I made the sad face I used to do, and he said, "What is it, darling, what is it?"

We agreed to meet at his home. At his home, the door was open, and I ran fast and covered my face so I wouldn't be seen. He was waiting for me, and we went straight to his room and closed the door. He said, "Tell me, what's wrong? What happened? Does your husband want to take you back? Did he change

his mind?" I said, "No, no, no. My friend wants to see you because she wants to know where I'm getting the money from.
Her man is white like you." He said, "No problem, let me talk
to her." I said, "I've got good news too. My husband wants the
money Friday!" He said, "How much?" I said, "Three thousand." He said, "Is that all? You've got it, don't worry!"

Rahima, I was so happy! When we knocked on Maryan's door,
she opened it. Her Italian man was there, it turned out he knew
Carlo—they were old friends. We fixed dinner and drinks for
the men. I drank tea that night and played good girl. We closed
the doors so nobody would see us. We talked and we talked, and
Carlo said, "Thank you for helping Aman—I really love her...."
He told Maryan he loved me a lot and he wanted to marry me
and take me to Europe. She said, "But she's too young!" and he
said, "I know. I'll wait as long as it takes."

Friday came. Maryan and I went with the money. Off we
went to my husband's house. My husband said, "We're all ready.
Let's get it over with." Maryan suspected him and she said to
herself, These are two of his friends. He could take the money
and say it never happened. So she said, "We need another witness." We don't have to get divorced in front of a judge. Your husband can divorce you wherever you are—he can even divorce you
in the street! He can just snap his fingers and say, "Go! You're
divorced." All you need are witnesses. Maryan said, "I need a
third witness. Can you call your watchman?" Because at least we
knew he was our tribe.

When he had brought in the watchman, he said, "Before I
divorce you, where is the money?" My cousin gave him just
what he had demanded: three thousand, one thousand for each
dalqad. She counted the three thousand shillings, all in hundred-
shilling notes, into the hand of the watchman, and the watchman counted them into my husband's hand. When he had the

money, my husband said my name and said he divorced me in all three *dalqad*s and there was no coming back.

He gave me all three *dalqad*s—if he had given me only two, there was a chance he could say he was still married. But he gave me three *dalqad*s, in front of the three witnesses and Maryan, and I was free! Then he said he would go to the judge to tell him he had divorced me, so the judge could take out what he had put in the book about me. We shook hands, and he said goodbye and good luck, and I told him the same thing.

Rahima—when I got out of his house, I was jumping up and down, and going "Lulululululu." Maryan and I jumped and we held each other, and we ran and then we held each other again. I was free! Free! Free at last!

And I was no longer *nashuusha*.

I spent the night at Maryan's house. We talked and talked and talked. We had a thousand shillings left, so she said that since Carlo didn't want it back, why didn't we go home and celebrate? But first, she said, we should stop by his shop and tell him the good news. He was very happy. We went shopping and bought clothes for our families—her mama, her sisters, my mama, everybody. We bought a sack of sugar and a lot of pasta and tomato paste and a lot of coffee and a lot of spices—we bought everything our families needed. She bought me a pair of gold earrings, the kind young girls wear, and they were beautiful. She bought me two dresses—very expensive, nice dresses, and shawls, shoes, and underwear. And then we went to my mama's house.

They were all surprised to see me. In the middle of the day, and with so many gifts and so much food! My mama said, "Where did you get all this? I don't want anything she got from selling her body"—as if I really were a *sharmuuto*! Maryan said, "Please don't speak like that, don't let the neighbours hear you.

It's not true what you're saying. *I* bought all of this. Be quiet, and listen to what your daughter has to say!"

I couldn't talk. I just cried and I held my mama. We all went into the house, and closed the door. Maryan told her I had been divorced the night before. My sister and my mama began to sing "Lululululululu" so the neighbours could hear, and Mama cried out, "My daughter is divorced! My daughter is divorced! My daughter is divorced!"

CHAPTER
19

I WAS HAPPY TO SEE MY MAMA
celebrate. I had given her a lot of scares because I was a young
lady out there by herself, running around. Mama invited the
neighbours and told them. We got some *halwa*, the sweet you eat
when you invite people over, and cookies. Afterwards we went
to see my auntie and her daughter, to give them a gift and tell
them the news. My mama and my sister went with us. My mama
asked where we got the money to pay my husband, and Maryan
said that she paid—her boyfriend gave her the money.

We stayed in Mango Village for two nights, and then we went
back home to the big city. I knew I couldn't stay in the village
after what I had been through. Maybe once a month, I had been
going back to bring Mama money—every time Carlo gave me
one hundred shillings, I gave her fifty. When I bought a dress for
myself I bought one for Mama. I knew what my family needed,
and I gave to them. Carlo would drive me, and he would park
outside, about a mile away, while I ran in. I would only go at

night, when everyone was asleep. If he couldn't drive me, I gave the gifts to a cousin or friend or a driver—anyone who was going to Mango Village.

I was always welcome, my mama would have taken me back any time. Mama always loved me. But I didn't want to shame her. So after the celebration for my divorce, we went back to Mogadishu. I spent the night with my old man. We stayed home and made love. We had a good time again, but it was…I don't know, a part was missing.

Not long after we were back in the big city, Carlo took me over to Maryan's house. She said she had to go somewhere and could we all go together. "Sure," he said, "come on." At night you can ride with whoever you want, because nobody can see you, so we all went together. (In those days, even in the big city, when you drove with whites you had to cover yourself with your shawl until there was nobody watching you, or until you were out of the city where you lived, and then you took your shawl off and you breathed!) I didn't have a shawl on, so I took my dress up and covered myself with it because I also had on a long slip. I lifted my dress up until it covered my face.

We stopped in front of a very nice house, in the area where all the consuls and ambassadors lived—a white, rich people's area close to the downtown. The house was brand-new and white. There was a watchman watching the house, and Maryan got out and talked to him, and he opened the gate for us to drive in. Around the house was a beautiful garden, with stone seats in it, and I was saying to myself, I wish this were my house! Maryan opened the house with a key, and I asked her, "How come you have a key?" She said, "It's my friend's house." I thought it was her white man's house. We looked around. She said, "How do you like this?" Everything—the house, the painting, the furniture—smelled brand-new. The living room was beautiful. I said to myself, Allah, I love this. One day please give me a house like this.

Maryan handed the keys to me. She said, "You can sleep here tonight—it's your house. This is your house." I said, "Please don't tease…." Carlo said, "Yes, darling, it's true. It's your house. I rented it for you." I jumped up and looked at him. He said, "Everything inside is yours. The key is yours, and you've got a maid in the morning who is going to come and do everything for you—all you have to do is sleep and come and go. The watchman will be here at six in the evening and he'll leave at six in the morning, the girl comes at seven in the morning and she leaves whenever you let her go." Food was everywhere, and they had even bought me clothes, towels, sheets, soaps—everything was there. Some of the stuff I didn't even know how to use! Everything was there, and it was so beautiful.

He wanted the two of us to spend the night there, but I couldn't tell him yes in front of Maryan, so I said no. We took Maryan home and I was so happy—I kept on kissing him. "Let's go back to the new house—to your house," he said. I was holding the key so tightly, as though I didn't want to lose it. I told him, "No, I don't want to go to the new house." I was afraid, because it was so big and I knew he was going to leave the next morning and I would be by myself. So I told him, "No, no, no, let's go for a ride and then go to your place, and some other time we can sleep at my place." So he said, "O.K." He was really sweet.

The next morning I went to look for some of my friends. I was looking for any friend, I didn't care, I just wanted to share my happiness. We rode in a taxi to my house—they couldn't believe I had a house! I couldn't even open the door—one of my friends had to open it for me. The house had the smell of new furniture. The refrigerator was full of drinks and the cupboards were full of food. There were flowers too. Nice! He had put the drink I liked—champagne—in the refrigerator, and we opened that and drank it.

Around nine-thirty, there was a knock on the door. Carlo. He didn't have a key—I don't know if he kept a spare one, but I doubt it. I introduced him to my friends, and I told them he was my boyfriend. Two of my friends laughed because they hadn't met him yet—the other two I had taken to his house. We sat and celebrated together.

I wasn't homeless any more so I could stay in my house, sleep as late as I wanted, go when I wanted to go. Before, I used to be on the go because I had to. Now I could go out and get my friends and bring them over. Finally two really good friends moved in with me, because they were running away too, and we stayed together. My house became all the girls' house. Runaway girls knew they could always stay with me.

Nobody in my family knew about my old European man; whatever I got from Carlo I would spend, but always I would buy something for the family and take it home. Mama was even able to go back to her business again, buying and selling bread. Sometimes I told her I was working for a family—a lie, but I was making peace, slowly, slowly, with Mama.

I loved to be with the young kids—after all, I was just a teenager, and I didn't have much in common with Carlo. Every night there was a party. Some of the city kids had cars, and everyone loved to drive. So many of us would squeeze into a car that we'd have to sit on top of each other, and we'd smoke, drink, and sing. All we wanted to do was have a nice ride, and sing. Someone would say, "Let's go over there," and all the cars would—whoosh! —take off and go to the same place.

One time I was by myself, walking home from a movie about ten o'clock in the evening. That late at night, it isn't easy to find a taxi, and you sometimes have to walk a little ways before you find one. There was a long, straight road, and in the middle of it was a sidewalk with plants on both sides. Big lights shone down over both sides of the street. It didn't bother me to walk—I've walked all my life. A black Volkswagen came slowly behind me. The driver told me to get in. I said, "Get lost!" He said, "Please, I'll take you for dinner. I'll give you what you want!" I looked at him and he was an old man. I told him, "Go to hell, old man! Go to your wife!" He kept on insisting and I kept on walking. This was in front of the Parliament, in front of the big hotels. When I got close to the taxi stand, I saw there weren't any taxis there. I waited for about ten minutes. The same black Volkswagen came, dropped a man off, and left. The man came straight to me, and when he came close I realized he was a policeman. I thought he was going to talk to me, but instead he came right up to me and slapped me, four or five times, in the face. I felt dizzy and I fell down. He started to kick me with his boots. The next thing I knew, there were people there, holding him back. I was still on the ground. Two men were saying to him, "Why? Why?" A young boy, about fifteen, helped me up, saying, "Sister, are you all right?" I shook my head, and finally I could see, and I looked to see who had done this to me. They were holding him and begging him. They couldn't fight with him, because he was a policeman. But the police were supposed to protect people, not beat them. Everybody was surprised—they thought I must be his wife or his daughter. He said no, he had to arrest me because I was a *sharmuuto*, I was wearing a short skirt. I was bad for the city, I was a shame to the city, so he had to clean me out. I *was* wearing a short dress with a shawl, but even if I had been a prostitute, he didn't have the right to slap me and kick me. I knew that the old man in the black Volkswagen had brought him, and that the old man must be a big man.

The policeman took me by the hand and dragged me all the way to the police station, which wasn't far away. The head of the police station was my mother's relative, but he wasn't there—he had gone home for the evening. The first thing they wanted to do was take my fingerprints. I had heard that once they take your fingerprints, you are a criminal. So I refused, and they began to whip me across the knuckles to make me open my hands so they could fingerprint me. While they were taking my fingerprints, the old man came and told them to put me in jail until the next day.

The jail was very dark—there was no light, and it smelled like pee. It was cold, there was nothing in it, nothing. All night I stood up, I sat down, stood up, sat down. I couldn't lie down. Rahima, I was scared. I didn't know what would happen. I didn't know if my family would find out. I didn't know if they would come and take me to the big jail. I had heard the new President was a fanatic, and he had ordered the police to pick up bad girls. Now, if I look back, I can see why he thought this would help the country. Young kids who needed money, they would do anything. And the whites who picked them up were a bad influence. They made little kids do things: oral sex and other bad things. I never did that. I guess they wanted to protect us, but they only arrested Somali girls, and sometimes boys—never white street girls, and never white men. The police didn't want us to become European—even a Somali girl in short pants, they'd arrest her. You must be bad if you were wearing European clothes. But that night in jail, I wondered, how could this happen? I was too angry to pray. They let me out in the morning. I never walked much after that.

Chapter
20

One night soon after my night in jail, I went to a movie with a group of friends and I met Roberto. He was a little older than me—he was between nineteen and twenty-two. I could see him, but he couldn't see me, because my face was covered—everything was covered, I had a long dress on, and a big shawl. He was so curious to see my face. He was half Italian and half Somali. He had just come back from Italy. His skin was not too white, not too dark, a handsome man. I told my friend to tell him in Somali, which he didn't speak that well, that if he wanted to see my face he would have to come to my house. He said, "O.K., O.K.!"

We took a taxi to my house. It was a nice, quiet, middle-class neighbourhood—no kids stoned you, because it was a white neighbourhood, and besides, it was night-time. I changed out of my dress, and put short pants on—I would never wear pants in the streets, only white girls could do that. But in your home you could do as you pleased. I was learning how to dance, and I had nice music. So I played some music, while my friends and I looked to see if he and his friends were coming. They came, and my heart—ah! We offered them something to drink, we smoked —I had some cigars, a friend of mine had brought cigars. We had cigars up there on the table.

They liked the house, and asked whose it was, and my friends said it was mine. They said, "Where did she get a house like this?" We put on some James Brown records, and we danced. When they left, Roberto asked if he could see me again, and I said yes.

Roberto worked with his father in a garage, fixing cars, and he went to school in the daytime. He didn't get finished until around ten or eleven; he always came late to see me. In the day, I would think about him. We started to see each other every night. When he asked me where I got all this money, I told him my father was rich and we weren't from the big city. I had just got back from Egypt, I said, and my brother was a captain in the police and he was paying for my house and my food because I was going to school, and I was going to get a job very soon, with the government, and blah, blah, blah. I didn't have the education to work, but if I had it, I would have liked to work for the government. The lie I was telling was the life I wanted to live.

I didn't go anywhere else; in the daytime I stayed in my house and at night I went out with him. Sometimes we didn't go anywhere, we just stayed in the house and made love. That was the first time I felt, I'm going to make love, make love the way…it was something I'd never felt with anybody else. It was just making love, love, love, love. I just wanted him to hold me.

I told all my girlfriends, "I love him." They said, "I thought you loved Antony!" I never forgot Antony, but I was feeling for Roberto what I had felt with Antony. I loved them *both*. I believed that you could love more than one person in your life, that Allah gave us a big heart to love as many people as we wanted.

Yes, I loved him. We always teased and pushed each other, hugged each other—he liked to play a lot. Once I called him "*Bastardo! Bastardo!*"—exactly like that. I saw all these Italian people calling each other *bastardo*, and I thought it was something common. I didn't know what it meant, but he knew. He got upset and slapped me and my lips bled.

It was when I was with Roberto that I began to meet a new class of people—high-class people. I had passed through the low and middle classes. I looked back at how I had started in Mogadishu, sleeping on the street, always dirty and scared and desperate. Slowly, slowly, I had made life better for myself. Once I met Carlo, I never had to go with any men for money. I had a nice house. And I had a young man who loved me. And together, we met all the big men in Mogadishu. We went to their beautiful parties in big villas, where they had every kind of drink, every kind of music, where the crowd was mixed, with elegant Somali women and important government men with interesting lives. That's when I felt I had reached the top.

Roberto began to leave work to be with me during the day. And in the evening I used to turn off all the lights, and when he asked me why, I told him I was afraid of my brother, but really I was afraid of the old man. I used to ask him to park his motorcycle somewhere else.

One night Carlo said he would come by, but I had plans to go to a party with Roberto. Before he came, I told my girlfriends to cover me up with two or three blankets to make me feel hot, so when Carlo touched me I would feel as though I had a fever. They put me under a bunch of sheets and blankets and I was really hot when he came. I said, "I'm sorry, I'm sick, I'm going to bed, I can't keep you company. I'll see you tomorrow night— do you mind leaving?" He kissed me and said, "You're sure you don't want me to take you to the doctor?" I said, "No, I took some medicine and I'll be fine. You can go home."

Rahima, he left—but while I was getting ready to go out with Roberto, he came back. I was out of bed and getting ready, when he knocked on the door. My friend said, "Who is it?" I ran back to the bed and covered myself up again. I asked him why he came back, and he said, "I brought you some aspirin." While I was thanking him, Roberto and two friends knocked on the door. Roberto came straight into the bedroom and gave me a hug and a kiss, and said, "What are you doing in bed? You knew I was coming and we have to go. Why aren't you ready yet?" He said it in Italian, which of course Carlo understood. I wanted to have Carlo leave before Roberto realized. But Carlo was mad—he had seen the young man kiss me—he stood up and spat in my face and called me a *putana*, and he told the others this was his house and they could get out.

Roberto looked at me—he couldn't believe it. He said to his friends, "Let's go," and they left.

I ran after him. Still wrapped in the sheet, I jumped on the motorcycle behind him and begged him and begged him to let me go with him. He was cursing me, he was so angry. At first we were going slowly, and he was talking to me: "Why did you do this? I wouldn't have even talked to you if I knew you were doing this. I thought you were honest." He called me a *sharmuuto*. And then a car came up close behind us, as though the driver was trying to hit us, and I looked behind us and saw that it was a white car—Carlo's car. So Roberto went faster and zigged and zagged and went into small sidestreets where cars couldn't come, and we disappeared.

He took me to the beach, where there was nobody around. I was trying to beg him and hold him and kiss him, and he was pushing me away. He started to slap me, but not like he had before—not in a joking way. This was real. He said, "That old man is going to kill me. I was in his house and going with his woman for more than a month. Why did you lie? Why?" He told me we were through. But I was still trying: "It's not true! He's not my man." He shouted, "You're lying again. See? He is your man. Don't tell me lies." When you're young you think you can convince everybody, you think you're so smart. I thought lies were the best way. But he didn't want to hear them. He said, "No. We're through. I'm sorry I ever met you." He was angry, very angry, and I was trying to make him calm and kiss him, but he was pushing me and slapping me. My face was full of pain— you feel as though you have a fever when they slap you. My eyes were watering, my nose was running. It was a very sad night.

He asked me where he should drop me off, because he was ready to go home. I knew I couldn't go back to my house, so I asked him to take me to Maryan's. He didn't say goodbye. He was cold, very cold. There was nothing I could do.

The next day Maryan and I went to his daddy's shop in a taxi. She told him I was waiting outside and wanted to see him. He came to me and told me to get out of the taxi—he wanted to talk to me. When I got out, he said, "Don't ever ever try again to come close to me or my house or my shop. Ever again. I could kill you. Don't ever come to me, and don't ever send any-body. If I want you, I know where you are. So leave me alone, and leave right now."

Rahima, I wished I had never been born. I felt very small. My heart was breaking in two. We went back to Maryan's, and the tears were just running down my face. She was holding me and holding me and saying, "Aman, be strong!" I went into the bath-room and washed my face with cold, cold water.

The next day Carlo came. Now I hated the old man, because he was the one who made me lose the one I loved. I told him I didn't want him—I didn't want to see him again, ever. I said he could keep everything he had given me, and I had paid him, because he'd been sleeping with me almost from the day I met him up until now. And now I would leave. But he kept on coming. He started to bring some of my clothes over, and gold—new gold—and money, but I didn't take it.

I made a deal with the old man, since I knew he loved me. I said I was going to make my own decisions about when to see him: "You come when I say come. When I say leave, you go. I can have any friend I want, man or woman." If he wanted me, he would have to agree. He said yes. I told him, all right, I would go back to him.

But Rahima, I hoped Roberto would forgive me. I went where I thought he would be. I went into a movie; if he wasn't there, I left and went into another one; I went to four or five movies a night. But when I finally saw him, he had a beautiful girl with him. She was half European, like him, and after a while I heard they were married.

CHAPTER

21

I WAS STILL WITH THE WILD GIRLS —high-class Somali girls, the ones who were just after a good time. They didn't have to suffer like me to get money, because their parents had money. One girl—her daddy owned the movie theatres, he was the top, one of the richest Somali men in Mogadishu. But you know what happened to him? All his children became no good. All his beautiful daughters—they went with white men. They didn't want to date Somalis. They thought that if they married a white man, they could live the way they saw their father's European friends live. These girls were educated, they had finished high school, they had been given all this freedom, but they still brought shame to their daddy. One of his daughters even became an alcoholic, and she died before she was twenty. She was a friend of mine. Now, when I look back, all the rich families I knew, their kids all ended up bad…alcoholic, or with white men. Rich kids, they're spoiled, I think. It's all easy for them, so they want to do everything they're not allowed to do. But back then I admired those girls so much. I kept the truth about myself to myself, and all those girls knew very little about me. Very little. I was living a double life, to support myself as well as Mama. No one could put me down. Because I was a girl from the bush, these city girls—they were my friends, but they thought they knew more than me. I was a fast learner, and I saw the system and how they used it. By this time, the only thing they knew more than me was from their education: they knew how to read and write. The way I dressed and the way I talked—you couldn't tell the difference between us. I could change my dialect, but if I spoke the way I really did, you could tell my tribe. All of the tribes have a different accent, even though we have only one language and one religion.

One day, one of my friends said, "You know, there's a new band coming from Aden, and they are really good." There was only one club girls could go to, and if you went you had to be careful and hide your face. We had heard about this club—some girls went there for lunch, but at night prostitutes went there. We went as a group—five girls and three boys. When you went to a club in those days, girls couldn't order alcohol. What we did was, the boys ordered drinks from the waiter and then passed them to the girls. They used to order hard liquor and ask the waiter to put it in Coca-Cola or Fanta so no one could see. I ended up with a whisky and Coca-Cola. I drank it, and then I felt very loose and ready to dance.

When the band took a break people went up to talk to them, to tell them they liked the music. Then the band went to other people's tables, and sat down and talked. One of them even spoke Somali. They spoke many different languages. And they came to our table. They were dressed beautifully, with jackets and jewellery and perfume—a nice smell. As they were walking over to our table, I was trying to decide which one I liked best. The one I chose was the one who sat down by me. I felt shy.

They ordered drinks, and after they drank with us they went on to greet other people. As he left, he touched my shoulder and said he would be back and I should hold his drink. He said it in English, but I understood what he meant. A friend of mine said, "Oh, you like him?" and I said, "Be quiet!"

At the next intermission, he came back and asked if he could dance with me. A lot of my people were around—he wanted to hold me tight, and we don't do that in public, so I kept myself a little away from him.

Before we left he asked if he could see me again. I told the friend I was with to tell him yes, if we were all going to see each other again, but I didn't want to see him alone. I didn't understand that much English, and his Arabic was different from mine. He said, "O.K., why don't you all come over to our house tomorrow evening?"

They had rented a nice villa, with beautiful bushes of flowers around the doorway. When we went there for dinner, there were twenty or thirty people there. After dinner, the band played for us and we all danced. Each of the band members must have had three or four girls around him, even though some of those girls had come with their own boyfriends. One of the other band members—the leader—was sophisticated, but I didn't like that type. Mine was friendly and open to everyone. His name was Paul. He and his friends were all from Aden, where there are Somalis, Arabs, Indians. He was mixed like that, Arab and Indian. He was quite thin with a narrow face, and he was white—not white, white, white, but quite white. There was trouble in Aden at that time, so a lot of boys had come to Somalia—soccer players, musicians, even ones who worked at the bank. Paul and his friends felt very lucky they had a contract to play in Somalia.

At the end of the evening, our group invited them out for dinner. The day came, and we took them to The Jungle Club—

the restaurant where you eat under the trees. They had never seen a place like this, where each tree was like a house, the branches thick with leaves, and all around us, so we couldn't be seen. The sky was full of stars. We brought our own music to listen to. The meal was very good—goat meat and rice. They had drinks too —soft drinks and liquor and camel's milk. We ate, we danced, and we talked under the branches of the tree. The sand was white and soft. You were free to do what you wanted.

Late, around five in the morning, we went back to Mogadishu. Paul and I talked a little bit—he told me about Aden, about how there were both Arabs and Indians there, and how he had a British passport because it had been a colony. Most of what he was saying I didn't understand. I understood a very, very little bit of English—just "How are you doing?" and "What's your name?" — not enough for a big conversation. And I understood a very little Arabic. He tried both languages—now one and then the other. We understood each other. I knew that I liked him partly because a lot of women liked him and I was still competing, trying to prove myself to the other girls, and Roberto. But I also liked him because he was foreign, he was new—different from the men I knew in the city.

And he liked me. Before we left The Jungle Club, we had kissed, we had talked. I saw him off and on at clubs. He kept on asking me to go out, he kept sending his friends to see me. But he was dating—he had a long list of girls. And I was also busy.

Each day I had four or five different appointments. Sometimes I had two dates in one night. I stopped dating Somalis, except for a few important people, but I partied sometimes with them. Then one night Paul and I stayed drinking and dancing and talking and I spent the night kissing him. That night we made love. And from that day, we became close friends. If he went out, it had to be me. If he invited someone to hear them play, it had to be me. If I didn't go to see him, he came and looked for me.

But still this wasn't what I wanted. Sometimes I disappeared and went back to Carlo for two or three days. Sometimes I got away and went home to Mango Village—I got tired and confused when all this still wasn't what I wanted, and I got tired of partying all the time. Rahima, I was very confused—when you're young and you've seen everything, bad and good, and still you're confused, you need a home to go to. I wasn't sure which way to go and which move to make. Everything I was doing was wrong, and I didn't know what else to do. All I wanted was simple— to make a nice life and be with a man I loved. But it was hard to get!

Paul and I, we saw each other more and more, and I became more relaxed. He made me feel good. He was always around me, putting his arm around me; he chose me over all the other girls who wanted him, and that made me feel like a queen—on top of the world. Even though I had had a lot of men, I hadn't had much respect, and he pulled the chair out for me—he was a gentleman. It was so nice, very nice, and I liked it.

I used to wear tight, tight clothes—pants, short skirts, and dresses. But I began gaining weight, and my clothes were too tight on me. I felt cold all the time.

The sister of a friend of mine had just come back from Kenya, and she had a lot of stuff to sell. She was slim; she was a tall woman, with a big chest but with a little stomach. One day, when she was getting dressed, I saw she was wearing one of those things and I asked her what it was. She explained to me what it did. If you had big hips, it made them small, if you had a big stomach, it made it small; and if you had a big bottom, it made it small; all at one time. I asked her how much it was and she said she was going to give me one free. I liked it, and I wore it. Now my clothes fit me again!

We went to a movie that night. In the middle of the movie I felt a terrible pain, as though somebody had pulled my stomach out. I couldn't breathe. My friend and her sister held me by the shoulder and asked me what was wrong. I couldn't say anything. I don't know if it lasted a second, a minute, an hour, but there was this terrible pain, and then it was gone. I told them I had to go, I felt like throwing up, I was sweating all over my face. They took me outside to breathe—even though the inside of the cinema was open to the sky, it was still too hot. I breathed, and sat, and I asked them to call a cab and went home. One minute I was in a hot sweat and the next minute I was cold. But the pain was gone.

Then, in an hour or so, the pain came back again—the same thing, I felt the same way. I cried this time. This wasn't like any other stomach pain, this was in my back, and in front, around my waist.

In the middle of the night I woke up. The bed and the sheets and everything I had on was sticky and wet. And something was making me feel like pushing, slowly, slowly. At first I didn't know it was blood, I just thought it was sweat. In those days, I never counted the time between my periods—I noticed them when they came and when they were over. I thought this might be my period, but I had never had pain like this. When I put the light on to go to the bathroom and looked to see what was wet on my nightclothes, it was blood. But this time it was a lot of blood. I went to pee, and there was a lot of sticky blood between my legs. When I looked in my bed, it looked as though they had killed an animal there. I said to myself, I don't think one person can lose so much blood.

I woke up my friend and her sister and she said yes, it was too much blood. They took me to the doctor. The doctor asked me if I was pregnant. I said no, I had never been pregnant. I didn't even suspect I was pregnant, because when I noticed that I was gaining weight and feeling cold, I thought I had malaria, because Mango Village was near the river and people always said that when you felt cold it was malaria. Malaria comes and goes just the way my cold feeling had. You have a fever and you feel cold, and sometimes you vomit. I never thought about a baby.

But the doctor checked me and he said I was pregnant. My friend and her sister had to leave, but I told them I was going to try to save the baby. That's what the doctor had told me, that he was going to try to save the baby, because I wanted it.

While I was lying in the bed I had been thinking, "Who's the father?" And I didn't know who it was, because I had slept with different men—not many, but several. But a baby needs care. The young boys couldn't offer that, they had nothing to offer the baby. So I decided to put it to Carlo, because he was the only man that I could say—I am his woman.

He came the next morning and I told him what the doctor had said: I was pregnant and he was going to save the baby. I told him it was his baby. I didn't know then there was a way he could find out—I didn't know about blood tests and all that. We thought they could save the baby, because they were giving me pills and injections. Carlo was always there, always there—he came to the hospital every day.

On the fifth night I had the worst pain yet. This time, it felt as though something wanted to come out—as though a baby wanted to come out—it felt as though my whole stomach wanted to come out, and I was pushing and crying, and pushing and crying, and then something came out, and when I looked at it, it was a big piece of blood that was all together, like liver—

a small piece of liver. I thought it was the baby. So I called the nurse and told her I had had the baby. She came and looked and said, "It's not the baby, it's a hemorrhage, and it's very dangerous." And the blood was just coming—hot blood. After a while I passed out. I woke up feeling as though someone was taking out my brain. When I opened my eyes and looked, there were three or four people around me and a white woman was in between my legs doing something in my vagina. Every time she touched in there—I think she had a spoon, because she was scraping—it felt as though she were scraping in my head, inside my brain. I cried, and they held me, they held me tight, until they were finished. I didn't have any more energy to cry or to stop them or to move even a finger—I was just flat, but I was there, with my eyes open, and there was nothing I could do. I wanted to stop them, but I couldn't say a word, that's how tired I was. I asked Allah, Why don't you take my life—kill me? because the pain was so great I couldn't stand it any longer.

When they were finished, my legs were shaking—my whole body was shaking, my teeth were chattering, d-d-d-d—I couldn't stop.

The next morning they told me I had lost a lot of blood and they had taken me to do an operation to take out the baby. I had lost the baby. I was glad I was alive. I didn't feel too sad, because I hadn't known who the father was. But I had a little feeling, like, why had I lost it?—and knowing how much I would have loved it if I had seen it.

I was very weak from losing so much blood. Still nobody knew where I was, not even my family, because I didn't want them to know, I didn't want anyone to know. I came out after eight days—I was normal and everything was all right, and I went on with my life. I saw Paul again, and I told him that there had been a family emergency, that my grandmama had died.

Sometimes it was my great-grandmama who had died—I always had some emergency in my family. This time, I told Paul I had to go home for the funeral. I started going out with him a little bit—not late and not drinking and dancing, because the doctor told me to take it easy and get rest and eat healthy food to get my blood back. I looked as if I had been in the hospital, but I was lying to him and saying that we had had a death in the family. Sometimes you look sick when there has been a death in the family. So he believed the story, and I told my friends the same thing.

CHAPTER
22

I WENT BACK TO MY OLD LIFE again, but now I was tired of this kind of life—very tired. I was too close to selling my body—too close. Now I could see the system, I had grown a little bit. All they were interested in, here in the city, was sex. Party, and after the party finished.... I wanted to be married, to show I could get married. So I said to myself, Unh-unh. This has got to stop. Either marry the old man or marry the young one, but stop bringing a bad name to your family and yourself. You've seen enough. It's not what you want, so leave it alone. But I knew it was hard to find a Somali to marry you after you had had all these men. Because everybody thinks you're a *sharmuuto*, and whoever marries you, people are going to say, your wife is that or this. And I didn't want to hear that.

I stayed in my house for a couple of days by myself, without going anywhere, thinking. I had a lot of time to think. Carlo came and stayed for a little bit. He wasn't what I wanted. So I chose Paul. That was, if he wanted me. If he didn't, I would have to marry the old man, because he kept on asking me when we could get married, now that I had grown a little bit and I was free. He even knew what I was doing, and after all that, he still wanted me. I said to myself, If it's not the young one, take the old one, and get your life straight.

Every time I saw Paul he said he loved me, so now I asked him, "What do you mean, 'You love me'? Do you love me just as a companion? Do you love me just to kill the time while you are in my country? Tell me where I stand." And he said, "You want to know where you stand? You know why I don't go with any other women? It's because of you." I said, "You're just teasing me. You're lying." He said, "What do you want for proof? Let's get married." That was the word I was looking for. I said, "You mean that? I mean that much to you?" He said, "Yes! I want to have a life with you and meet your family." I wanted to say, "All right," fast, but I said, "I'll think about it."

By now I was speaking a little better English and a little better Arabic, because I was speaking both these languages every time I saw him. Communication was much better. We saw each other every day, and every time he said, "What do you think? Shall we do it? Please, let's do it." Begging. When I said, "All right," he said, "Good!" and jumped up and down. So we told his friends and my friends, and after three days we got married. I asked him, before we got married, what religion he was, and he said he was Muslim, even though his father was Christian, but he lied. Later, I found out he was Christian. He pretended he was Muslim so he could marry me. I could not have married a Christian.

We were married by a *sheikh*, in his home, but it wasn't a traditional ceremony like my last wedding. We went to a place outside Mogadishu called Agaaran. Many runaways went there. I covered my face, my shoulders, my hair, and I bent my face down. Then my friend, a man, told the *sheikh* what we wanted, all that we wanted—to get married. There were five people there, four of our friends and a witness. In less than an hour we were married, and we were out.

I knew we couldn't stay in my house. We decided to look for a house together. He had a little money saved, and his mama sent some money from India, where she was living with her daughter, and I had a little money. I had never saved money, so mine was really nothing. We found a nice home, in a compound with shops and seven houses, and rented a one-bedroom place with a living room and dining room and a kitchen. And we got on with our life.

Beautiful. New marriage—no messing around. We were always together. Friends came to see us, invitation here, invitation there. Life was—at last —the way I wanted it.

After two or three months, the man the band members were working for cheated them and didn't pay them. Two of the band members went back home, but Paul stayed in Somalia and looked for new work. I became pregnant. He looked for a job, but there was no job, because he was a foreigner. He couldn't get a regular job in an office, where you just go and apply—no. You had to know somebody in the government—you had to have somebody to help you, and he didn't have anybody. But he was tough, and he was always looking. Besides, friends were helping us. In the compound where we lived there was an old Italian man. I had known him before, and we became friends, and after a while he became like my father. He had a shop and a house together, and I used to go and sit in the shop. He was a wonderful man and he helped us a lot.

Rahima, my husband couldn't find a job. I couldn't go to Carlo for help. After I left him, I avoided seeing him because I knew I had hurt him. I saw him a few times—in the distance— and I would run away and hide. I couldn't ask my mama because she didn't have any money. There was no way I could ask my father. I had never really made peace with my daddy, and now I was afraid to see him. He would have killed me, because even though my husband was supposed to be Muslim, he was still considered an infidel, since he was white. Every daddy wants a good marriage for his daughter. But your daddy can only control your first marriage, then the second one is your own, it's up to you.

So the only people Paul and I had now were Allah and a few friends and this old Italian man who lived in our compound. The time came when we couldn't pay the rent. We couldn't pay the light bill. The old man paid for us. He paid for our food, he gave us cash, he took us out to eat. A few other friends helped us too—especially Paul's Arab friend Sulayman, whose wife was half European and half my tribe. When I became pregnant, I was shy to go out to parties, and my husband didn't have a job, so a lot of our friends dropped us.

When I was about seven months pregnant, Paul got a contract to play in a new club outside the city. The owner was a big policeman. It was a nice place, with good food and trees around. But my husband had to bring some more musicians, because all he had was himself and an old Italian who played the saxophone. So he went to India, where his mother was living. He stayed a long time and found two other musicians to bring back with him.

After he left, I hated the house. I felt lonely, and scared, and I didn't want to stay there by myself. My whole body began to swell, especially my feet. People said it was because I missed my husband. This was the first time I was going to have a live baby, and I knew this one was his—ours—so I wanted him to be there. Since I had become pregnant, I loved him a lot. Fifteen days passed after the time I was supposed to have the baby.

The day Paul showed up, it was about ten in the morning. I was at my friend's house. I couldn't believe it was him. I wanted to get up, but I was too heavy—I was very skinny, with a stomach bigger than the rest of my body. He came and kissed me and helped me get up. All that time he was gone we hadn't talked on a telephone or communicated by letter, because we didn't have a telephone and I didn't know how to read and write. But he had written to a friend about what he was doing.

Paul had brought some gifts for Sulayman, so we went over to his house and had lunch. The men ate in one group and the women in another, because it was the custom, and he lived with his mama and daddy and brothers, all of them together. So while we were eating—we women were all eating around one plate on the floor—I leaned forward to reach the food and I couldn't straighten up again. I had a pain in my back. I ate the rice, but I knew something was wrong. I was excited and happy to see my husband, and I wanted to see him alone and just talk to him. So I told him I wanted to go. As we left, everyone said, "Hey, are you going to have the baby tonight? Because you were missing your husband, that's why you didn't have it before, and now that he's here, are you going to have it tonight?"

Still I didn't know I was in labour. I had heard that when you are in labour, you have pain in the stomach. I thought there was something wrong with me because of this pain in my back. Two more nights passed like that. We put our mattress outside the door, because it was hot and there was a nice breeze. When the pain came, my husband massaged my back with oil and brought me a basin to throw up in so I wouldn't have to go to the bathroom. Now the pain was coming back about every hour.

The third evening my friend came to see me. She saw me in bed with the basin and she asked what was wrong. I explained, and she said, "You're having the baby." I told her, "No, I feel pain in my back, not in my stomach." She answered, "That doesn't mean anything." She had had two babies—she said boy babies give you pain in the back, and girls in the front. I said I didn't want to go to the doctor and have him put his finger in my vagina. I hadn't been to the doctor once, and I was nine months pregnant. I even fell a couple of times in the street and passed out. A lot of the time it was so hot, and I had to carry water, cold water, with me all the time. I hated the hospital they were going to take me to—it was an old hospital with old nurses and old doctors. There was a new hospital, with young doctors, but a lot of people died there and everyone said the old hospital was better. So I said, "It's not time yet." But she said, "Shut up."

In the hospital, the nurse took me in to examine me, and they waited outside—my husband, and Sulayman, and my friend. Then the nurse sent me outside to wait for the doctor. They had a long bench outside and we sat down on it. After a while I couldn't sit down. I felt as if I wanted to doo-doo, as though someone were pinching me there with a stick, and I had to get up. I honestly thought I was going to doo-doo all over myself. I felt ashamed and humiliated and couldn't understand why.

When the doctor came, he said there was something wrong and he would have to cut me. But I refused to even let him examine me; they didn't have the medicine that kills the pain—you are alive when they cut you. He saw I wouldn't let him cut me, so he invited my husband and our two friends and all the nurses he could get to hold me. They held me, and he cut me, and he was putting his hand in my vagina doing something. The labour pains were gone, and this was a new pain—the doctor pain. I was crying for help.

None of this my family knows. My mother, my daddy, my brothers and my sisters—none of them. That day I came to love my mama so much, because I knew what she had been through to have me. What pain! What pain! Mothers, we have to give them more respect and more value, because to carry a baby and to have a baby is very painful, it's very painful. When I was in labour, that's when I really began to value my mother. Because before that, I didn't know all she went through. And she hadn't been in a hospital. She held on to a rope and somebody had to get up and hold her. I don't know how she did it, maybe she lay down. But wherever you are, the pain is the same.

It was terrible. Then the doctor wanted me to push, but I didn't have any power to push, so they started pushing down on my stomach, and they almost broke my chest—I was very skinny. Anyway, with the help of God—thank you, Allah—I had the baby.

They sewed me up, alive again. There were eight people holding me. And he cut me in so many places—at least two or three places. Each cut took four or five stitches—imagine, they were sewing me just like clothes. I was tired and was saying, "Allah, take me away...."

The baby they brought me was red so I refused him: I didn't think a red baby could be mine. I hated the baby, because he had put me through all this. They told me it was a boy, and I said, "I don't care." Now the pain of the baby was gone, but the pain from the stitches felt like a snake was in there eating me. Throbbing, everything was throbbing.

In the morning they brought the baby back, and I loved him. But when it came to giving him milk with my breast, he was biting me and my nipples were very little and he sucked very hard, as though he were going to eat me, and his tongue felt like a knife and it hurt. They were forcing me: "You have to give him milk." He was red, but he was beautiful with a lot of hair. He was skinny like his daddy. And I started to love him. When I woke up, the first thing on my mind was him: "I want to see my baby." When I was in pain I didn't care about him, but now I couldn't wait to see him. I called the nurse and asked her to bring him. The baby was hungry, he almost ate me up. The nurse was there and she said, "It only hurts the first time. The pain will go away. Your baby needs milk." I tried again for the sake of the baby, but it was too much, it felt as though he were pulling my heart out. So I pushed him away and told them I could not do this. They took him away and gave him some milk. And they brought him back, after they bathed him and combed his hair. My husband came, and Sulayman; they brought me gifts and took pictures, and then they left.

After two days, my husband had to go to Aden to get the two new band members. He left while we were still in the hospital. The old Italian man was godfather to the baby, so he came to take me home. After we had been at home for two days, I sent someone to tell my mama.

My mama came and my sister came. My mama had been slowly accepting my marriage, but Hawa accepted it right away. My daddy and his family considered me a *sharmuuto*, and I was as good as dead as far as they were concerned. For them it had started with me going to the movies, and then Antony and then a marriage to an infidel. My father had tried to help me when I left my first husband, but I ran away, they brought me back, I ran again.... Now, when I think of my daddy and mama, I know that that was painful for them...the pain I caused them, the shame I caused them. But I was a survivor. I didn't want to sit there and wait. I wanted to go and get it. Be the strong one.

Mama and my sister brought me fruit and oil. Mama was happy to see my baby. Hawa stayed for two days and then she had to go back to Mango Village, because she was married and had a family, but Mama stayed with me. She was the mama for both of us. She even started to whip me when I refused to give the baby milk. Even after ten days, it was still painful for me to feed the baby and my nipples were always bleeding.

My husband came back with the two boys and took them to a house he had rented for them, close by the club. A woman who has just had a baby has to stay in the house for forty days, according to Islam. So I didn't go anywhere for forty days, and then, when the forty days were over, I went out. The place we lived was near the garage where Roberto worked with his father. I usually took a taxi, but this time I walked, pretending I was walking to a little shop just past the garage. I put on my best dress, and it was evening, so I went with a friend. I told my friend I needed to get something at the store, which I did, but my real intention wasn't that—my real intention was to see Roberto. It was the first time we had spoken since the day he left me. He congratulated me. Very nice words: "I heard you had a baby boy—a beautiful baby boy. I'm glad for you." He had loved me, but he was happy now with his wife and his life, and I was happy with what I had. I told him to come and see us some-time, so he could see the baby, and he said he would—one day he came to see the baby and even brought me a little gift.

The band started playing in a lot of places, and Paul was bringing in big money every week. I used to go with them. Mama stayed with me and took care of the baby because I was still young and wanted to go out to parties. She knew that. We had a maid coming in to do the cleaning and cooking, we had every-thing the way we wanted it. Our friends started to come back again. This time, even more friends—black, white, you name it. In the discos and in the clubs, all the young people wanted to be friends with us. It was a good life.

We were part of a very good group. But there was a girl who had been trying to be friends with us and to help us when we were broke. She used to give us money, and in those days she came to visit us all the time. She had a house, and a man who came and went and helped with the expenses. She also went to the club to get the white men. She was about twenty-six, very tall—over six feet—and skinny, except she had big breasts. My husband knew she was a prostitute. She came to our house sometimes, but she didn't go out with us—we didn't go out with prostitutes in public.

The band played only once a week at the main club. They had contracts at other places, but not enough to keep them busy all the time. One night the band wasn't playing, so I stayed home. And they went out—my husband and his Arab friend Sulayman. They left around six and came back around twelve. I asked him what restaurant they had gone to, and he told me they had gone to the only club that had music on weekdays, the club where the prostitutes and the white people went. He and Sulayman had gone there to drink some beer and dance. I asked him who he saw, and he said So-and-so and So-and-so, women who knew me and my husband, the women we called prostitutes.

Paul was still asleep in the morning, so I thought I would visit some of the women we called prostitutes. All of us had the same name—*sharmuuto*—it didn't matter whether you sold your body or stayed with one man or were married to a white man— once you left your daddy and your mama's house and you weren't married to a man of your same colour, Somalis saw you as a prostitute. But in between us, we had different levels. And this was very important. Sometimes I used to visit some of these women—we would play cards and talk. I liked them, and I used to go to their places when I got lonely, and talk to them. They told you what was out there and what they had been through—all the pain they had been through and how they became this way.

I took a taxi and went to the house of one of the prostitutes. When they saw me, they thought I knew what had happened. They said, "Aman, I'm so sorry…I don't know how you found out…it just happened last night…. Who told you?" And I said, "What are you all talking about?" They said, "You don't know?" I said, "Don't know what?" It was early to arrive at their house—it was around ten in the morning, and they usually sleep late because they are up late at night—so they thought I knew what had happened. They stopped talking. I got mad. I begged them to tell me, but they refused. They said, "We told her, 'Why are you bringing him here?'" I knew they were talking about my husband, but I didn't know who the woman was. When they refused to tell me, I left.

I went to the house of the girl who used to visit us. She thought I knew what had happened too. "They told you! I knew they were going to tell you." So I answered, "You better tell me everything." And she told me—she told me she had slept with Paul. She even gave him money.

I couldn't believe it. How could he take money from a woman? I didn't know what to say to her. I didn't know what to do. There was nothing to do. She was still sitting there saying, "I'm sorry, I like him, and he loves me too. I was drunk…." Why would she sell her body to one man, just to give money to another man? I said, "Why did you pay him, when we've got money and we don't need it?" She said she had always helped us when we were poor. But I said, "Why would you give it while you were sleeping with him, as if you were paying for him?" I couldn't understand. When you are surprised like that, you can't even get angry. So I left and went home, woke up my husband, and asked him. And he said it was the truth—she wanted it, she forced him; she paid him and forced him to take the money. But still that didn't make any sense to me. I said, "Why are you doing what she wants if you don't want it? I've got a thousand men out there who want me and I have never done anything since I married you. Your wife just had a baby, and she's beautiful, she's young. We've got our life together—you've got a good contract and good money. Why did you have to go with this woman?" He said, "She forced me. I was drunk…." I got mad at last, but after a week we made peace again.

A few days later I went to my mama's home with the baby. I told my husband we were going to stay five days in Mango Village. The baby wasn't feeling well, so I thought a change in the weather would be healthy for him. But I only stayed three nights; I came home on the fourth night and left my son with Mama. It was around nine in the evening when I came through the back door, carrying a big bag of fruit to put in the kitchen. Besides, I had walked a little distance and my feet were dusty and I didn't want to get the living room dusty—in the back we had a little area where you could leave your shoes, and a rag to wipe your feet before you went into the rest of the house. I came all the way into the kitchen and put the basket full of fruit into the refrigerator. I heard soft music coming from our room. We had three bedrooms now, because after I had the baby we moved to a bigger home. Our bedroom was way in the back. The door to it was open. So I walked, without shoes—no sound —and there was a noise, like somebody breathing hard. I said to myself, Who could be in there? I walked in, and my husband and that woman were making love.

I just felt flat, like ice. I stood there and looked at them making love. I thought I should go back in the kitchen and get a stick to beat them. Then I said to myself, Stick is not enough —get a knife! While I was standing thinking, she saw me. They saw me. They jumped, and he pushed her away. None of us could speak. We looked at each other. Then he grabbed the sheet and covered himself with it and began apologizing: "It's not what you think. It's not my fault...she came...." She started telling me, "He's lying, he came with his friend, he was begging me for two nights!" Her clothes were on top of my baby's bed. I grabbed the clothes and threw them in her face and told her to get out of my house. I even gave her fifty cents to ride the taxi. She dressed so fast and ran like a rabbit.

When I was young, I didn't understand jealousy—when other women spoke of keeping their men from other women or said they were jealous, I nodded, but I never felt that way. I might feel anger, but once we made peace I was no longer angry. But this was too much for me. All the women he slept with, it was always their fault. Why not his fault? I knew what went on out there, because I had been out there, and I had never forced any man—they had all forced me. So how could it be the woman's fault? I said, "Wait a minute. You've gone too far. It's not her fault. It's your fault."

Finally we made peace. But now I had learned how to be jealous. This girl was from one of my enemies' groups, and I knew how they were going to laugh at me. And she knew what my husband had—that was killing me more. She knew how he made love. Every time I thought about that, I couldn't stand it. Whatever love I had for him, it was dying—slowly, slowly.

I had wanted him to feel free, but not that free! I went every Friday to the club where his band played, so most of our friends didn't know what was going on. One night Pasquale—a young Italian man—told my friends to tell me he liked me. They told him I was married. His father was a very big man who owned a lot of buildings, hotels and homes. Pasquale began to take me out. He was young and wild and had a nice car, a Jeep. It was just funny to be around him, he was a happy guy. He loved the same things I loved. We loved driving around; we liked singing;

we liked talking; we liked making love. And he liked a lot of company, and I liked that too. Even though he was Italian, he could speak Somali because he'd stayed so many years. He spoke very good Somali. We could talk about anything, movies, people, we just talked and laughed. Paul and I, we didn't go anywhere with each other—no friends' houses, no going out to eat, nothing. We would come home, and he would hit the bed and I would hit the bed.

After a while, I realized I was pregnant. Paul and I had made love after we had had the baby and after we had had the fight, but we hadn't made love since I had met Pasquale. I told Paul I was pregnant and he said, "Wait a minute…we haven't made love for a long time…it can't be mine." I said, "No…remember, we made love not even a month ago…." So he said, "O.K. But we've got our son and we're too young and we can't afford another child—why don't you take some medicine and lose it?" I didn't know such things existed. I said, "What are you talking about? I'm not going to kill my baby!" He was angry, but he accepted it.

CHAPTER
23

Oɴᴇ ᴇᴠᴇɴɪɴɢ, ɴᴇᴡs ᴄᴀᴍᴇ ᴛʜᴀᴛ the President was shot dead. Everybody was scared. There was a lot of grief. The day they buried him, the people in the Parliament sat down to discuss who would be the next President, and they couldn't agree. Around four or five in the morning we heard a big noise I had never heard before, like an earthquake. The whole house was shaking. It was the noise of the military tanks going by outside to arrest the ministers. In the middle of the night, Siyaad Barre, a young man who was in the military, had taken over the country.

All my neighbours came out into the courtyard. We asked each other, "What is it?" We went to the house of a man whose wife was a policewoman—a lovely woman, the kind of woman who always knew what to do when there was trouble. We asked her what had happened. She said, "I don't know, but I think it's a revolution." We said, "Why?" I had never heard of a revolution before.

We were always at war with Ethiopia and Kenya over land. The white men had divided Somalia five ways, and given one part of Somalia, called N.F.D., to Kenya, and another part, called Ogaden, to Ethiopia. You can tell the land should belong to Somalia because it's Somalis who live there, moving with their herds. No Kenyans live there, except the military and the police. Kenyans know that the land and the people and everything belongs to Somalis. The white men gave them that land, but it belonged to us. If it really was Kenyan land, Kenyan people would live there. So I was used to fighting and hate over this. When I heard the news, my first thought was that maybe Ethiopia or Kenya had taken over the country while we were sleeping.

I wondered where our military was and why they hadn't fought. The policewoman said, "No, it's our military that took over." I said, "What for?" She explained to me, "You know your uncle is a Minister and your other uncle is a Deputy, under the republic, but it's not going to be like that any more." She said colonels and military captains were going to be ministers now. We would now all be under the military.

I knew the military were very bad. Even the police were bad. Ever since that policeman had grabbed me off the street and thrown me in jail, I hated the police. I knew what they were like, and the military was worse than the police.

Nobody wanted to sleep, because it was already morning by this time, and we didn't want to go outside the compound, because we were scared. We sat in the courtyard and prayed. After the noise stopped and the sun came up, people began to go outside to see what had happened. The street was full of people, they were all asking each other and telling each other what had been going on. They had arrested all the big people in our area.

At first there was just a lot of confusion. There were soldiers everywhere. After a few days, we began to feel as though we were not free any more. It was like the military owned us. You couldn't do what you wanted. There were no lights on in the streets. You could not go out at this hour. You had to stay home. If you were out you were arrested, you were abused. The military started raping women. And they started arresting people—the older people who had money, or those men who were chiefs—anybody who was related to the previous government. It was worse for Somalis, because they were getting arrested and beaten. The foreigners, all they got was "Leave immediately." But for Somalis, they would knock on your door, taking your husband or your brother or your father, and it was just horrible, just horrible. It was no good. Evil could happen to you for no reason at all.

They expelled most of the foreigners from the country, giving them different deadlines by which they had to leave, some only twenty-four hours. They gave my husband ten days—they gave him extra time when he said he was married to a Somali woman. Me and him, we weren't getting along that well, but he said, "Let's all go together." He thought he could get me and our son put on his passport at the British embassy. So we went there and they told us they could put the baby on his passport, but they couldn't give me a passport, because I wasn't British. They said I had to have a Somali passport. We didn't even know where to start, because I had never needed a passport before. I had to go to Mango Village and get a birth certificate made, and bring this paper to this office and that paper to that office. I was running all around, fast. And we began to sell our furniture and give some of our money to my family. My husband said he could take our son with him and wait for me in Aden, and after I got the passport I could come. But I told him no—I would bring the baby with me.

Before the revolution happened, we hadn't been talking. We were mad and jealous of each other. But now we were working to-gether, because this was a much bigger disaster than our quarrels.

We made peace, we forgave each other, we told each other we loved each other. And I meant it, because I realized my family was the only thing that mattered to me.

The next morning, my husband left. I had sold everything. I had even given the key to our house to my husband's other friend, Ismail, because Paul trusted him. He was a traffic policeman, and my husband gave him the musical instruments to sell for money to buy a ticket for me and my baby as soon as we had a passport. Ismail promised to help us until we were able to leave the country.

Every day I went to Immigration. And every day they said, "Come back tomorrow. Your passport's got to be signed. The man who has to sign it isn't here." The next day I would be given the same story. It was scary, because the place was full of soldiers and they treated you very badly if you were trying to leave the country. I had gone there nine different times. My suitcases were ready. I had bought some clothes for my baby and myself, and gifts for my husband's family. All I had was a little pocket money, because I had given the rest of my money to Mama. She had taken the baby to Mango Village—the military weren't there, so it would be safer.

Finally Ismail, who had sold the band's instruments to get the money for my ticket, came to Immigration with me to find out what was going on. He went in by himself and left me outside. They told him the truth—that they had no intention of giving me a passport. He came out and told me what they had said, but then he said he knew some big person who would be able to get me a passport, and told me not to worry.

I went to his house several times, but there was nobody there. So I went back to Immigration to find out what was going on. They let me inside to talk to the man who was supposed to sign the passports. He said, "Sit down. Listen. You want a passport?" I said, "Yes," in a soft, sweet voice. He said, "Where do you want to go?" I said, "With my husband, to Aden." He said, "Who's your husband? Is he an infidel?" I said, "He's white, but he's Muslim." He said, "Look, I know there are a lot of *sharmuuto*s like you in this country. We're not pimps, that we should give you passports so you can go and sell your body. I'll do you a favour and tell you not to show up any more around here, if you don't want to go to jail. Go find a man who is black like you and leave the white ones alone, and stop being a *sharmuuto*. Go find yourself a nice man and stay in your country, and don't ever come back here."

I couldn't wait to get out of there. I said, "Thank you. Thank you." I was crying when I left, and I didn't even look back, because I thought that if I did they might come after me and put me in jail. My husband was gone—I couldn't go after him. He couldn't come back to me. My money, my house, my furniture —everything was gone. And I was pregnant, and the child had no father.

I thought about Ismail. He'd promised Paul he would help me, so I went to see him. A man opened the door, and I told him who I was looking for. He told me to come in. After I had had something to drink, they told me Ismail had just flown to Rome for a honeymoon with his wife.

While we had lived next to the old Italian man, we had used his telephone; my husband's family used to call from Aden and leave messages. So now I went to him and told him what had happened. He told me not to worry—I had just turned seventeen; I was still young. He'd seen how strong I was; I would make it. He would help me, and Allah would help me.

I had the number of the telephone where Paul was going to be. So we called. I told my husband what had happened, but he wouldn't believe it, because when he left, everything had been almost ready, and now I was calling and telling him that nothing was possible—everything was gone—the money was gone—because Ismail was gone with the money and I couldn't get a passport. He hung up the telephone before I even finished explaining everything. I thought it was disconnected, but he didn't call back.

The old Italian man told me to call him, maybe it had been a bad connection. We called back, but he wasn't there. I left a message saying I would be waiting at the telephone. I waited a long time.

I went to the Italian man's house the next day and the day after that, but still my husband didn't call. On the third day the old man told me to call my husband again. I called and got him. I said, "Why didn't you call me?" He said he couldn't believe what I had said. "What you told me isn't possible. I believe you that Ismail has gone to Europe, but I don't believe they refused to give you the passport, because if they had they would have said no in the first place, when I was still with you. The passport had the picture on it; all they had to do was sign it. What would be the sense of their saying no—I don't believe it. That's the reason you didn't want me to take the baby with me: you knew you were going to stay. You probably have another lover and the baby isn't mine. But I'll send you a letter saying you are free. From now on, you are a free woman! And one day, I will see my son. Sooner or later, I will see him. Goodbye, and don't call me, ever." And he hung up.

At first I didn't cry. I was too upset even to think. I walked and walked. I ended up way on the other side of town. It was late, almost midnight—luckily the military had moved the curfew to twelve o'clock. When I realized how far I had come, Anna, a friend of mine, came to my mind. I decided to go to her house. I told her everything, even that I was pregnant, which she hadn't known before. I was ashamed. How was I going to stay in this city where I knew everyone? Here I had thought I had finally made a life for myself, and now what I had worked for was gone. I would start over, but I didn't know how. The only thing in my mind was just to leave—"to go somewhere where nobody will see you again and nobody knows you". That was my only idea. I told her that I couldn't stay in this country. I didn't know how to start again—I was pregnant and I had a little boy and I had sold or given away almost everything I owned. She said she wanted to leave too. With this military, you couldn't do anything—they were raping the girls and women and putting the men in jail. They hadn't killed anybody in public yet, but the situation was bad. The streets were nearly empty. There was almost no traffic because most of the people who had cars had been white or had worked for the government.

There had been many foreign companies in the country, all of them looking for oil. By now, most of those companies had left. It seemed most of the whites had been told to leave, and most Somali men had been put in jail. There was nothing to do but leave. If you didn't have a passport, the only places you could go were the neighbouring countries. My country and the neighbouring countries were all at war with each other, but I knew if you had money you could get into those countries.

Anna and I both agreed, "We have to leave, we have to leave." She said, "Let's go out and have one last night of fun." We found Pasquale—he was still here. He was tough; even though this revolution was frightening everybody. He said we should get dressed and go out to eat as though life were normal.

We ate in an empty restaurant, the only customers. On our way back, the military stopped us. It was ten minutes to twelve and we were trying to get back to Anna's house before the midnight curfew. When we came near the roadblock, the two of us girls bent way down in the car so no one could see us. But they stopped us anyway. They saw us and told us to get out of the car, just the two of us—me and Anna. Pasquale said, "Why?" The soldier told him to shut up, that it was none of his business, that all he wanted was to arrest the two *sharmuuto*s, and he told us to get out. So Pasquale got out too. They told him in Somali, "Go! You are a white man. Go!" And he said, "No, I'm not going"—in Somali. They couldn't *believe* this boy spoke Somali. He was a fighter. He didn't care if he got arrested or beaten. He said no, he wasn't going to leave us—we hadn't committed any crime; we had all three gone to eat out; it wasn't midnight yet; we weren't five minutes from home; we hadn't done any harm to anybody, so why did the girls have to go to jail? He said he was responsible for us, because he had taken us from our families, and he had to take us back. Finally he said, "If you are going to arrest them, you have to arrest me too, because I'm not going to leave. If you're going to kill them, you have to kill me too. If you're going to beat them, you have to beat me too. Anything you do to them, you have to do to me too, because I'm not going anywhere."

There were a lot of soldiers with big guns. The roadblock was at a four-way stop and all four corners of the intersection had guards. They all came and were surrounding us and pointing their guns at us as if they were ready to shoot us. My legs were shaking. I knew what they could do; I had seen girls after they had raped them and beaten them and taken their money and their gold.

The four men who had been talking to us went away and talked among themselves for a few minutes; then they came back and said, "You all can go. But don't ever go in a white man's car or with a white man again, and don't be out after eleven. You are young girls, and you should be ashamed to be in the street living this kind of life." So we said, "All right, sir, we will, we will, thank you, thank you." Pasquale started the car and we jumped in and we left. When he dropped us off at Anna's, all three of us —we were still shaking. Anna and I told him to be careful on the drive home, and he said he would be.

Even though he was kind when I saw him, Pasquale never said he loved me—and with all the troubles and confusion, I couldn't tell him about the baby. Anna told me about an Italian man who lived in the middle of the city. He was married to a Somali woman and he owned a bar. She told me that he did abortions in one of the back rooms with a piece of wire from a bra. She said he did the operation every morning for two or three days, and after about the third time you would begin to bleed heavily and would lose the baby. At first I agreed to try it, but after she told me what he would have to do and after I thought about the pain and about Allah—because the Qur'an says that if you kill someone, the punishment is hell-fire for ever—I couldn't go through with it.

I kept going to our old Italian friend to see if he had any message for me from Paul, but he never did. Then one day, he said he had a letter for me.

Anna and I ran back to her house. She read it to me. It said: "Aman, how are you doing? I'm fine. Everything here is O.K. I hope everything is better in Somalia. I hope my son is safe and everyone else is too. I don't have a job. I don't have any money. I'm staying with my family. I hope to see you again one day, you and the baby, and especially my son. Take care of yourself. And please, my son is still young and he is with you, and I know he's going to be Muslim, because you are Muslim, and I don't know when I'm going to see him, so please send me my gold neck-lace." He had had a thick, heavy gold necklace with a big cross on it that belonged to his father, which they had given him when his father died, and he had given it to our son when he was born. Now he wanted his gold chain back. His letter went on: "Don't be in the street all the time, because it's shameful for my son. I don't know what you are going to do with the other baby—give him to his father or keep it, I don't care, because I know it's not mine. I can't come back. You're divorced. You're through. You can take this letter to any *sheikh* or any embassy or any government office you want. It's your divorce paper."

It hurt. Not the divorce—I knew a long time before that our marriage was in trouble. But his cruel words really hurt.

I didn't send him anything. Nothing at all—no letter, no telephone call, no gold chain—nothing. I just said to Anna, "Me and you, we have to find a way to go out." We had decided to go to Kenya. A long time ago I had tried it, and I had always liked the idea of Kenya—I knew people who had gone there and they said it was a beautiful place. But I didn't know how big it was—I thought I would be in Nairobi as soon as I reached the border....

Now there was a little more peace, because people were getting used to the situation and were learning to live with it. But the military were still everywhere, in control—they went into any house they wanted and in the street they arrested anybody they wanted. When we were downtown where the soldiers were, we always hid if we were riding with somebody. We didn't walk in the streets. Some of the stores were closed—so many people had left for ever.

There were still parties sometimes, but we were always very quiet. At one party I met a man who worked for an oil company—Mario. Every weekend he drove me to Mango Village, to see my mama and my son. His family lived in Mango Village too—his stepfather, an Italian, worked for the sugar factory. His mother was a beautiful Turkish woman. She would cut my baby's hair—she was always happy to see me. When we were in Mogadishu, I would stay at his house, since I no longer had my own home. I stopped spending money on myself—what I didn't give to Mama I saved. Mario told me to save it—I would need it. He saw how bad the situation was, and it was getting close to time for him to leave too. He had found out he was being transferred to Mombasa, in Kenya. He didn't know I was planning to go to Kenya too. He asked me, why didn't I follow him when he left, and stay with him in Mombasa? I guess from there, whatever would happen would happen.

I was full of love and I didn't have anybody to give it to. So when he asked me to come after him, I said I would think about it. For the next two days, all I did was think. I thought about going back home to Mango Village and getting a job—maybe one in the sugar factory. But when I thought about staying around the people where I grew up, and how small I had become, and how everybody knew me, I knew it would be very embarrassing for my family. No one else in Mango Village had a white baby except for one old prostitute, and I knew what they called her. And I had another one coming. How could I face that? I couldn't even face the big city. I really thought about going back home, but then I said to myself, No, I can't do it. I knew I had to go to Kenya, and I was glad Mario would be there too. I told him I was going to go to Kenya for sure.

The next week I took him to the airport and he was gone.

Now it was my turn to look for a way to leave. I looked around and looked around. On the twelfth day I found Laila, a Somali girl from Tanzania. She was desperate to go to Tanzania because that's where she grew up and her family was still there. Her brother had made her marry a Somali man and she had become pregnant. She didn't like her husband, and she had left him and come to Mogadishu. She had been selling her body, and she had managed to save 175 shillings. That wasn't even enough to go halfway, but she didn't know that. We met while we were both at the truckstop, asking about trucks leaving. She spoke good English and Swahili and Somali.

I was relieved when Laila told me she spoke a language they speak in Kenya, and she also wanted to go. Now we had each other, thanks to Allah. And we were both about the same stage of pregnancy.

We found out that there were no trucks going straight to where we wanted to go, so we had to take them from place to place. The trucks didn't go all the time, because the roads were rough and it was the rainy season. We went to the truckstop every day. Finally we found a truck.

After we made the arrangements with the driver, I went to see my mama and my son for the last time.

You know when you leave and you talk to your family: "If I go, do this and this…if this happens, do this and this and that…." I told Hawa how to treat my son…and how to treat my mama, because I used to buy all my mama's clothes and support Hawa. I told them if anything happened to me, you have to do this and that. I knew I couldn't take my son with me to Kenya, because I knew what I was facing—a very rough situation. I didn't know where I was going, and what would happen to me. I knew he was safe with Mama, and once I was settled I would be able to get him. So I left Mango Village and came back to Mogadishu.

The day before the truck was due to leave, I went to look for Anna and told her we were ready to leave the next morning, early—at about eight o'clock. She said, "All right. No problem." We went out that night. We went to The Lido—that notorious club—and I danced the whole time, because I knew I was leaving the country the next day. I knew if I stayed I could no longer be my own person, somebody would control me. I didn't like the military, I didn't like what they were doing. There was no way to stay.

In the morning Laila and I went to the truckstop. Everybody who was going was there. But Anna didn't show up. We waited and waited; we waited for more than two hours, but she still didn't show up.

And so we left.

CHAPTER
24

THE ROAD WAS VERY BAD ON THE way to Kenya. From Mogadishu to Baidoa, it took us three nights. We slept in the big truck. The truck was taking pasta, tomatoes, oil, sugar, and coffee down to Baidoa. My friend and I sat in the front with the driver, and the back was full of food. The road was wet and muddy, and we had to get out and push the truck…push, push…keep doing that until it got dark. It was a lot of pushing….

But I forgot about the fighting and hate, because soon we were away from all the signs of battle, in the country. The countryside was beautiful, and it smelled like flowers. It was the rainy season—the good season in Somalia—and everything was green. It was cool, not hot, and the breeze smelled so good—I was back in paradise.

We spent the night in Baidoa, and the next day Laila and I found a different truck. We drove on and spent the night in Lugh, a town on an island in the Jubba River. The time before when I had tried to go to Kenya, when I was running away from my husband, I hadn't come this far. It was interesting to see all this new area of the country. My country and Kenya had had a big fight, and now on the trip we saw burned trees, burned cars, even burned villages. Every little way that we drove we saw some sign of the fighting, and I had never seen all this before. There was a lot of military equipment just lying in the road. I asked why the Kenyan people were treating my people so bad, and why they had this hate. They said that when Kenyans and Somalis were fighting, the Kenyans lost many of their people. But I think there's another reason also. It's another hate, like, why are you better? They think Somalis look better, they think we have more power, they think we have more money. They think we have more beauty than they have. So I think they're just insecure and jealous. Also Somali women don't like to date Kenyan men. If they ask us for a date the girl automatically says "No!" They get mad because we make them feel low. And in a way they're right, because Somalis don't mix with some other Africans, like the ones I told you about—the ones we call Addon. But all I knew was that Kenyan people could be very, very bad with Somalis.

The next day we came to the border town. We were so close —we could see the buildings in Kenya. While we were looking around at everything—walking around—we met this lady we knew from back home. When I saw her, Allah! I thought I saw my mother. I knew her daughter from when I had been a street girl in the city. Her daughter was half-caste: half Italian, half Somali. She had gone to Nairobi, and the mother was trying to get a paper so she too could go to Kenya. At that time you had to have a get-pass, a permission paper, to get into Kenya. She had been in the border town for three months, waiting for that paper. She asked us what we were doing there, and we told her we were doing the same thing—trying to go to Nairobi. So she took us back to her house. On the way she explained everything to us.

She said it wasn't a simple matter to get your pass. You couldn't go right to the Kenyan District Commissioner or his assistant, the District Officer. You had to pay money to some other people first, and they would talk to the District Commissioner for you. She said she knew who we should talk to, and she would help us.

She took us to the Kenyan side. You could go for the day, but you had to be back at night. We went straight to the D.C.'s office, and she told us to wait outside under the big tree. She went inside and came back after a while with two men. She introduced us to them, and she told us what they could do for us: they could get everything done in three or four days. We agreed we would talk that night, they would come over to the lady's house and tell us what to do. So we said, "O.K. Thank you."

They showed up when it got dark. I thought we were going to give them the money and they would go and take care of our papers, and when they had got them they would come back. But they wanted to talk to us before they left, so they expected me and Laila to walk with them outside.

I told them I was tired, and I couldn't…. I understood when a man said, "Walk with me…"—I'm not stupid. I said, "I'm sleepy, I'm tired—and I'm pregnant." To his face. Because I knew he wanted something from me. "I need the sleep and the baby needs the sleep, so why don't we do our business, and then you all can go." He didn't like it, I could tell, but he said, "Give us three hundred shillings." So I went into the room, counted my money, and came back and gave it to him. They said they would come back tomorrow with the paper. They would take care of everything.

The next night they came. They weren't pleasant and smiling the way they had been the first time—it was as though they had bad news for us, it was as though the money was too little. I'd noticed that every time the men came, my friend's mother went away, leaving the four of us together—knowing that we were both pregnant, that we were paying a lot of money to get this paper and we didn't want to pay with our bodies too. I told her, "Please stay with us the next time they come." But here they were and she did the same thing—she left. When she was gone, the men came close to us. I didn't speak Swahili, but I told them I wanted to see my husband. I don't know what Laila told them in Swahili, but finally they both left. The third night they didn't show up.

The following day we went to see them at the D.C.'s office, and they didn't want to speak to us, they were busy. They told us people had been watching us—they knew we were trying to buy our way into Kenya and the police wanted to arrest us. They tried to scare us. My friend's mother told us the men had let her know they wanted to sleep with us—if we wanted the paper, we should go to bed with them, that they were doing us a favour for nothing. They said the D.C. and the D.O. were taking our money and they wanted to get our bodies for doing us this favour—it was the least we could do.

When they arrived that night, they told us they wanted more money. So we gave them two hundred shillings more, for a total of five hundred. The lady was taking money from us every day for shopping too, so our money was running out. That night they took the two hundred from us and they didn't stay that long. Seven days and still no paper. The next time we saw them, we were too nice. One of the guys took me outside. It was dark—not that dark—you could see because the moon was up. I was standing against the fence. He did it standing up. He came, and I wiped it off. We waited for the two of them inside to finish and then we went inside. It was like business. I said, "Now you've got what you want—when do we get the paper?" I was angry. "Tomorrow?" He said no, it would take two or three days, but this time we would get the paper—he and his friend liked us, he said, and they wanted to help us. After they left, we washed ourselves and our clothes.

The next day we went to the Kenyan side, but we didn't go to the D.C.'s office, we went to the market, hoping we might find somebody to help us. We went to one shop to buy soda, another one to buy snacks. And we met three young men—clean with nice khaki safari suits on. Something told us to stop and talk to them. They were from Nairobi, and were there for six weeks of military training. We trusted them, and they said they would come to see us.

They did come to see us, and we drank tea. We told them what the problem was—everything. That's when they told us what was *really* going on. They told us how it worked: the men who worked for the D.C.—even the D.C. himself—slept with girls, and they also took the girls' money and shared it. It was like a game to them. One of them said we should take our stuff to their tent little by little and not tell the lady anything. She was probably on the side of the two men, thinking if she helped give our bodies and money to them, they would help her get a pass. Later, I found out they were right—that's exactly what she was doing.

We brought our things slowly to their tent, so she wouldn't realize we were leaving. One of the men had found a truck that was going to Nairobi. He brought the driver to his place, and gave him the money, and everything was set. I wasn't feeling very trustful, because of everything that had happened, but we were ready to leave. We left the lady's house and went to the boys' tent to wait until evening. When it got really dark, the boys, Laila, and me, we all pretended we were going back to the Somali side, but we circled around and went to the Kenyan town and started walking. We walked and we walked and we walked, for almost an hour. We had to be far away from the border so when the truck stopped no guards—nobody—would notice. I knew sometimes people didn't get picked up, and then you are dead, for real. Eaten by a lion or hyena, or killed by the Kenyan police. If the police caught you trying to sneak across the border, you'd get beaten, or robbed, or they forced you to work on farms, they used you as labour…if you were lucky. Otherwise they just killed you and got rid of you.

We were also scared because we didn't know where we were going, but we were convinced now that we were really on our way. Finally we stopped, but not too near the road. The boys told us that when the truck came, it would blink its lights twice to signal us. We waited and waited, and finally the truck came and blinked its lights twice. We ran to the road. The truck stopped. I kissed every corner of those boys' faces. We said goodbye and good luck. And then we jumped into the truck and drove away.

CHAPTER
25

WE DROVE AND WE DROVE. WE were in Kenya now, in N.F.D., and it was still Somali people. We stopped at small places where you could eat—meat, rice, and milk. The food was different. Somalis have one religion and one language, but each tribe has its own accent, and the culture is different, so the food is different too.

At last we came close to a village and we spent the night in the truck. In the morning, the driver went to the police station. All cars coming into Kenya had to register at the police station. Before he went to register, he drove us to the other end of the village. There were a lot of big, tall trees, and he told us to climb one of the trees and wait. If we stayed in the street, people passing through could tell we were different, could tell we were escaping. So to avoid problems, we should climb the tree. Remember how my grandmama had hid in the trees? That's what we did! We climbed the tree around ten o'clock and we stayed there until three.

It got hot, and I was dizzy. When I opened my eyes—ouff!— the whole tree went around, around! We were thirsty...we were hungry. I could feel the baby inside me jumping, kicking.

We closed our eyes, and prayed to Allah that the driver would come back.

When he came, he brought us food and water. We drove on to the next town, Wajir, and he had to register with the police again. He asked for money for gas and food. He took us to his sister-in-law's house, and told her to give us something to eat, and said for us to wash up: "You all get ready, we'll be back," he said. But he never came back. He took all our shillings, and —he's gone. I asked the lady, "What's wrong?" She said, "My brother-in-law is in trouble because of you. Now the police will come." We were scared of the police—the way they treat you after they arrest you. Where could we go?

She told us we should find Asli, an old lady who was in the same tribe as Laila. She couldn't go with us, because if the police saw her with us she would go to jail too. So she sent a four-year-old boy to show us where Asli's house was.

Together we had three big suitcases and bags—too heavy, especially since we were both pregnant. I asked them to please give us a hand. If we left, we wouldn't know how to get back, and we couldn't lose our things. So the little boy gave us a hand. He took the small bags. I took a big sheet out of my suitcase, and wrapped the suitcase inside it, and then tied the ends of the scarf around my neck…the way we carry in the country. And the other suitcase Laila carried in her hand. We were tired! At one point I wanted just to leave the big suitcase in the middle of the street. Then I said, "No, this is all I've got, I'll take it with me."

We knocked at Asli's house. She asked who it was, and the boy said, "Hello, Auntie," and she opened the door. Laila told her who we were—we were telling everyone we were sisters. Asli let us in. I gave her some gifts: earrings, a scarf for the hair we call a *shaash*, and some sandals.

We told her we wanted to go to Nairobi, but the trucks don't leave every day, only every other week. She said soon we'd find a truck passing through, and until then we could stay with her. We started paying her ten shillings a day…sometimes a little more, just to please her. The Kenyan government wanted every home to report every guest, but we didn't have a passport or a get-pass, so she couldn't let them know we were her guests.

This is where she used to hide us: in the big oven where she baked bread. In the morning after she baked bread, she used a long shovel to take out the hot charcoal, and let the oven cool off. When someone knocked on the door, that's where we went. If she was baking, we went under the bed.

There were some single boys renting rooms from her, and they wanted to talk about tribes. I'd get confused trying to keep track of all the different names and groups. Asli asked me if I was really Laila's sister, because I didn't speak Swahili and I didn't seem to know the same people. They were all talking about family they knew, and they became like a family. I felt a little outside of them.

Soon Asli figured out I wasn't her tribe, and she asked me, what tribe was I really? I should leave her house and go to another woman's house, since I wasn't her tribe and I didn't know the language; she said she didn't want to have me there—she didn't want trouble because of me. She told Laila I'd cause her trouble too, since I didn't know the language.

I hoped Laila would tell her, "No, we've gone all this way together, we'll stay together"—because that was the plan we had made in Somalia She didn't have enough money and I had helped her by paying for our drivers, tips, food, and gifts. So I hoped she would say, "No, no, Aman and I, we'll go all the way together." But she didn't.

Asli got an old lady from my tribe to come over. You could tell she was poor—her clothes were ragged and dirty, she looked very poor. When I asked her who she was, she said I was too young, I wouldn't know any of the people in her family. I told her my father was chief, and I knew most of my tribe. She told me her story.

She'd lost her boys and husband and all her cattle—her house was bombed. Kenyans had bombed where she lived because they knew a lot of Somalis were living there. She lost everything. She even lost one of her eyes. She told me she lived where her land was, where her house had once been. She didn't even have a bathroom, she had to use the bushes for a bathroom. There's not even a *daash*—nothing. Her house was like the ones in the country I told you about—a bush house made of a branch frame and woven mats. The D.C. had to help these people after they bombed them, so she survived on the little food they gave her. She told me I was welcome if I wanted to live there with her, she didn't mind, but she didn't have anywhere to hide me. If I even went to pee, anybody could see me, and they would report me to the D.C. because she wasn't allowed to have an unreported guest. She was in the same situation as Asli—if she was caught hiding illegal Somalis, she'd be in trouble, fined and sent to jail.

So I said, no, I can't do this. Why should I put trouble on this innocent lady? I'm supposed to go with her when she has nowhere to hide me, and she wouldn't be able to get a car to take me to Nairobi. I said, "Thank you, but I'm in trouble, I'm going to stay here, and if they catch me and take me to the police, I'll tell them how I got here and they can find that driver who stole my money."

I thought if I put trouble on somebody, I should put it on the one who deserved it, not this nice old lady. I gave her twenty shillings and a *shaash*, and I told her—"Thank you, Auntie. I really appreciate your help—now go." Asli got mad. "No, Aman, *you're* going!" I said, "I'm not going without Laila. Where Laila goes, I go. I've given her money to help me get to Nairobi. She's going to take me."

The poor woman left, and Asli was telling me, "You better go!" I knew she was scared, because if she shouted, the police could hear. I refused to leave. I said, "Bring the police here. I'm not going anywhere!"

While we were arguing, there was a knock on the door. She told me to go in the oven. I said, unh-unh! I might never come out. She might never open it for me. I said, "No! No more in the oven! I'm going to the police anyway, why should I hide myself? I'm not going in there!" She became even more mad, but she called out, "Who is it?" in Swahili. When she saw it was a friend, she opened the door.

A man came in and asked Asli what all the yelling was about. She said, "This devil came from Somalia, she doesn't want to leave my house! I don't want her in here. I called one of her family. She didn't want to go with her." The man asked me what was wrong, so I told him everything…. I told him it wasn't fair, I was a young girl like Laila, what's the difference just because I'm not her tribe or I don't speak Swahili? Laila's in trouble. She doesn't have a paper, even if she says she's a Swahili. Where is the paper? She's Tanzania Swahili, not Kenya Swahili!

I told the man, "Look, one of your tribe took my money and left me here. This lady said she would help us until we got a car to go to Nairobi. The moment she finds out I'm not her tribe, she wants to put me out. I've been paying her every day I've been here. I was giving all this."

He nodded and said, "This is not fair." He talked to Asli and said, "You can't just put them out. Just because she's not our tribe. She's still Somali." She said, "No, it's because she can't speak the language and she doesn't have a paper and I don't want to be in trouble with the police."

He said, "If that's the case, wait. I'll take care of it. Can you hold on until I come back?" He asked us our names—I told him my name, Laila told him her name too, and her daddy's name. He was back in less than an hour, with a piece of paper signed by the D.C. It said: "Aman is the wife of [his name]. Laila is the sister of [his name]. Laila has picked up Aman from [his town] and is bringing her back to Nairobi to stay with [his family]." He gave us a get-pass as well—so now we had permission to pass through the streets. He told Asli, "Be kind and as soon as possible I'll have a truck show up, and they're out of your house. Please take care of them." She said "All right." Now it was fine, because we had the paper.

He told me, "Don't worry, Aman. Laila speaks the language, you don't, so I want you to hold on to the paper. The paper is yours. If they ask you anything, just tell them I'm your husband. I work for the government, I'm a driver for the D.C., so they know where to find me." I was very happy.

And the same night, while we were eating dinner—maybe an hour and a half later—police were all over the house. I don't know how they even got there—it was like they parachuted in! They took all twelve of us—everyone in all the rooms—except for Asli.

We went to the police station, they put us in line, and they asked us for our papers. Six of Asli's cousins didn't have any papers, but I'd never heard her ask them to leave, though she was putting me out! Anyway, I showed the police officer my paper and he said, "Why didn't you show the paper before they dragged you all the way here?" I didn't say anything. I just sat back and made my stomach bigger than it was! Ha!

Laila, she talked to him in Swahili, and she said, "Yes, me and my sister-in-law came from the country, and we were just passing through, hoping to make it to Nairobi in the morning, waiting for a car to pick us up." So he told the police to take us back. Asli's six cousins, they never came back.

We stayed another nine days, until a boy found us a truck. It was evening when we rode off. I'll never forget. The driver had some *qat*, and he asked me if I knew how to chew it. I said, "No"—people in the north mainly have it, I'd seen some in the south once—"but I want to try it. I'll do anything. I'm happy!" All of us chewed some *qat*. We sang. We drove all night long.

The next morning we came to this place called Habaswein. That's where a lot of people got killed. It was about one hundred miles of desert. It was dusty, and the grass was dead and dry. There were no trees and no buildings, so you could see for a long distance. It's a point where they have a roadblock, and I think they cut the trees down on purpose so they could see anybody trying to sneak in. It's just miles and miles and not one tree. We could see everything...way, way, way into the distance. And the hot sand looked like water, it shone like water—Allaaah!

A lot of people got eaten by hyenas and lions. A lot of people die in Habaswein. I saw a woman's hand. The rest of her body must have been eaten. There was a ring with a green jewel, and a watch. Just one arm only.

We went to the police station. We showed our papers, and then went to a small restaurant, but I couldn't eat because the *qat* killed my hunger. Then we drove to a city close to the river. Our driver knew the D.C. there. We went to his house and they killed a goat for us to eat. After we'd had a good meal, we finally slept. The next morning, we left after breakfast.

The first thing I realized was that I really was in a different country. As we went south to where the Kenyan people lived, the land began to have more grass. In Somalia, the grass has all been eaten by animals, but here there were farms in neat green squares. The trees weren't close together like in Somalia, just one here and one there.

And the women were different. They didn't wear scarves on their heads. They wore their wrap-dresses tied above their breasts, and left their shoulders bare. I said, "What are these women?" I thought they must have shaved their heads, because their hair was short like a man's. Our driver told us, "Ah, these people, they're the Kikuyu tribe." He could recognize tribes, but to me everything was strange. I'd never seen a black woman with short hair, and carrying a baby with the wrap tied around her chest instead of her shoulder, which didn't look very secure. But they could carry baskets on their heads, and they didn't fall off.

The thing I noticed next was the cold. I said, "I'm not smoking a cigarette, when I talk why does smoke come out of my mouth? What is this place! Aaaah!" And the driver told me, "It's the cold." "What is this place!" I said, "I'm cold, and my mouth and my nose hurt!" The driver said, "You've got a lot to learn!" We saw a mongoose coming out from behind a tree. It was the first time I'd seen that in all my life.

And then, before midnight, we were in Nairobi! The driver took us to a motel. We rented one room, with two beds in it—ten shillings for the first night. We had no money, so he paid for us. We thanked him, and he left.

In the morning, when we woke up, I was hoping it would be easy to find who we were looking for—Laila's people and my people. Laila knew a couple of people from her family were here, but nobody knew where they were. We couldn't eat breakfast because we'd have to pay. We just washed and said, "Let's go to town!" I had gold. I told Laila we were going to take the gold with us and sell it, so we could have money and we could eat and pay for the motel.

We couldn't pay to ride the bus, so we walked. It was a long way. In the street they were selling roasted corn, orange sections, small mangoes, sweet potatoes…. We bought one orange and we split it in half and ate it on our way.

We went to the town, we went, went, went, all over the town. Nobody looked like they were Somali. Laila said, "We better find some Somalis!" We were looking for *any* Somali this time. We couldn't find them. And it was getting hotter…ahhh, my baby was kicking, kicking. So I said, "Forget about Somalis, let's go find a jewellery shop so we can sell what I have wrapped in this old cloth—my gold." We found a store and we went in. I opened up the cloth and showed the owner. He liked it. He asked me, "Where is the receipt?" (He asked Laila, in Swahili, and Laila asked me.) I said, "Why do you want the receipt? This is my gold. This is my gift that my people gave me, different people gave me, so I don't have the receipt." I didn't even know you had to have a receipt. He refused. We went to another one; the same thing. We went to another one; the same thing. They refused. What do you need the receipt for? I tried to explain, with a little English and no Swahili and a little Arabic…. I was mad, sad. We left.

I don't know what happened, on the way back, but downtown I fell. Passed out. When I woke up, I was sitting on the floor, water was all over me, and an Indian man was giving me water. Laila was explaining our situation—we just came here, we hadn't eaten, we'd been looking for somebody all day long. He took us to a small restaurant he owned, and he was kind, giving us *mandasi*—which was like a sweet donut—and milk until we weren't hungry any more. We thanked him very much and walked back to the motel. We weren't talking to each other, we were just tired. Back at the hotel I slept in my bed, she slept in her bed, and it was quiet.

After about an hour, we heard a Somali voice. We couldn't believe it! She jumped, I jumped. I said, "Did you hear, Laila, a Somali? Shhhh!" There were two Somalis talking! We didn't know which room the voices were coming from. We jumped out of our beds, opened the door, and ran out, listening at every door. We found the voice, and knocked on the door. Ouff! What a joy! It was as if I saw my brothers, the face of one of my people! We started to cry when we saw those faces. They asked us, "What happened? Why are you all crying?" We were just so happy to see somebody who spoke our language, somebody who was like us.

CHAPTER
26

They took us to the Garden View Hotel, where a lot of Somalis were staying. At the bar, I saw two girls I knew from Mogadishu. They'd also left because of the military. They told me Luul—a girl who was like a sister to me, someone I really admired—Luul was in Kenya too, but they weren't sure where. The girls told Laila the area where her people were. I didn't go back to the hotel. I stayed there with them. Safe.

Next morning I went back to the hotel and I got my things, and I told Laila to take her stuff and one hundred shillings that the Somali men had given me. After what she did with Asli, I didn't trust her any more. She was safe now, she found her people too, we were both safe. Bye-bye! I never saw her again.

After three days, I managed to pawn a pair of my earrings for bus fare. Remember my friend Mario? I went to Mombasa, where Mario was supposed to be. But when I got to Mombasa, guess who I found—Luul! She was still the same: elegant and pretty, with dark hair to her shoulders, and glasses. She was educated—she could read and write English and Italian. Everybody loved that girl. She told me the Inspector-General of Kenya was in love with her. I told her I was looking for Mario. She knew him, and she told me, "Aman, his company was moved from Mombasa to Tanzania."

But she said she knew a man who worked for the same company, and she'd even heard that Mario had asked him to send a telegram if I showed up. She said, "I know he wants to see you." We sent him a message. We stayed in Mombasa about twenty days, waiting.

It was important to have Kenyan papers—not just the pass I had, but papers that said you were Kenyan—otherwise, everywhere you went, police bothered you. Luul said if I gave her some money, she would take it and fix the paper for me. Again I went to a pawn shop. This time I sold my gold. I got about three thousand shillings, and Luul and I went back to Nairobi, where she had a friend who could fix the paper for me.

In Nairobi, Luul rented a room in an expensive hotel downtown. Everything was different in Kenya. I didn't like their food…I began throwing up…I held my nose…everything smelled bad to me…I went to their restaurants…I had to use a fork…. The fork to me is dirty because other people use it…everything seemed dirty to me there.

I couldn't stay. Luul was too busy partying all the time. She was not helping me get the paper like she promised…and the money! She had money, but the hotel was taking most of it. She only came in to take a shower, maybe sleep a couple of hours, and go. I stayed most of the time in the hotel. I met some Somali men and I became their friend. I told them how I wanted to have Kenyan papers so I could stay in Kenya and not be arrested. I told them I wanted to go to Tanzania to see my uncle. One of my friends told me I could take my permission pass and the letter to Immigration and get an emergency document—it's like a small passport for one year. He said he would go with me to Immigration, he made an appointment, and the next day we took a cab and went.

I waited in line, and talked to a policeman through a small window—telling him how much I wanted to go to Tanzania. I gave him my paper. He took my picture. And in less than an hour, I had a one-year passport! I couldn't believe it! When I went back to the hotel, I gave the boys one hundred shillings for helping me. Luul came and I told her I was going to leave, now that I had my paper. She couldn't really believe I would leave, go to a country where I had never been, where I didn't know the language. She said I should go with somebody. She found Khayrta —a girl going to Tanzania, who said she would take me with her. I had to wait a couple more days and she could leave with me.

Since I was leaving, I felt a bit better. I thought I should at least see the town. Luul took me to a club called Starlight. The man who owned the club was an Englishman with blond hair. I was hiding my pregnancy—I felt ashamed. He asked me if I wanted to be a model. I said, "What's a model?" He said his friend in England would take my photos, and send me all kinds of places, and my picture would be everywhere. I thought, my picture in the paper, and everyone would see me? I thought becoming a model was like being the biggest prostitute, so I said, "No! Nobody's going to take my picture! No!"

I went to Tanzania with Khayrta, Luul's friend. The bus took one night to get to Dar es Salaam. The road was rough, with a lot of bumping, and it was bad when we got there. We went to an area where Somalis live in old mud-and-wattle houses, with only a little space between them. There were no trees. It was mostly women there, women who had businesses cooking and selling food, or renting out rooms. Drivers stop there to eat

Somali food and chew some *qat*, relax and maybe rent a room. There are also some girls who are single: they go to a bar, go with white men, and everyone calls them prostitutes, but that's the way they survive. They all live in the same area. Khayrta lived with the girls there. So I stayed there.

I saw Mario one day, at a club. He saw the way I was hiding my stomach, always holding it in. He said, "Are you pregnant?" And I said, "Yes, I am." He didn't ask who the father was. We didn't talk that much. Then he left. I guess I knew. I was suspecting something like that would happen. It was painful and it was shameful, but it passed, it passed.

By the time I was nine months pregnant…ahhh! I still didn't have a place of my own. I was still with the Somali women. I felt shame because of my stomach, so I stayed home and chewed *qat.* It made me feel strong. It's not like drugs, it's natural leaves, you don't get drunk—you get smart and strong, it gives you energy when you're sleepy and tired.

I would clean the home of these women, and cook for them. In return, I had a place to stay, and they were giving me pocket money. I didn't have a special place where I slept. It was like this: if I'm staying in your room, if you come with a man I have to leave, and sleep with the others. So I slept room to room. And one day, after lunch, I felt these stabbing pains in my back, every half hour. I thought, it's just started, you've got a long way to go, so don't say anything. With my first baby I had labour for three days and three nights, so I thought this would be the same. This pain was coming all day, but I didn't mention it to the girls. Just chew my *qat*, and drink tea, and talk, and after seven or eight, when they went out again, I took a shower. The pain is coming closer and closer! Haahhh! I threw up, but this pain won't go away. And all the girls are gone…. I stay with my pain and the pain is increasing, increasing, increasing….

Around three in the morning, the girl whose room I was in came back with a seaman, a white man. She told me, stay out so she can do her thing. She gave me a pillow and a mat to sleep on. I put the mat out in the *daash*. I tried to sleep, but I couldn't. I kept coughing, coughing. After a while, the white man came out. He asked me what was wrong, if I was in trouble. So I told him, no, I'm sick. He helped me, held my shoulder, and I went in to the bedroom and I told her, I'm in labour. She screamed, "What!" I said, "Yes, I am." She asked me, "Since when?" I said, "Since yesterday, after we had lunch." She asked why I hadn't told her. I said, I've got a long way to go anyway. I know because my other son I had for three days and three nights, so since it just started yesterday, I've got a long way to go.

She told me to lie down on the sofa and she gave me a big sheet. I was shaking…I covered myself…and she gave me something to drink. The man left and she called a neighbour, another Somali lady, who was from a place very close to Mango Village. She knew my family. She called a taxi and took me to the hospital. It was early in the morning.

They spoke Swahili with the nurse, and told her what was wrong with me…labour. The girls had to leave. Nobody could come in the room with me. They said they would come back at four o'clock and visit me. After they left, I felt scared. The two nurses were speaking in Swahili. There were many other women in labour, and each woman had a bed. They gave me a bed, and I didn't feel pain any more. Every time I heard a woman holler or cry, I jumped out of bed and went to see what was wrong with her, to see if the baby was about to come, to see if she needed the nurse. If she was really in pain, I lifted her sheet, hoping the nurse would see her baby is about to come. And that's the first time I saw a woman, a not circumcised woman…you know the part of the body where the baby pushes out…it's different. It reminded me of when our cows used to have babies, it's similar. Since we've got a small one and sewn, when I saw this, I thought, they've got a lot of cow pussy. That's what it looked like to me.

That part of a Somali woman is covered and closed—it looks better. I have brothers, cousins, and friends who have dated European women, or women who have a clitoris, and they say we have the best one—they say it's smaller, hard, it's clean and it's less wet. I know myself we smell better and are less dirty than women who are uncircumcised.

You know, Rahima, I've heard many Europeans, many white people no matter where they come from, they're trying to educate Africans about circumcision. But would they accept it if I educated them to circumcise? This is my culture, my religion, and I don't believe another nation can take away another nation's culture. If Somali women change, it will be a change done by us, among us. When they order us to stop, tell us what we must do, it is offensive to the black person or the Muslim person who believes in circumcision. To advise is good, but not to order. These days in my country, they're doing it in the hospital so there is no pain. I hope more women will do it that way for their daughters.

Now I stayed all day in that hospital, without my pain. All I heard was women around me—when they cried, they said, "Mama Yangoye." That means, I think, my mother, my mother… they were calling their mothers. But where I come from, when you're in labour you call for the Prophet's daughter, Fatima. So I thought maybe Mama Yangoye was Fatima's name in Swahili.

My turn…my pain comes. Aahh! And this time it's really— shuhh!—strong…one after another. So I went into bed and held it. In Somalia, when you're in labour, if you cry it's shameful, so you have to hold it. I put a sheet in my mouth, and bit down on it, and I was holding the bed. And I was just trembling and shaking. I prayed in Somali. But the pain was not going away. Then I realized, maybe here they don't understand your language! Remember all day long they've been saying, "Mama Yangoye"—maybe that's what you should say! And I was too shy to say it, so I covered myself with the sheet and I whispered to the head of the bed, "Mama Yangoye!" The pain is still there, but I feel the baby coming out and it has no room. It feels like my skin is breaking, and I hear *guh, guh, guh, guh*. I can't stand the pain any longer, so I take the sheet off and I yell and yell, yell, in English and in Somali. There was an Indian doctor passing through, and he saw me. He had scissors in his coat pocket. He brought out the scissors, and he just *kuh, kuh, kuh*, started to cut. I had the baby. A boy.

In Somalia, when you have your baby, they put the baby up in another room, and bring it to you in the morning. I expected everything would be the same here. The nurse took the baby away, and took me into another room. They cleaned and sewed where he had cut.

When I went to the hospital, all I had on me was a sheet, a scarf on my hair, and a little wrap-dress. Nothing else. My money was tied in my wrap. They put me in a wheelchair, and they brought me my baby. But the little baby was naked, no clothes. In Somalia they give you clothes! So I wrapped the baby with part of the sheet I had. I thought the nurse was going to take me to another room, I thought I would be given a bed. But when she took me to a room, the bed was full and there was no mattress on the floor. She just put me in the room and told me, "Find a spot and stay there." On the floor. I thought she was coming back with a mattress or clothes.

I sat in the corner, with the baby in the wrap. I was hungry. Whatever food I'd had yesterday, I'd thrown up last night. The

Somali girls came by at five o'clock, but the staff told them I was not ready yet—they should go and come back tomorrow.

The hospital was not giving me anything to eat, or anywhere to sleep. They put me in that room and left me there. So I stay, stay, stay…stomach was empty…I wanted something to drink, something to eat, but nobody was giving me anything. I couldn't talk Swahili with the other women. I knew some English, but none of them were speaking it. Later I realized this hospital was a poor hospital, a government hospital for all the country and poor ladies who cannot afford a hospital. Allah! That night! I'll never forget.

When I stayed there, and I realized nobody was going to help me, I folded my sheet, and I put half of it under me, and I covered my baby with the other half. My stomach was so empty, I took my scarf and I tied it around my waist. It was getting dark. I opened the door to see what was out there. There was a guard. I spoke to him in English. I told him I wanted something to eat; he said there was nothing to eat, the kitchen was closed for the day, everybody already had their food. I told him I'm hungry, I just had a baby and I'm dying for food. Please! I have money! But I don't know where to go. Help me! I'll give you the money, and you can go and get me some food. He said he's not allowed to do that. I told him, "Call me a cab and I'll go get some food." He told me I was not allowed to leave the hospital.

I almost died that night. When the baby cried, I wanted to give it some milk, but nothing would come out, nothing! I was so tired, but I couldn't sleep on the cement. Finally the morning came. I was the first one out the door. I saw a small pushcart with food. I bought up almost everything he had and went back to my room and sat on the floor.

Finally they brought me some hot soup, and as I drank it I felt the milk coming. I gave to my baby. I kept folding the sheet over, looking for a clean place, because I was also using it like a diaper for the baby. The girls came at four o'clock to visit me. I was bleeding, the sheet was dirty. When they saw my situation they went back home and brought back clothes for the baby and for me. I stayed three days in that hospital room, and then the girls took me home.

One of the girls gave me her room for forty days, and after forty days I was on my own.

After that, I moved to a room in a hotel. To pay the bills, and to feed my baby, I had to do something. I did the only thing I knew how to do. I went to bars with men. I wanted to do like the other girls did, but I couldn't—I couldn't say, "Give me some money and then I'll go to bed with you." I just chose one man, and if I thought he could give me some money I went with him, and hoped that he'd give me some the next day. If he didn't, then the night was lost. I felt like I was filled with shame. I was doing it a different way, but I was one of the prostitutes.

After three months, I took my baby to the doctor for his first shot. My baby, he was laughing and happy and strong the morning I took him to the clinic. He had a shot, and as soon as they gave him the shot, he turned red. He started to cry, and he got a fever. The same week my son was dead. He'd been in the hospital about seven days, and they couldn't save him. When the baby died, I became sad, lost....

CHAPTER
27

I COULDN'T GO BACK TO THE BARS.
I thought of Mama—how she always started something new. I would start something new.

There were many women who were traders, in those days. They didn't sell in the market, they travelled to the neighbouring countries, buying and selling to shops. Men were the drivers. Many of these business women were Somalis who were part of a network. I knew a man whose family was smart, good workers— they owned transportation trucks and had a contract for an Italian company. After the mourning for my baby was over, I began to meet him for coffee or lunch. He had been interested in me before and I never gave him a chance, but now I could see who he really was. He was like me, uneducated, and he felt outside his family and he wanted to do things his own way. He wanted to prove himself to his family. He was a lovely man, a kind man. He wasn't handsome or tall, but that didn't matter to me any more. We married—a small ceremony with just a few of our friends. He worked for an Italian company who hired drivers because the roads were so bad between Tanzania and Zambia. He bought his own truck and slowly, slowly he began to have other drivers working for him. After many years, he opened his own transportation company and they became one of the biggest companies in East Africa. He was a hard-working, honest man.

He helped me start a business. I told him, "No more sitting around—I'm not going to be a housewife." I had always wanted to start a business, like Mama had, but when I was a single, young girl there was no way I could do that. And I was with the white men. But now I was married to a Somali man, so the other businessmen could say, "Oh, she's the wife of…" and they would want to help me. Now I was part of a Somali family.

Everyone helped each other do a clean job—no cheating, no cheapness. I would buy spices from Arab or Indian stores in Dar es Salaam, and bring them to towns in Zambia where they didn't have that type of spice. I even went to Zanzibar! They had the best spices there. When I brought my spices to Zambia, I could make two thousand shillings in one trip. And when I was in Zambia, I would buy old cars and drive them back to Dar, where I would sell them and make another twelve thousand shillings.

Women didn't compete with each other. If you had good stuff, there was always a store that would need what you had. My husband's cousin, she and I became partners. We went to Zambia; we went many, many places, all the way to Zimbabwe, Mozambique, and Malawi. It was hard work, but we helped each other and I liked it.

During this time I still sent money home to Mango Village. I heard it was getting harder and harder to live in Somalia. My cousin at home had a telephone. Everything was now controlled by the military, but Mango Village had less military because there were no powerful people there—the military didn't bother with the small villages. It was still not safe for me to go back; I was afraid of what the military would do to me when I got to the city.

When my husband's company was starting to do well, and my business was also going well, I sent Mama enough money to buy some land in Mogadishu. But Hawa wanted her to stay in Mango Village, and Mama wanted to stay close to her. She bought a group of four mud-and-wattle homes, and she rented two of them out. Part of me missed my son, but part of me was happy he was living there. Now, when I look back, I can see we had everything back home, in that one place. You've got your farm, you've got your home, you've got your animals, you've got your family around you. In Mango Village, where I grew up, I had everything.

But after a while I decided I could get my son. I had a wonderful life in Tanzania. It was a peaceful country and the people were kind. Tanzania and Somalia are like twins—the same food, the same religion, the same kindness. It wasn't like Kenya—the police didn't hassle Somalis, the people didn't have the hate for us. I had a good husband and a good job, now I would be able to take care of my son. So I knew I would have to be brave for him. I went back alone and it was scary again when I got to the city—it was the way I was afraid it would be. It was all there: abuse, rape, arrests, taking money from your home.... It was horrible. There were roadblocks everywhere, and they were searching and searching and suffering the people. The military they did as they pleased. They had an excuse, which was "Because I say...."

Remember my friend Anna? The one who never showed up to meet Laila and me at the truck stop the day we escaped to Kenya? After I left, she wished she'd left with me. She went through hell, hell, hell. Raped, beaten. She lost her teeth. They told her husband to leave the country because he was American, but she couldn't leave the country, she couldn't get a passport. She was in and out of prison. I hated to see my country that way. I love my country. I love my culture. I want to see my country back together, and my people back home.

When I arrived in Mango Village—Allah! It had been four years since I had been there—it was still green and beautiful, with the river, and all the fruit and plants everywhere. It wasn't as dangerous as Mogadishu because we didn't have the money, the power, and the belongings. The military was only arresting the strong leaders, the senators and ministers. The chiefs still solved problems and paid back for damages done to another tribe. The government couldn't take that away; the only person that could take that away was the tribe.

My son was living with my mama in her new home. When I got there, I saw him playing outside with Hassan's son. He was so big! I cried and hugged him. He hugged me like he knew me. He was healthy and he was safe. Mama took care of my child the way she had taken care of all of us. She was still a big, strong woman, but she was getting older. I loved her so much, and I wanted to give her what every child wants to give their parents— the most important thing you can do—I wanted to send her to Mecca. And that's what I did before I left Africa. I sent Mama to Mecca.

We have five duties in our religion—to believe in Allah and the Prophet, to pray, to help the poor, to fast during Ramadan, and the fifth is to go on the Haj. All Muslims have to take this journey once in their lifetime—a trip to the sacred city of Islam, the Prophet's birthplace, in Saudi Arabia. Every child wants to send their parents on the Haj if they can afford it. Now I could buy her an airplane ticket. Still I would like to go for my father, who is now dead, and then for myself before I die. All the bad things I've done—wash them right out, and come back clean. Everyone must send their parents before they go. It's respect to do this. It's love. I was able to do that for my mama and she loved it.

This is where I would like to end my story. I struggled, and I survived. I made it this far, but many girls I knew—they didn't. I hope for myself and for my people we can give a chance to our daughters so they don't have to run away to find freedom, but can learn, stay in school. It's like my grandmama used to say—we should trust and respect each other: girls should listen to their parents and respect their parents, but also there should be respect given to girls. It's about trust: they should get love and a little freedom—otherwise the daughters will suffer like I did. Because this is my story, but it is not just my story. It is also the story of many, many other girls.

Afterword

Some Background to Aman
by Janice Boddy

The area where Aman grew up is part of the Somali Democratic Republic. But Somalia as imagined by Somalis is inaccurately described by current political boundaries. It spills over into adjacent states and includes Djibouti (formerly French Somaliland), the plateau region of eastern Ethiopia known as Ogaden, and the Northern Frontier District of Kenya, N.F.D. Approximately one-third of all Somalis live in these areas,[1] explaining why Aman occasionally says that her people are found on both sides of "the border". The present partition of their lands is the consequence of colonial wranglings—involving the Ottoman Empire and in its wake Britain, France, Italy, and Ethiopia—that began in 1875, crystallized around the turn of the century, and effectively ended in 1960 with the joining of British (northern) Somaliland to Italian (southern) Somalia, and U.N.-mandated independence.

The Somali People

By far the majority of those who live in the contemporary republic of Somalia (or republics, in view of the north's recent secession) belong to a single ethnic group. Their homogeneity is

:markable in Africa, where countries whose borders were determined by Europeans insensitive to local realities usually incorporate diverse peoples, languages, religions. Though lifestyle, custom, and dialect—what Aman refers to as "accent"—vary from north to south and hinterland to town, Somalis share a cultural heritage. "They speak the same language, respond to the same poetry, derive their wisdom (and their experience) from the camel economy, and worship the same God."[2] Their sense of cultural identity is the product of a history in which the themes of descent, Islam, and herding interweave.[3]

Somali society is based on pastoral nomadism, a lifestyle well suited to the country's semi-arid climate, where drought is frequent and rainfall highly localized. Despite rapid urbanization since the end of the Second World War, some 80 per cent of Somalis still live in rural areas[4] and over 60 per cent make a living from animal husbandry in some way.[5] Somalia is virtually unique within Africa for the central role that pastoralism plays in the national economy.

Contemporary Somalis are the direct descendants of camel herders who entered the Horn of Africa at least two millennia ago, people known to linguists and historians as Eastern Cushites.[6] Current scholarship suggests that a group of Cushitic herders from the highlands of southern Ethiopia spread first along the Tana River to the north Kenya plains.[7] There they split. One branch moved gradually northeast into southern Somalia, where they developed a mixed farming and pastoral economy[8] like that existing today in the crux of the Jubba and Shabeelle rivers. (This fertile region inland from the coast, known as the Benaadir, is where Aman grew up.) From there some of the herders moved north again, presumably in search of water and pasturage; by 1000 A.D. they occupied the entire Horn.

On reaching the shores of the Red Sea and Indian Ocean, they came into contact with Islam as practised by Arab and Persian settlers engaged in maritime trade. Legendary intermarriages between Somalis and saintly Arab families took place in the eleventh and thirteenth centuries, ensuring Somalis' wholesale adoption of Islam and furnishing Arab patriarchs for at least two of the six Somali clan-families.[9] Conversion, coupled with the pressures of herding and population growth, set off a reverse, now proselytizing, migration southwards that was still under way when Europeans arrived on the coast towards the end of the nineteenth century.

Two things are worth noting at this point. First, despite Arab contact the word *Somali* appears in no Arabic documents before the sixteenth century, yet as early as the fourteenth such documents refer to identifiable clan-families or "tribes". This suggests that Somali political unity may be fairly recent, or more fiction than historical fact,[10] a point clearly relevant to late-twentieth-century events. Second, what historians call "migration" or "expansion" when describing the movements of herders often refers less to co-ordinated, large-scale relocation than to the cumulative effect of seasonal scatterings and reunions: gradual realignments, whether peaceful or not, of households, animals, and the resources that sustain them both.[11]

While pastoralism is the salient feature of the Somali economy, it has not meant complete self-sufficiency. In precolonial times grain was obtained from Ethiopia, cloth and other commodities from the coasts. In addition to livestock, hides, and butter, goods caravanned from the interior to the sea included coffee, ivory, frankincense, and myrrh;[12] there was also some traffic in slaves destined for Arab lands. Along the coasts from the thirteenth century onwards, settlements of Arabs, Persians, and Islamized Somalis grew into powerful mercantile city-states —of which Mogadishu, capital of the present republic and Aman's last home within it, was one.[13] Several of these eventually came under the political umbrella of the Omani commercial empire,[14] which, in the first half of the eighteenth century, succeeded in wresting control of the Indian Ocean trade from the Portuguese.[15] Descendants of early Arab, Persian, and Portuguese merchants occupy distinctive quarters—like that in which Nuur's family resides—in Somalia's coastal cities today.

Colonial Intervention

When Britain, in 1839, established a coaling station at Aden (now in Yemen) to provision its new steamer service operating between India and Suez, its supplies of meat and produce were obtained by treaty with northern Somali clans. The strategic significance of Somalia increased dramatically with the completion of the Suez Canal in 1869, setting off a scramble for the Somali coast, and eventually the hinterland as well. Dominion over Indian Ocean commerce swung back to European hands, and the fleet with a refuelling base in livestock-rich Somalia had a critical advantage. In the tangled diplomatic intrigues that ensued—involving European powers, Ethiopia, and the Ottoman Khedivate in Egypt—Somalia was divided into spheres of foreign influence. Britain secured most of the northern littoral. France took the northwest headland that is now Djibouti. Italy, which had earlier established itself on the Red Sea in Eritrea, acquired control over most of Somalia's Indian Ocean shore. The southernmost part of Somali territory, much of it now in Kenya, also went to the British. Ethiopia, reacting to the European presence and unsuccessfully seeking an outlet to the sea, moved east, seizing the important Somali pastureland of the Ogaden steppe.

The area traversed by pastoral Somalis—unhindered prior to

colonial division—included wells on the coastal plains, and rain-fed pastures in the interior uplands that held no permanent water. Somali livelihood depended on moving between these zones with the seasons. European presence was confined to the coasts and not, at the turn of the century, particularly disruptive to herding. But Ethiopia—uncolonized itself—played an alto-gether different role. Its periodic forays into the Ogaden were devastating. In 1890, with Italian sponsorship, it had secured ad-mission to the Brussels General Act. This gave it the right as a Christian state to unrestricted purchase of European weaponry,[16] and ensured its superiority over Somali herdsmen armed with bows and spears. But imported guns eventually fell into Somali hands both within and outside the Ogaden,[17] a development vital to the battle Aman recounts between her grandmother's tribe and the tribe on whose lands they'd been permitted to live.[18]

The forced and arbitrary division of land and people by col-onial powers now separated families, and severed their water sources from their traditional areas of grazing. This, coupled with the sheer carnage of Ethiopia's advance[19] and its destruc-tion of Muslim sanctuaries, spawned a Somali nationalist resis-tance led by the religious sage and respected oral poet Sayyid Mohammad 'Abdille Hasan (dubbed "the mad mullah" by the British). Somali violence was directed first against Ethiopia, later against the intrusive Europeans as well.[20] In European So-malia it was known as the Dervish[21] uprising, and began in the north in 1899 with raids against Somali lineages and clans friendly to the British. It soon spread to the Italian zone, to be broken only in 1920 by British aerial bombardment of impor-tant Dervish strongholds, joined by a devastating epidemic later that year. It was during the turmoil of the early-twentieth cen-tury, fraught with clashes between opposed Somali groups and sporadic guerrilla resistance to "infidel" control, that most of

Aman's grandmother's family were killed, and she and six sisters and cousins began their long walk to marriage.

Herding, Marriage, Family, Clan

Pastoralism in Somalia is both a livelihood and an ethic: despite differences of clan membership, wealth, or class, Somalis share a set of values finely tuned to the requisites of a harsh, unforgiving desert. Their culture is rooted in the regular movements of families with their herds to maximize sparse supplies of water and vegetation. Movement is enhanced by a flexible social organization that facilitates the dispersion of people when required, yet enables collective action and encourages mutual aid. The key to this system is genealogy.

Virtually all Somali citizens say that they belong to a vast extended family, a single genealogical tree whose every twig can be mapped in relative time and, at least roughly, geographical space.[22] Their sense of common identity owes much to the broadly held belief that "all Somalis descend from a common founding father, the mythical Samaale to whom the overwhelming majority of Somalis trace their genealogical origin."[23] As with other Muslim peoples, this genealogy conventionally leads to Arabia and the lineage of the Prophet.

For practical purposes each Somali belongs to one of six clan-families, which some (including Aman) refer to as tribes.[24] Four are overwhelmingly pastoral, or "northern", and constitute the majority (around 85 per cent) of Somalia's population; Aman's is one of these. Two others are "southern" and associated with mixed pastoralism and farming. Members of a clan-family trace their relationship back some thirty named and remembered generations to a common ancestor. The clan-family is a massive federation of kinship groups that are widely dispersed and rarely operate as a unit.[25] Instead, common interest and mutual aid fall to its temporally graduated subunits, each representing a different level of kin segmentation: the clan, whose members trace their relationship to a common ancestor through as many as twenty named generations of forebears; the primary lineage, descendants of a clansman who lived some six to ten generations ago, who normally do not marry among themselves (i.e., they are exogamous); and, politically most significant, a relatively stable subdivision of the primary lineage that is the compensation-paying group.

This last is "a corporate group of a few small lineages reckoning descent through from four to eight generations to the common founder and having a membership of from a few hundred to a few thousand men."[26] Its members are committed both by common descent and revisable contract to share responsibility for *diya*—"blood money"[27]—usually measured in camels, should one of their members murder, injure, or insult someone from another such group and be held to blame.[28] A *diya*-group both pays and receives blood money; it consists of kin adjured to avenge injustice against their own with violence if no exchange of camels is agreed upon, and to defend each other materially or aggressively when they themselves do wrong. Thus when Aman is judged at fault after fighting with another child in Mogadishu and breaking her teeth in the fray, representatives of their *diya*-groups in that city meet to arrange an indemnity. Although *diya*-groups include women, the emphasis on men in the previous quote is not entirely quaint. For membership in Somali descent groups is reckoned patrilineally, devolving from a father to his sons and daughters, much as family names are transmitted in Western Europe and North America.[29]

Pastoral Somalis do not adhere to the strict conjugal preferences of other Muslim groups, for whom unions of close cousins—especially the offspring of brothers—are much desired.

Though marriages between close kin are not proscribed and do occur, people tend more often to marry outside their primary lineage and *diya*-group, and may be encouraged to wed even farther afield, into other Somali clans or clan-families, so as to expand the family's roster of potential allies.[30] Yet women remain lifelong members of their natal descent groups; at marriage they do not transfer allegiance (or adopt their husbands' names), nor do their husbands' groups assume full responsibility for their behaviour or for wrongs committed against them. In Somalia even today patrilineal groups are political groups; politics *is* kinship.[31] Married women living in their husbands' territories, towns, or homes are ambassadors of their own lineages abroad, and are enjoined to good conduct lest they tarnish their families' reputations. If, however, they bear children to their husbands' groups, they are also likely to develop some loyalty to these through their sons, at least for as long as the marriage survives. Thus a Somali matron is pulled in several directions, as Aman's mother's life clearly attests. In this society bonds of blood supersede those of conjugal love; the former are immutable, the latter temporary, and numerous divorces result from tensions that arise when wives are forced to choose between the two.

In Somalia, as elsewhere in the Islamic world, a man is legally permitted up to four wives simultaneously if he can provide for them equally well; siblings by different mothers are in some ways rivals for their father's attention and the resources he commands. Co-wives must therefore remain vigilant to ensure that their huband's assets are equitably shared. Disputes among co-wives are another source of marital tension leading to divorce or to division of the composite family and its herds into matrifocal groups that begin to move independently of one another. In this case the husband rotates residence among his wives.[32]

Indeed, the mother-centred family is the mainstay of Somali society, and it is hardly surprising that strong social and emotional ties tend to develop among maternal offspring, giving even households like Aman's, in which siblings have different fathers and disparate lineage loyalties, the close-knit quality evident from her account. Aman's immediate family takes shape as an unofficial matrilineage that contradicts the strong patrilineal emphasis of formal Somali kinship. Such views of the world provide an alternative, female perspective on social reality too often neglected by historians and anthropologists in favour of tidier, official versions supplied by the dominant group—in this case older men.[33]

Usually when parents in Muslim countries divorce, their children, most important their sons, remain with the father or, if they are very young, return to him when somewhat more grown up. Children, after all, belong to their father's, not their mother's, descent group;[34] it is from him that their social identity—their "name"—derives. But Aman's mother keeps her children with her after each divorce. She has good reasons for this: women are socially responsible for raising children, and mothers justly fear for offspring entrusted to the care of unscrupulous co-wives.[35] So Aman's household—her mother, mother's mother, and two half-siblings by fathers other than her own—is theoretically unorthodox, but not all that unusual. Apart from Aman's full sister, Sharifa, lost to malaria at an early age, all the people in her household are members of different descent groups: Aman's grandmother does not belong to the same lineage as Aman's mother, and her brother and sister belong to different lineages as well—in all, five different lineages, though not perhaps clan-families or even clans. The point is this: while Somali descent is patrilineal, kinship *per se* is broadly bilateral; in addition to her own, Aman counts members of her mother's and two grand-mothers' lineages as her kin.

Though one's most clearly defined rights and duties lie within her patrilineage, all relatives have a general obligation to aid each other, especially in times of need. In fact, one's closest personal ties may be forged with maternal kin, who neither compete directly for her family's resources, nor bear corporate responsibility for her actions. And specific matrilateral ties (i.e., through kin "on mother's side) have collective—lineage to lineage—implications: her mother's entire lineage stands in the relationship of mother's brother or mother's sister ("uncle" or "aunt") to Aman on the basis of her mother's marriage to her father.[36] Because kin traced through women are "friendly" but wield no formal authority, a woman or junior man can appeal to them when seeking sanctuary—in Aman's case, when running from an unwanted marriage enforced by her father's sons. There is something more: when Aman seeks out a cousin of her brother in the city, she activates both matrilateral and marital ties—ties to her brother through their mother, and to Hassan's lineage through Mama's former marriage to his father. Marital relationships and the matrilateral ones that flow from them crisscross and link the ever proliferating and segmenting lines of patrilineal kin. Important regional networks of mutual aid are based on such ties, and on "neighbourhood" or physical proximity as well.[37] All these things place structural limits on official patriarchy as a political force.

Aman's story clearly demonstrates the importance of family, especially lineage and clan membership, in Somali society. Even young children know their genealogies, hence their formal political affiliations, and with time they learn their informal ones as well. I. M. Lewis, an anthropologist whose *A Pastoral Democracy* is

the canonical work on northern Somali social order, describes
the significance of this knowledge:

> As Somali themselves put it, what a person's address is in
> Europe, his genealogy is in Somaliland. By virtue of his
> [or her] genealogy of birth, each individual has an exact
> place in society and within a very wide range of agnatic
> [patrilineal] kinship it is possible for each person to trace
> his [or her] precise connection with everyone else.[38]

Each such connection is marked by a kin term that denotes its
moral valence, so that agnates—male and female patrilineal
kin[39]—separated by two generations (before reaching a common
ancestor) are known as "true cousins", by three generations as
"second cousins", by four generations as "third cousins", and so
on, each remove reflecting a corresponding diminution of solidarity.[40] Yet morally closer terms—those for full brother or sister, for example—may be applied to distant kin of any kind
when the speaker is invoking intimacy and obligation.[41]

Personal names in Somalia are social and, to some extent, geographical addresses, for they too contain genealogical information. A child receives a personal name shortly after birth, to
which is added her father's personal name, and after that her father's father's personal name, and so on, up the patrilineal lad-
der to the purported founder of her clan and, beyond that, her
clan-family. In cities and towns, those who are members of the
same clan and, within it, the same lineage, tend to reside in the
same area or quarter. This explains Aman's ability to track down
kin on whose hospitality she can depend merely by asking
strangers where a certain "name" can be found. In any en-
counter with fellow Somalis she is able to locate herself and

others in social space, to know just how closely connected they are, the history of their groups' interrelations, the extent of their moral and material allegiance.

Somali emphasis on patrilineal descent entails a corresponding emphasis on "purity" of birth that enjoins strict control of women's sexuality.[42] Marriage with non-Somalis is proscribed, even when both partners are Muslims, for those who have Somali mothers and non-Somali fathers can claim no membership in a Somali clan: as they cannot be placed within the Somali moral universe, so perforce they exist outside it. Offspring of a Somali man and non-Somali woman *can* be placed, but their marriage is hardly better received. Because they are not bound by the reciprocal rights and contractual trusts of Somali descent, non-Somali citizens and foreign residents are looked down upon, regarded with suspicion.[43] When Aman falls in love with Antony she unwittingly resists the Somali system, thereby illuminating its ideals, and the means, the gender practices and constraints, by which kin solidarity is maintained.

It is a surprisingly small leap from gender and kinship to nation-state: solidarity based on the ideology of common descent makes it difficult indeed for Somalis to accept the national boundaries that were established during colonial times and are now recognized internationally. In the hope of creating a country that encompasses all Somalis, Somalia has periodically become embroiled in border wars with neighbouring Kenya and Ethiopia, where many of their kin reside.

Still, kin solidarity is not absolute. Every ancestor in a genealogy represents a point of potential fission as well as unity.[44] The lineage system in Somalia is therefore referred to as "segmentary",[45] and considered well adapted to a mobile way of life. It is characterized by something of a paradox: the very forces—of loyalty, mutual interest—that draw people together can also set them against one another in rivalries between clans or the sub-groups within them. There are two reasons for this: loyalties are relative, nested within ever broader and therefore more diffuse kinship segments, and the system as a whole is fiercely male-egalitarian. Brothers may be allies by virtue of their common father in a quarrel, say, over grazing rights that erupts between them and their father's brother's sons (as the sons of equals); they may be enemies (as equals) in a dispute over their common patrimony. And it is hardly unexpected that when divisions appear among the sons of a polygynous father these typically follow matrifocal paths. A person's political allegiance is owed first to the immediate family, next to the immediate lineage, then to the clan of the lineage, and beyond this to the clan-family or tribe. Ultimately, one's loyalties rest with the nation itself.[46] Each level of segmentation defines where one stands in relation to others; enemies and friends are contingent, rarely permanent. A well-known Arabic saying makes the point: "I against my brother; I and my brother against my cousin; I, my brother, and my cousin against the world". Patrikin who are supportive in one context can be predatory in another, as when members of Mama's lineage threaten to seize the animals that she and her siblings legitimately inherit from their father.[47] The result of all this "is a society so integrated that its members regard one another as siblings, cousins, and kin, but also so riven with clan-nish fission and factionalism that political instability is the society's normative character."[48]

Because all men are considered equals, there are no clearly defined positions of political authority, and a lack of political centralization is the rule. Lineages at different levels of segmentation are led by their elders in an informal council of adult men summoned as needs arise.[49] Yet Aman describes her father as a chief, and speaks of lineage chiefs in the cities and towns.

Some *diya*-group councils do elect or acclaim a senior man on the basis of his personal qualifications—wealth, prestige, wisdom, ability—to act as spokesman or representative; where such a figure did not exist, colonial officials often arranged to have one named.[50] But such men have no independent prerogative.[51] Nor do elders among the less nomadic Somalis of the south wield any permanent authority.[52] The title of "chief" that Aman assigns to certain men should not be regarded as implying a hereditary, fixed political position; a "chief" is in essence a charismatic leader, one who exercises power *through* people rather than *over* them.[53]

Kinship in Somalia is the means by which politics are done and resources ranging from livestock to government building contracts get distributed. People are therefore anxious to know who in government is related to whom and how. Aman told me that in the elections of 1969 she and everyone else she knew voted for members of their own clans or primary lineages. With the exception of southern agricultural clans, for whom ties to the land are politically more significant than precise genealogical calculation, Somalis hold authority to derive from numerical supremacy alone.[54] Prestige and power flow from brute strength. Raqiya Abdalla, a Somali woman and former Director of Culture in the Ministry of Culture and Higher Education, notes that "with frequent local disputes over land, water, women, invaders and other rights, it is essential for each family and lineage to be as large as possible, and its strength is very much dependent upon the number of [its] sons".[55] No wonder that Aman is concerned with the size of others' descent groups relative to her own, and sometimes speaks of wishing to avoid her family's "enemies". No wonder, too, that Aman's father's father "started him marrying young". Even in the modern Somali state, the size and repute of one's lineage largely determines the resources or positions to which one can aspire. Colonial policies are partly to blame; yet since independence in 1960 the composition of both civilian and military governments has reflected the numerical influence of clan coalitions, rather than individual merit.[56]

Lineage exogamous marriages—the norm—critically, if imperfectly, balance divisive tendencies by forging links between kin groups who are otherwise remotely related and indeed potentially hostile. As women circulate and maternal ties develop, distant lineages are entwined in immediate kinship that may defy the rules of patriarchy should it become the basis for political and economic alliance. A family's claims to "nobility" —influence and prestige—are traditionally supported by the fact that it has contracted marriages with clans geographically and genealogically removed from its own, for as Abdalla puts it, "only rich clans could have such distant relations."[57] So to speak of a "sexual politics" in Somalia is to speak not only of politics between women and men, but also of politics among *men* (or their respective lineages and clans) conducted *through* their kinship links with women—daughters, mothers, sisters, wives. The critical importance of women to Somali interlineage relations is evident in the constraints on their sexuality, among these, circumcision. Even purely patrilineal relations are forged through women, since membership in a lineage devolves to succeeding generations through the bodies of men's legal wives.

Marriage is not the only force that binds antagonistic descent groups; there is also Islam. Male Somalis traditionally divide along a single axis: the majority are "warriors" or secularists, and a minority are religious men (*wadaad*s and, in Aman's account, *sheikh*s). Much as the hero Sayyid Mohammad 'Abdille Hasan sought to transcend clan divisions by appealing to the common beliefs of Islam, male religious experts ideally act outside the system of kin politics. They are excluded from direct involvement in fighting and expected to mediate, not resolve, clan disputes. The religious role thus complements the secular; where the latter is associated with social division and individual worldly pursuit, the former is associated with the unity of Somalis as Muslims and their membership in a universal community that submits to Allah's will. *Wadaads* and *sheikhs* solemnize marriages, lead weekly prayers, direct all religious ceremonies. *Sheikhs*, who are better educated, also teach Arabic and the elements of Islamic theology and law.[58] A religious man is expected to lead an exemplary life, to follow more strictly than others the Prophet's way. Yet the position is not without contradiction, for he owes his security of life and livelihood—he also owns livestock, trades, or farms—to the *diya*-group to which he belongs. In fact the lines between secular and religious spheres are blurred, since charismatic political leaders often attract their followings because they are learned in Islam.[59] Mama's first husband was such a man, from a sheikhly family of the southern coast.

The divisibility of kin groups into small, relatively independent units, and the potential for these to unite in common cause, well suits a life demanding quick response to environmental fluctuations, an ability to take advantage of seasonal and scattered reserves. Camels (dromedaries) are the Somalis' most valued livestock, since they can survive without water—the scarcest of local resources—for up to a month while continuing to produce milk, a major part of Somali subsistence. They also provide meat and transport. Cattle, goats, and sheep are kept as well, but require more frequent watering: once a week for sheep and goats, every three days or so for cattle. The division of work is keyed to these differences. Typically, boys and young men move with the camels far and fast to waterless grazing, while their mothers, younger brothers, and sisters travel more slowly with the flocks through pasturage closer to sources of water. A man's flocks are apportioned among his wives, who make the exacting decisions about their care. His camels are collectively managed and are often pastured with those of kinsmen in his *diya*-group;[60] his rights in them are not absolute, since the animals are used to pay joint compensation or the herds increased by indemnities received.[61]

Most nomadic hamlets, like the one into which Aman was born, have only two to four mobile houses, each associated with a matrifocal family, whose menfolk are usually brothers, or fathers and sons. However, for a variety of reasons, the families who travel and live together may change from season to season, and even those from different *diya*-groups might co-reside.[62] During the rainy season—when the desert blooms, grazing is plentiful, and both herds and flocks can subsist in proximity— clans congregate for feasting and sociability. They reaffirm old ties or create new ones through marriage. Herdsmen sacrifice to Allah, poets banter, and young men and women dance: this is the season of happiness that Aman describes.

Camels and Poets

Camel herding is considered the "most noble Somali calling";[63] owning large numbers of the beasts is the clearest sign of wealth. Camels are slaughtered for religious feasts and to provide hospitality for honoured guests. They are the objects of feuds, but also the subjects of serious verse. They are praised and sung to as they march to the wells, while they are watered, or while they rest. Terms describing camels and camel husbandry provide a metaphoric language through which poets, lyricists, and dramatists speak of intimate love and thwarted desire, marital fidelity, jealousy.

Place names frequently reflect pastoral concerns: *Candho-qoys*, the place of "moist udders"; *Geel-weyta*, the place that "weakens camels".[64] Pastoral vocabulary is also used extensively in business and bureaucracy. The Somali word *raadraa'*, literally "to trace lost animals or to track down stock thieves", figuratively refers to modern research. *Layis*, which denotes the breaking of a young camel, also signifies student exercises in a school workbook; *gaadiid* means both burden-bearing camels and the fleet of government limousines.[65] *Hugaan*, a term for rope used to lead a camel, was applied to the Bureau of Ideology (*Hugaanka Ideolojiyada*) under the socialist regime.[66]

Camel imagery pervades Somali culture, present and past. It is the basis for Somali aesthetics and social style. Animal husbandry is essential to people's sense of self, just as the exchange of livestock is crucial to mending and weaving their relationships. Aman's mother's concern for her animals, her abiding desire to replace those lost through drought and disease, reflects a deep sense of loss and is by no means idiosyncratic.

When the British adventurer Richard Burton visited northern Somalia in the mid-nineteenth century, he observed that

> there are thousands of songs, some local, others general, upon all conceivable subjects, such as camel loading, drawing water, and elephant hunting; every man of education knows a variety of them.
>
> ... The country teems with "poets"... [and] every man has his recognized position in literature as accurately defined as though he had been reviewed in a century of magazines—the fine ear of this people causing them to take the greatest pleasure in harmonious sounds and poetical expressions, whereas a false quantity or a prosaic phrase excite their violent indignation.... Every chief in the country must have a panegyric to be sung by his clan, and the greatest patronize light literature by keeping a poet.[67]

Verse is the most prestigious and political of Somali oral genres. On private and domestic levels, people explain themselves to others in verse,[68] or use it to contract and terminate marriages. Poetry is also used to publicize events, or "as propaganda for or against some person, group, or matter of concern.... Truly memorable verse persists for generations...and in many cases is known throughout the length and breadth of the Somali Peninsula."[69] The rhetorical arts in Somalia are like news media elsewhere: they are the principal means by which information is disseminated, but also publicly controlled, manipulated by group interests.

Poetry is also the medium of political debate, an exercise in public relations by a poet's political patrons, laudatory perhaps or bitterly satirical, but eminently persuasive. Verse is customarily excepted from the rules of insult and indemnification. Thus its "exchanges of banter could be extremely aggressive without incurring censure, [moreover] praise could be showered on someone, even on oneself, which otherwise might be embarrassing to utter."[70] Public officials are especially watchful of urban bards, whose talents can be used to direct public opinion against government; those who resist accepting government patronage risk harassment, exile, even imprisonment.[71]

Poetry may be the quintessence of Somali verbal skill, but in Aman's prose narrative a rhetorical turn of mind is no less apparent. Her story, of course, is compellingly told, but that is not all. Aman, like all Somalis, has a deep respect for the power of words, their efficacy and effect, for speaking itself as an art. Attending parties in Mogadishu, she becomes a conversationalist gifted in the art of repartee, the elegant turn of phrase.[72] That she chooses words with care is evident from the pseudonyms she uses for herself and her interlocutor. "Aman" means "trustworthy" in Arabic; using it, she persuades us that she now tells the truth about herself, where before, as a young woman alone in the city, she lied. "Rahima", the name she selects for Lee Barnes, means "compassionate"—tellingly, the term is derived from the Arabic root that also supplies the word for "womb".[73] Aman's younger cousin, who helped us with this book, affirmed that Aman is well regarded by her family as a storyteller and wit.

But perhaps most important, Aman frets over what others say about her, for words can surely damage or enhance her "name" —her own and her family's reputation. Aman rebels, does what she wants, feigns disregard, but worries all the same. That she *is* concerned with what others say, because of her own or her mother's potential disgrace, is obvious in her delight at being demonstrated a virgin when she marries for the first time.

The Position of Women: Gender, Honour, Female Circumcision

In an unfinished foreword to Aman's narrative, Lee Barnes wrote:

One important influence on Aman's life was her culture's traditional practice of clitoridectomy and infibulation of the vagina, or "female circumcision".... In Aman's culture, the removal of the clitoris and labia minora and the sewing up of the vagina until it is all but closed are performed in a single operation when a girl is about six to ten years old. This operation has a profound influence on a girl's development as a woman and as a sexual being, as will be clear from the narrative. Aman's relationship with her first husband, her running away, the manner and occasion for her being "disvirgined", and her subsequent relationships with men were all profoundly shaped by her experience with circumcision. The subtle and not-so-subtle intertwining of sadism and sexuality in a culture that practises female circumcision will also be clear from Aman's many experiences with men of various ages from her own culture.

Lee went on to point out that Aman's story is that of a Somali girl who grows up not in a "traditional" setting, but during a time of rapid social change. Her experiences of men and sexuality would have been highly improbable for her mother, even more her grandmother, a comparison that Aman's account of their lives invites.

According to Somali custom, women's social status is inferior to men's, and both sexes are firmly schooled to this from birth; both are also raised to believe that gender inequality is natural, as counselled by Islam.[74] But whether women are legally equal, are complementary, or subordinate to men is currently a heated debate in the Islamic world. More women are literate now than ever before; those who have read the Qur'an for themselves hold that their inferior position is dictated not in the Qur'an, but in subsequent patriarchal interpretations of this holy text that have become Islamic law.[75] Whatever their position in theory, in practice women are expected to submit to the authority of fathers, brothers, and husbands, and are enjoined to display modesty and exercise self-restraint. In other Muslim societies this has led to the division of communities into sexually distinctive spheres of action and physical space. But a herding lifestyle, with its need for flexibility and mobilility, makes such sustained division impossible.

The bush house or tent is the primary abode of a nomadic Somali; it and its companions in a tiny hamlet are protected by a simple thorn-bush fence. Unlike houses in towns, such structures are neither permanent nor capacious enough to allow for strict sex separation. When nearby grazing is exhausted and it is necessary for a family or hamlet to move, it is the women who are responsible for dismantling the huts and rebuilding them at the new site. Women's other tasks—equally critical to the household's well-being—include making utensils out of local materials; weaving rope, mats, and rugs; fetching firewood and water, often from great distances; loading and unloading the transport camels with every move; processing pastoral products such as liquid butter for trade as well as for use; and, not least, caring with their daughters for the family's sheep, cattle, and goats. Much of their work requires them to be out and about in public; the same is true to an extent in towns. Nor are they typically veiled from head to toe, as this would impede their activities. Segregation and veiling in the black garb called a *shuko* are therefore rarely practised, save among wealthy urban Somalis, or for light-skinned, beautiful daughters—like Hawa—with prospects of lofty marriage. Both are customary, however, in the enclave of Arabs—including the family in Mogadishu who employed young Aman as a maid.

Women and men contribute complementary skills to the Somali household economy; but while the labours of both are crucial to a family's prosperity, much of the hard physical work falls to women and the young. Boys and unmarried men who herd camels lead a frugal, arduous life. In the dry season they subsist mainly on milk provided by the animals in their care, which during periods of drought may be in scant supply. They undertake frequent long treks to secure water for the camels and find them grass, all the time remaining alert, ready to defend the herd.[76] Since camels are the principal form of wealth, feuds between kin groups over the animals—promised in bride-wealth, withheld from compensation, stolen or retrieved—are common.

Married men's roles in clan politics can take them far from home for extended periods; married men also manage the camels, engage in trade and purchase provisions, clear wells, and assist in watering the flocks. And however co-operative the herding enterprise appears, only senior men exercise rights of disposal over family property.[77] Females and junior males are therefore subordinate to these men; their security of livelihood depends upon their relationships with fathers, husbands, brothers, paternal uncles. But unlike junior males, women cannot aspire to become socially dominant themselves. Strictly speaking, a woman has no legal identity: she is forever a minor, an adjunct to her father's name. She is represented by male kin at virtually all important undertakings. Though women may own and dispose of property in their own right, they rarely have an opportunity to do so, since Islamic inheritance rules are seldom fully adhered to in their case. All lineage property is overseen by the elder men: land, camels and other livestock generally remain with the patrilineal group on the death of the holder, to be apportioned among his sons.[78]

Somalia is clearly a male-dominated society, yet women wield considerable influence within the household and, through this, can influence public affairs. In fact, women's rights are considerable. In marriage they are entitled to adequate maintenance and are free to return to their natal families should they feel misused; their brothers are duty-bound to provide for them in that event. They are accustomed to travel unchaperoned on their own initiative, and since they are *entitled* under Islamic law to own, inherit, and pass on property independently, could presumably try to enforce their claims in religious court.[79] While marriages are normally arranged by families, such intervention often follows a courtship initiated by the couple themselves, and elopement is neither unknown nor unforgivable.[80] Aman's first marriage is a case in point, though she later rejects her husband and so mocks her family's efforts to accommodate her initial desire to marry him.

Arranged marriage is accompanied by the transfer of bride-wealth, which some observers regard as degrading to women. But as Aman says, "It's respect." Somali marriage involves more than a relationship between spouses; it links in mutual obligation two families who are not otherwise close kin, a fact that marriage payments solemnize. That it is families and indeed their wider descent groups who are joined is evident from the fact that when one asks who has requested a woman in marriage, the name of her husband's lineage is usually given, not merely her husband's name.[81] Before marriage negotiations formally begin, the kin of prospective spouses will have made extensive inquiries into each other's wealth, strength, and influence, evaluating political prospects as well as the character and health of the intended mates.[82] Aman naively seeks to bypass these family obligations when she tries to conceal her first marriage from her father and to keep any forthcoming wealth for herself.

There are several kinds of marriage payment, and they move in both directions. It is customary for the groom to give the bride's family a token present of livestock or money once the engagement is set; he is expected to gift his future bride with clothing and jewellery as well. Under Islamic law, the marriage contract must then be formalized in a brief ceremony before a *sheikh* or religious expert; in it the husband agrees to settle a portion of his estate on his wife for her use in the event of divorce. This wealth, called *mahr* in Arabic, may take a variety of forms —money, animals, jewellery, land—and becomes the wife's personal property. But it is seldom paid to her immediately, being kept in trust by her husband until such time as the marriage dissolves. And if it is the woman who seeks a divorce, she must usually forfeit her *mahr* in order to assure release—as happens to Aman's mother and later to Aman herself.

When an engagement is arranged, the *yarad*—bride-wealth paid by the groom's family to the bride's—must also be negotiated. Elder kinsmen of the couple decide on the amount of property involved. While camels are the preferred form of bride-wealth—thirty is a respectable number, but a hundred may be required for a particularly desirable match—in agrarian communities the property transferred might include a plot of land, whereas in cities and towns, money, land, or buildings may be preferred.[83] The amounts decided reflect family status and the esteem in which the bride and her family are held by the groom and his kin. Bride-wealth is transferred on the day of the wedding feast, which takes place sometime after the formal marriage contract was signed.

Once the marriage is firmly established and early divorce seems unlikely, the bride's father returns a portion of this property to the husband's family as her dowry. It is also customary for a woman to be given a substantial gift of livestock by her father or brothers whenever she returns to visit her family.[84] Presumably such transfers take place in lieu of her proper inheritance, just as the right to be maintained by her brothers if divorced is guaranteed at the expense of her future claim.

It would seem that despite their subordinate position, women are well cared for in Somali society, and certainly for some this is the case. But the system is open to abuses, for occasionally, through poverty or greed, daughters are given in marriage against their will, often to elderly, even brutal and offensive men who offer a bride-wealth too tempting to refuse.[85] Sometimes a young girl goes through a series of such relationships, being repeatedly widowed or divorced before marrying someone she approves. Reforms to family law in 1975 (after the period of Aman's narrative) established that marriage was to be by mutual consent, and gave women the right to claim not only their due inheritance (half the portion assigned to a brother under Islamic law) but equal shares with men. However, the reforms were opposed by the religious establishment and they have yet to be complied with to the full.[86]

One might think that the elaborate property exchanges and broad social links that marriage entails would make Somali marriages highly stable. But this is not the case. Divorce is fairly common and, according to Somalis I've spoken to, more frequent in the south than in the north.[87] Under Islamic law, it is more easily obtained by the man, who has only to repudiate his wife thrice before witnesses for their union to be dissolved. The woman who seeks a divorce must either provoke her husband to do this or petition the religious court; but in the latter case, her grounds—sterility, sodomy, nonsupport—must be fully substantiated. A desperate wife may seek to remedy her situation by fleeing; if, however, her brothers have an interest in maintaining the match, they will make every effort to find her and return her to her husband. Upon divorce, the right to allocate her fertility and labour in marriage reverts to her lineage, though she can expect to have more choice in the matter of a second husband. Thus Aman, wanting to be adult and control her own life, says that she made her first marriage in order to become divorced.

A girl's or woman's position in her family and the family of her husband affects the practical enforceability of her rights, and this position depends in no small way on her behaviour: she must exercise self-restraint, demonstrate patience and responsibility, show obedience and deference to senior male kin, display an attitude of spontaneous self-denial and sacrifice.[88] Most important, she must comply with the ethic of kin solidarity. To understand the implications this has for women, one needs to consider the concepts of honour, nobility, and reputation or "name", as well as the Somali ideal of independence.

Early in her narrative Aman recounts a legend that reveals a telling caste division in Somali society between those who are free-born or noble and those who are known as *sab*, former bondsmen—the Midgaan, Tumaal, and Yibir.[89] The *sab* are dispersed among Somali clans but do not marry with them, and are distinguished from noble Somalis by their trades—they are blacksmiths, leather-workers, shoe-makers, hunters, hairdressers and, according to Richard Burton,[90] circumcisers and infibulators—activities that the pastoralists scorn.[91] Unlike "free" Somalis, the *sab* were once attached to pastoral kin groups; some effectively remain so today. As clients the *sab* are what no Somali wishes to be: economically and socially dependent. So too are those who once were slaves, the people of "African" descent whom Aman calls Addon. For Somalis, pastoralism means liberty, dignity, autonomy. Women, though less able to demonstrate these ideals than men, nonetheless uphold them. A popular story portrays the noble view:

The sheep asks the gazelle why he runs away from humans, especially considering he is always starving. If he did follow humans, the sheep argues, the best pasturage would be available to him. The gazelle responds, "A sheep cannot understand. My family and yours are not alike. We are the children of liberty and open space. As for me, I prefer to die on my own feet while running away before being gorged with food by a master who would kill me when I became fat or who would kill my children. My heart is not the heart of a sheep."[92]

The tale is particularly acute when viewed in terms of Aman's and her mother's married lives.

To explain women's willing participation in a system of values that they themselves can never fully uphold and, on the face of it, diminishes their worth, we must turn to the ideology of honour.[93] Honour stems first and absolutely from nobility of ancestry, which women and men share by virtue of their common descent. Honour is also associated with autonomy, as expressed in the egalitarian ethic of segmentary kinship. But true autonomy cannot be realized by all: within the family and the lineage, females and junior males—hence most Somalis—are dependents, politically weaker than the patriarch, unable to control resources in their own right. The social reality of hierarchy contradicts the fundamental value of equality. But some reconciliation of the two is found in the notion that the authority exercised by superiors is a reward for moral worth, rather than acquired by force or ascribed by sex and position. Authority thus depends on being accorded respect by others, most importantly by followers, dependents. It must be earned—deserved and kept. It can also, therefore, be lost.

Respect can be earned by demonstrating personal assertiveness, when, for example, one successfully resists others' demands on one's property, as Mama did in the wake of her father's death. But it also derives from wealth, for generosity and hospitality are means to make others dependent. Since women, however assertive, control few productive resources, they are less able to achieve this authority than men.

Equally important, however, is the ideal of self-mastery, expressed by both stoicism and emotional and physical restraint. And embracing these concerns is a specific concept of "reason" —'aql in Arabic—widespread in the Islamic world. 'Aql means social sense, the ability to recognize and follow both cultural ideals and Allah's laws.[94] Children are born with little *'aql* but, unless infirm, are bound to develop it as they mature. Those who show their emotions for others display a want of *'aql;* the man who fails to conceal his feelings for a woman is seen to be controlled by another person, and loses the respect of others. As I. M. Lewis observes: "No man whose conduct reveals that he is emotionally dependent upon his wife, or wives, can hope to enjoy a reputation for male hardihood."[95]

Women manifest social sense, and so partially resolve the contradiction between their acceptance of the ideals of honour, and their incomplete ability to realize them, by deferring to those in authority *voluntarily*. Lila Abu-Lughod, an anthropologist who has studied these issues among Egyptian Bedouin, points out that "what is voluntary is by nature free and is thus also a sign of independence. Voluntary deference is therefore the honorable mode of dependency."[96]

Voluntary deference implies modesty and propriety: a woman is shy, "ashamed", or bashful when among those more powerful than she, and she behaves towards them with courteous submission. As Aman says, "You don't look big people in the face. You look down." Thus modesty and *'aql* are intimately linked: the good woman is reasonable, well-behaved; she acts properly in social life and is finely attuned to her relative position in all interactions. She comports herself modestly, with effacement before superiors, yet she is not passive or unassertive in all social situations: with equals she is, and is expected to be, bold, wilful, independent. Passivity is therefore not so much a feminine personality trait as a tactical behaviour to be used in appropriate circumstances, a behaviour that young men also evince in the company of older men. And conformity is less a sign of weakness than of social knowledge and inner strength. Raqiya Abdalla, the former Director of Culture, describes the ideal Somali woman as "able, possessed of initiative, strong—but with the strength of a 'feminine' type, i.e., she must not try to assume masculine attributes and, most importantly, she must in no way challenge men's authority."[97]

In deferring to superiors, in comporting herself modestly in public, a girl or woman validates her father's claim to honourable status, his "name". Their relationship is complementary: he exhibits noble virtues, protects, and provides for her as his dependent; by her modest bearing she shows the world that he is worthy of her respect, a respect given freely, without encumbrance. Aman's behaviour should be measured against this ideal; though her father fails their relationship in important ways, he and his sons expect her to act as though he has not.

In Somalia, as elsewhere in Islamic North Africa, women's sexuality is thought to prevent them from achieving the same level of moral worth as men, because it ties them more closely to nature and the material world. Female fertility is highly prized; it is associated with plenty, prosperity, and life, with the continuation of the lineage through the birth of sons, and with the virtues of pity, mercy, and compassion. Nevertheless, women are considered socially less developed than men. They regularly and involuntarily menstruate; they give birth and lactate; when pregnant they publicly display their sexuality, their ties, that is, to other humans.[98] All these natural conditions that women cannot control are seen to represent weakness and a lack of independence, the antithesis of the social ideal.

Their bodily functions make it difficult too for women to demonstrate piety in keeping with Islamic rules. They are forbidden to enter a holy place—a mosque or a saint's shrine—while menstruating and for forty days after childbirth, because at such times they are "unclean". They are considered more "polluted" than men by sexual intercourse since their pollution is internal. According to Aman, a Somali woman newly married at the start of Ramadan is not allowed to fast, for she is expected to be sexually available to her husband and cannot therefore achieve the state of ritual purity required. Social views of women's inferiority and religious views of their essential nature support each other and are merged in Somali thought.

Ideas about sexuality likewise combine social and religious concerns. On the social side, sexual attachment poses a major threat to patrilineal allegiance. However deep the conjugal bond, loyalty to one's husband or wife should never exceed loyalty to one's lineage and natal family. Thus marriage seems to have the characteristics of an uneasy truce: each partner views the other with suspicion; each seeks to gain something from the other without relinquishing ground. And a married woman must behave honourably, with dignity, for she represents her family in the alien camp. Her strength "must be of a kind capable of concealing her man's weaknesses."[99] She must be a paragon—physical and social—of Somali womanhood. Some lines of a traditional Somali poem in which a husband dispenses advice to his new wife are instructive:

The wife of a husband of low birth never smells well, for she never burns incense for herself.
After she gives birth, she becomes even worse, and her husband abandons her.
[Therefore], be generous with water to your body and soul....
As long as you remain with me never cease to use the incense burner....
Clean your mouth and teeth, and always use your eyeshadow,
One should never find you untidy....[100]

In Somalia and throughout northeast Africa—among, for example, the northern Sudanese villagers with whom I lived—married women who fail to conform to such strenuous ideals, who are overworked or unable to make known important personal concerns owing to the strict constraints of propriety, may claim to be unwell. There is no dishonour in illness, whereas there may be in forthright behaviour or anger, particularly when expressed by a woman.[101] According to local wisdom, her sickness may be a sign that a spirit has entered her body in a bid to experience the good things of human life: perfume, gold, incense, fine clothing, jewellery, meat.[102] Known as *zar* spirits in Sudan, and *saar* or *zar* in Somalia, they are considered to be a type of jinn, the "genies" of Arabic folklore; since jinn are mentioned in the Qur'an, their existence and abilities are irrefutable facts of life.[103] Once in control of its victim, a spirit is extremely difficult to dislodge; it can, however, be placated by gifts and ritual procedures after the patient has mounted a ritual "cure" under the direction of a cult master or priestess. Such a cure is staged for Aman's mother, who in middle age is diagnosed as possessed.

The purpose of this ceremony is to invoke and identify the troublesome *zar* from among several potential candidates, each with its own name, society, religion, and occupation. Cult members drum and sing the spirits' personal refrains. At some point the woman's spirit responds by causing her to fall into trance, whereupon it manifests itself through her body and makes known its demands. The rite does not so much resolve the problem—it has none of the finality of an exorcism—as open up lines of communication between the possessed and her ethereal possessor. Spirit and host strike a bargain: the *zar* will cease to make the woman unwell so long as she obtains certain items that it desires, regularly attends spirit ceremonies, and periodically performs ritual acts such as burning the combination of incense proper to the spirit's identity on its special day of the week.

In these societies where women are hard-pressed to voice discontent, spirit possession mobilizes kin support and may enable husbands and wives to address issues they would otherwise find it difficult to discuss. But a *zar* affliction is expensive, and husbands are not always sympathetic to the possession diagnoses of their wives. And the Muslim religious establishment regards the cult with suspicion, maintaining that it is reprehensible to traffic with unscrupulous jinn. Yet neither husbands nor religious clerics deny the powers of spirits; ultimately their belief grants the *zar* legitimacy as a form of honourable redress.[104]

The honour of a family is vested in the behaviour of its womenfolk. A wife's poor social comportment reflects on her husband, but he can divorce her in the end; on her father it reflects indelibly. A daughter's sexual misconduct, especially, implies a lack of solidarity and discipline, weakness both moral and political, on the part of her lineage's men; her action is a public statement that her superiors are unworthy of her respect. The violation is punished, sometimes by the woman's death, and Aman is not being melodramatic in her fear that she may be killed. This extreme retribution indicates the extent to which female sexuality is intended to be put to social use. Social concerns are echoed by religious ones. Raqiya Abdalla writes: "Islam regards female sexuality as active and as a lustful instinct which consequently must be controlled."[105] In some societies controls include the precautionary measure of female "circumcision".

Although female "circumcision" is practised in many African societies[106] and, even in its most radical form—removal of the clitoris and labia, followed by infibulation (occlusion of the vaginal opening)—is often linked to Islam, rationales for the surgery vary widely. The procedure I observed in Muslim Sudan is virtually the same as the one Aman describes, but their social and cultural contexts—hence the meanings of the act—differ in important ways.[107] And historically the practice antedates the birth of Islam. Indeed, Muslim fundamentalists regard it as a barbaric "innovation" (*buda'*) and have called for it to cease. Nevertheless, the dovetailing of patrilineal and Islamic values—the insistence of both on male superiority—supports the continuation of the practice in Somalia today. In the early 1980s female circumcision was almost universal among Somalis, and infibulation was the type of operation usually performed.[108]

Social controls on women's sexuality are somewhat paradoxically accompanied by a liberal view of sexuality in Islam. The Qur'an describes the sexual impulse as a natural appetite to be satisfied, albeit in moderation and in a faithful marital relationship.[109] Neither sex should behave licentiously, yet a double standard of morality customarily exists. Among urban Somali men, especially, early sexual experience is a source of pride, a demonstration of their virility (if not their self-restraint). But for unmarried women, sexual experience is a source of shame and a symbol of degradation.[110]

Female virginity is highly valued in Somali society. It is strictly enjoined both for reasons of family honour and so that parentage will be clear. Excision of the clitoris and infibulation of the vagina are designed to reduce sexual sensitivity, hence erotic activity; in the majority of cases they ensure virginity at first marriage. As Raqiya Abdalla notes:

the principal effect of the operation is to create in young girls an intense awareness of [their] sexuality and anxiety concerning its meaning, its social significance. In general, the practice emphasizes punishment and control, clearly indicating to the little girl a sense of the mystery and importance of sex, and, at the same time creating a fear of the evils of unchaste behaviour in her.[111]

She goes on to emphasize that the relationship between virginity and infibulation in Somali society is closely linked to the vigour and continuity of moral standing, which has consequences for political status and economic gain.

The infibulation scars are a seal attesting to the intangible but vital property of the social group's patrimony, the honour of the family and patrilineage. This seal and a woman's sexual purity, must be transferred intact upon marriage into another lineage. Should either not be intact, the girl will be totally unacceptable to that lineage as the family involved would eschew ties with a lineage without honour. Preservation of purity and honour is thus essential if her patrilineage is to maintain its social status, broaden its kinship ties and *enhance* its patrimony. This is the economic rationale for the custom.[112]

Still, this external, visible virginity is not innate but made; it can also be remade, restitched to conceal her sexual experience. Women contemplating remarriage, prostitutes seeking a new life, parturient women wanting to please their husbands, may all avail themselves of this option.

Although the procedure has frequent medical complications and eradication of the woman's sexual pleasure may ensue, there is clearly much at stake in any battle to abolish the practice. Government reforms have been agonizingly slow to address the issue.[113] Men and women fear—with some justification—that if their daughters are not circumcised they will not marry; if a daughter does not marry, it is because she is unacceptable to other groups, and if so diminishes the honour of her own. It is not difficult to see how women in such a context might come to regard as natural and inevitable a practice that plainly does them harm. Being circumcised is a matter of pride and, as Aman's experience makes clear, often willingly or at least ambivalently undergone. By having the operation girls can actively demonstrate their worth as patrilineal kin. To the girls and their mothers, it is the proper thing to do, and even sceptical fathers hesitate to meddle in what is a woman's affair. Compliance is assured not by force, but by the power of social norms, so that a girl whose infibulation is merely delayed risks the painful rejection of her peers. And the infibulated woman's body is aesthetically valued: it is clean, says Aman, closed and smooth and hard. This web of implicit knowledge holds the individual, shapes her sense of self and social reality; it is seldom resisted or contested without cost.

That said, growing numbers of Somalis, women and men, are aware of the custom's damaging consequences and want it discontinued, preferring the less radical *sunna* operation, wherein only the prepuce (foreskin) of the clitoris is removed (in some cases merely nicked or pricked with a pin).[114] Since infibulation is a mark of ethnic distinction, and has acquired significance as an act of anti-Western, anticolonial resistance,[115] impolitic foreign pressure to abandon it could actually retard its demise.[116]

Aman's horror of being "disvirgined", as she aptly puts it, her loathing for the man who would perform this task, and her early sense of intercourse as an economic transaction—such feelings are echoed in three case studies of Somali women that Raqiya Abdalla includes as an appendix to her book *Sisters in Affliction*. Witness the case of Ardo:

The first nights of my wedding were really awful and filled with fear. The custom in Benader region is for the men to defibulate their brides with their penis. Except in very rare cases it is an insult if they use an instrument or if (as in the northern region) the midwife defibulates. Anyway, I refused to submit or co-operate with my husband. I shouted and fought him, and bit him seriously. Five days after my wedding, the man was still not able to have intercourse with me. Then I was forced to go to the hospital where they opened my infibulation. After that I got an infection and was sick for a few days before the man forced me again.

I was never happy with that first husband and I continued to hate him and fought with him in every sexual contact. I finally left him, and refused to go back, until he agreed to divorce me.[117]

The poignancy of Aman's story is deepened by the knowledge that it is not unique.

Though there are numerous contradictions for women within the lineage system, its alternatives may be worse. In urban areas there has been a breakdown of arranged marriage. This, while personally liberating, has had a price. For few such marriages last, and rural young who move to the city and wed without consulting or even informing their kin give up the supports that family offer in the event of divorce.[118] Rural women who have offended their patrilineages can seldom marshal the economic means—such as animals or land—on which they and their children might subsist.[119] Beyond their traditional roles, Somali women, particularly if uneducated, like Aman, have few options. Prostitution, of course, is one; it has increased dramatically since the Second World War. Though regarded as depravity by the religious, it is also widely seen as a form of rebellion by women unwilling to play the marriage/lineage game.[120]

Alternatively, an independent woman might get on through petty trade, as Aman's mother does for a time, bargaining one item of domestic consumption into other more lucrative ones. This style of earning a living, common among women in the underdeveloped world, demands constant work, much energy, quick, sure judgement, and luck. Little wonder then that a chord repeatedly struck by Aman is the quest for material security. The preoccupation is not confined to Somali women; it has become increasingly prevalent in urban Africa since the 1950s, with the progressive erosion of women's traditional supports.[121]

The resource Aman relies upon is her sexuality, reclaimed from her descent group, daringly proclaimed as her own. Aman lives by her wits in the city, intending to use men, rather than be used by them. She walks a fine line between honour and promiscuity, seeking to protect herself and her family (and herself *from* her family) by lying, concealing her true name. And yet, however bold her rebellion, it is tinged with the realization that she is ultimately no less dependent on men—or immersed in Somali values—than before.

Colonial and Postcolonial Somalia

To understand Aman's world one must also consider its broader social and political context—the reality of colonialism. The two decades following the demise of the Dervish resistance in 1920 were a time of colonial consolidation; they mark the period of Mama's early life. In the north the British maintained a strategic presence but showed limited interest in developing the colony economically; the area was seen as an asset to be traded for future political advantage. But in Italian Somalia, where Aman and her mother grew up, the situation was different.

In order to relieve mounting population pressure at home and to enhance its prestige in the European community, Italy planned to export commercial farmers and entrepreneurs to the fertile riverine area of southern Somalia. In turn, Somalia was expected to produce primary goods for the parent country.[122] Although the Italians had hoped to extend their authority deep into the Somali hinterland, in fact they proceeded gradually; the Italian presence was most strongly felt near the coast.

Under the Fascist administration that began in Italy in the 1920s, and even before, large-scale plantation projects were undertaken for growing bananas, cotton, citrus, and sugar; roads were built and the infrastructure for a settlement of Europeans was laid. To offset problems in recruiting labour from a largely nomadic populace, Italian and (mainly southern) Somali families were established in labour colonies and voluntarily bonded to irrigation consortia under terms that provided both wages for plantation work and land allotments for personal use. When Somalis absconded to take care of their interests at home, forced recruitment made up the labour shortfall. Those of lower status, particularly the descendants of slaves (Addon), were the first to be conscripted.[123]

In the period before the Second World War, Italian Somalia's towns grew, and basic health and educational services were established, paid for mainly by Rome. A system of rural administration was set up, whereby district residents (or commissioners) were weakly seconded by "chiefs" and elders on government stipends. Most of these men were vehicles for government directives, but some who proved loyal and co-operative received Italian decorations and largesse.[124]

Chiefs were assisted in their role as agents of the Italian resident by an armed rural constabulary, which, by 1930, was 500 strong. A sizeable police force of 1,475 Somalis, led by 85 Italian officers and subalterns, provided direct support to the administration. (The number of police was later reduced as the colony's military grew.)[125] Somalis did not take kindly to the imposition of Italian rule. Their valued independence had been compromised, and making matters worse, they had become subject to infidels.[126]

In 1925, Jubbaland, the coastal portion of the ethnically Somali Northern Frontier District of Kenya, was ceded to Italy by Britain. Soon after, the Italians established firm hold over their northwestern regions, with the hope of expansion into Ethiopia. To this end they infiltrated the Ogaden, where they colluded politically and materially with Somalis seeking reunification with brethren in the other partitioned zones. The Ethiopians, for their part, armed Somalis hostile to Italy's ventures, in the hope of countering Italian aggression and winning Somali territory for themselves.[127]

By 1934, preparations for Italy's invasion of Ethiopia from Somalia and Eritrea were well under way. After futile wranglings among the European powers (which amounted to unacknowledged support for Italy's imperialist aims), Ethiopia was invaded in 1935, and conquered the next year by an Italian army assisted by some 6,000 Somali troops and many thousands of Italian-trained Somali irregulars.[128] Their push to the border was complemented by aerial support.[129] It was during the turmoil surrounding this event that Aman's mother was hastily married to an older man with other wives, to prevent her from being pressed into concubinage by white soldiers. For a brief period thereafter, Italian Somalia included the Ogaden and the regions inhabited by Somalis on the upper Jubba and Shabeelle rivers, which united clansmen who had been arbitrarily separated by the colonial boundary some forty years before.

Under the Fascist regime, trade and commerce were strictly controlled. A system of government monopolies and state supported organizations favoured Italian endeavours; indeed, Somalis and other colonial subjects were legally barred from participating in any sector of the economy where they might rival their colonizers.[130] Between 1935 and 1940, the Italians increased large-scale agricultural projects, and built new roads and markets. Thousands of Italian emigrants and ex-servicemen became involved in the Somali economy as plantation farmers, merchants, mechanics.[131] The clubs and organizations of Fascist social life had been imported from the mother country, and "permeated the life of the Italian community to an extent which, particularly in the local context of Somalia, seems today ludicrous in the extreme."[132]

With the influx of Italians came regulations designed to preserve their racial status and enhance their dignity as "Aryan" conquerors, including policies that denigrated the Somali language and promoted adoption of the "civilized" Italian tongue. Italian concern for racial purity was clearly a match for the Somalis' own, as events in Aman's life attest. Mixed liaisons, while common, were officially discouraged, and interracial marriage was forbidden. There was no Somali presence in government and administration save at the very lowest levels. Social ties developed, regardless, across the racial divide, and many Somalis benefitted from new economic and educational opportunities under the regime. Between 1930 and 1940 Mogadishu more than doubled its population, due in part to the discharge of thousands of Somali soldiers. With the growth of urbanization and the spread of Western influence—to say nothing of Somali historical consciousness, fierce independence, and solidarity—a modern nationalist movement was born.

In 1940 Italy joined the Axis powers, and Somalia entered the Second World War.[133] The Italians captured British Somaliland that July, but seven months later it was recovered. The Allies went on to liberate Ethiopia (on behalf of Emperor Haille Selassie) and occupy Somalia. The loss of Mama's brother during a bombing attack dates to this period; her marriages to Somali military men in the Italian colonial army took place around this time as well. After the Italian defeat, all of Somalia except French Djibouti came under British military administration, and remained so until 1949.

The Italian population in Somalia numbered 8,000 in 1941; many women and children were repatriated under the British, and by 1943 that figure had fallen by almost half.[134] Given the constraints of the continuing war, the British were forced to rely on the administrative expertise of Italian civil servants and technical officials who had shown no Fascist sympathies; the remainder were interned. The Italian police force was disbanded and replaced by Somalis under British officers; a police school was opened to train Somalis for higher ranks. Italian laws were replaced by British; Italian provincial administration was supplanted by one set out along British lines, using indirect methods of rule, and the basis for local self-government was established. Aman's father, acclaimed by his descent group as their representative, was thereby empowered to assist the administration in enforcing law and order, for which he received a government salary. More schools were opened, though principally for boys, and nationalist aspirations continued to grow. Somalis respected the British for having ousted the seemingly invincible colonial masters and for relaxing their discriminatory rule.

At the end of the war the Four-Power Commission (Britain, France, the United States, the Soviet Union) assumed responsibility for disposing of the ex-Italian colonies. Britain's bid to re-unify Somaliland (excepting Djibouti) under its control was rejected by the three other powers; with U.S. backing, Ethiopia gained Eritrea and took back the Ogaden; Somali lands reverted to their former masters. Northern Somalia was returned to Britain in 1948, and, despite vigorous Somali opposition, southern Somalia went to Italy as a United Nations trusteeship for a period of ten years, after which the country would become independent. It was during this trusteeship that Aman was born in 1952.

Under the U.N. mandate, Italy's powers in Somalia were curtailed and a move towards democratic self-government was begun. Yet friction between the Italians and Somalis remained, for the new administration was supported by a strong military force that made the handover appear to be a military occupation.[135] Nevertheless, with UNESCO involvement significant advancements were made in education, and new state schools replaced the Catholic mission schools of the colonial era. From fewer than 2,000 in 1950, the number of children and adults of both sexes in primary schools had increased to roughly 31,000 by 1957.[136] But the population was well over a million.[137] Despite the progress, few children in Aman's age group went to school or remained there for any length of time.

During the Italian Trust Administration, irrigation-farming was extended and wells were drilled in grazing lands, signalling a shift away from exclusive concentration on the settler plantation economy. Plantation agriculture was revived for crops such as cotton, sugar, and bananas, but ownership of estates and control of marketing remained largely in the hands of Italian colonists.[138] Despite the expanding economy the country remained desperately poor, and most Somalis lived much as they had in the past.

Politically Somalia was moving towards independence with the step-by-step replacement of expatriates by Somalis in the civil service and police. By the end of the trusteeship there were only about 3,000 Italians remaining in Somalia, most of whom were permanent residents engaged in commerce and employed by foreign-owned enterprises; the rest were in the administration.[139] Party politics (heavily influenced by clan membership) were officially inaugurated with a municipal election in 1954, followed in 1956 by the first general election of a legislative assembly, based on universal male suffrage. Candidates were required to be literate in Arabic or Italian; at the time there was no official script for the Somali language.

Importantly, when Aman speaks of having been illiterate, she is referring *not* to the fact that she was unable to read and write Somali—without a standard script, few people could, though various adaptations of Arabic lettering were used by some. What she means was that she was not literate in Arabic, Italian, or, later, English. In fact, it was not until 1972, a couple of years after her departure from Somalia, that the socialist revolutionary government decreed a form of writing for the national language based on Roman characters, and embarked on a successful literacy campaign.

On July 1, 1960, the colonial period ended when a newly independent British Somaliland united with Italian Somalia to form the independent Somali Republic with its capital at Mogadishu. Despite the nationalist fervour that accompanied unification and the growth of political parties—as well as the increasing urbanization, Western influence, and class differentiation that Aman so clearly details—loyalty to kin and clan was still the predominant political force. The composition of the new cabinet was based on a delicate balancing of clan-families and the clans within them. This pattern came to be standard in democratic Somalia; since the government controlled or assigned significant resources, it was necessary for the various descent groups to be sufficiently represented therein. And, not surprisingly, an abiding concern of the new government (enshrined in the Somali constitution of 1961) was to bring the Somali territories in Kenya, Djibouti, and Ethiopia into the national fold.

Regardless of national politics and pan-Somali aspirations, most Somalis continued to eke out a living from their herds and their land as before. Two extremely poor rainy seasons were followed by calamitous floods in the autumn of 1961 that brought widespread hunger and disease.[140] Aman's horrific description of accompanying her mother to a famine relief post at that time is all the more chilling in light of recent disasters in Ethiopia and Sudan and the current Somali situation.

For newly independent Somalia, the problems of combining two judicial systems, currencies, military and civil-service organizations, local and central government institutions, systems of pay, taxation, and education were monumental. People spoke both colonial languages in business and government, as well as Arabic. When the northern administration first transferred to Mogadishu, Italian (and Italian speakers) took precedence. However, during the 1960s English began to gain ground, fuelled by the government's inability to settle on a script for Somali.[141] English-language hegemony only intensified the enmity between north and south, which was originally aired in an abortive military coup by British-trained junior officers in 1961 and which continues to this day.

Given its hopes for a unified Somalia, the elected government sought to quadruple the size of its army—5,000 strong at independence—and turned to the United States for aid. But the

U.S. was then allied with Ethiopia. Though the Americans helped upgrade the Somali police force, their proposals for the army were rejected as inadequate. In 1962 the U.S.S.R. stepped into the breach with sophisticated weaponry, military advisors, and loans—along with ideology and political rhetoric. In succeeding years Somalia became involved in significant border wars with Kenya and Ethiopia. Then, in the 1967 presidential elections, a pro-unification (southern) president was matched with a prime minister from a rival (northern) clan who advocated renunciation of Somalia's territorial goals and an end to border disputes in return for considerable U.S. aid. The political situation stagnated.[142]

Politics were nonetheless fraught with clan factionalism and corruption, a situation that persists in amplified form today. Several scholars blame the inherent "anarchy" of the Somali segmentary kinship system.[143] Some Somali politicians concur, and have called for the elimination of tribalism.[144] But the trouble may lie less with Somali political culture *per se*, than with its inappropriate adaptation to economic and social contexts far different from those it was designed to address.[145] Prior to the establishment of the nation-state, Somalia did not experience the level of violence that presently exists. The mobility, egalitarianism, and contractual code of conduct that characterized kin relations made it difficult for one group to dominate others. Moreover, all adults were engaged in subsistence production, and all groups had access to its means or could gain them through alliance. But as Somalia became increasingly integrated with the global economy, through plantation agriculture and waged work, property relations were transformed. Society became more deeply stratified. Pastoralists no longer supported only themselves; their surpluses were now extracted to support a growing class of merchants and state elite, who controlled valuable resources. Competition for access to commodities, services, government jobs, and foreign aid became increasingly pronounced. Yet the rhetoric of kinship was retained, invoked by the multiclan urban elite in their competition for state resources. In short, clan became partially conflated with class.[146] This is the world Aman enters when she runs away in Mogadishu. Her story vividly documents the breakdown of traditional mores, the safeguards of contract and Islam that once guaranteed social security, and the rise of class stratification in the urban milieu. In the 1969 parliamentary elections there were sixty-four parties in a population of scarcely four million, each representing one of the sixty-four important lineages and sublineages.[147] These parties did not represent divergent ideologies, a fact made clear when, following the election, all opposition members but one crossed the floor in order to be on the winning side.[148]

A few months after the election, the president was assassinated by a soldier while reviewing troops in the north. Murderer and president belonged to rival subclans of the same clan, and the death was retribution for losses sustained by the soldier's kin in pre-election violence. Parliament met to choose a successor, but with limited success, given the acrimony of debate and the deep rifts it exposed. On October 21, 1969, the combined forces of Somalia's army and police force seized power in a bloodless coup under the leadership of Major-General Mohammad Siyaad Barre. Some have found evidence of Soviet involvement in the take-over, which a year later resulted in a socialist regime ostensibly committed to overcoming the divisiveness of clan loyalties through administrative impartiality.[149]

After the coup, the democratic constitution was suspended. Members of the old government were harassed or jailed, and expatriates were required to leave. It is here that Aman's life in Somalia comes to a close, with her husband's expulsion to Aden and her own harrowing escape to Kenya. Somalia's story continues, of course, with both social triumphs and political strife. The 1975 reforms to family law challenged gender inequalities; the literacy campaign of 1972–74 established Somali as the country's official language and formalized its official script.[150] In 1977 the Siyaad Barre regime embarked on a futile campaign to recapture the Ogaden, which lost it credibility at home and curtailed its Soviet support. The regime began to rely on brute force to maintain power; opposition was cruelly silenced, human rights abuses became commonplace. An attempted coup, civil resistance, and guerrilla attacks brought bloody reprisals against civilians at the hands of the Red Hats, the government's crack troops. Retaliation was directed against powerful Somali clans— the Majeerteen in 1979, the Isaaq in 1988, the Hawiye between 1989 and 1990.[151] The atrocities rival those in the former Yugoslavia: the destruction of water reservoirs leading to the deaths of over 2,000 from thirst, rapes of women in targetted populations, summary executions. In the last two weeks of January 1991, a pitched battle between government forces and the United Somali Congress (USC) rebels—dominated by the Hawiye and led by General Mohammad Farah Aideed—resulted in the fall of Mogadishu and the flight of General Barre south, where he and his supporters tried to regroup.[152]

The USC failed to unite Somalia; they split over the installation of an interim president, Ali Mahdi, who was rejected by Aideed and the leaders of other armed opposition groups. The USC divided along lineage lines into factions headed by Ali Mahdi and General Aideed, which fought each other in Mogadishu with serious loss of life.[153] That story continues as I write.

Notes

FOREWORD

[1] Several recent works written from women's perspectives address this point. See, for examples, Abu-Lughod 1986, 1993, Boddy 1989. See also Shostak 1981 and Smith 1981 for other African women's oral autobiographies that challenge conventional wisdom.

[2] References to my work can be found in the bibliography.

AFTERWORD

[1] S. Samatar 1991:6; Ahmed I. Samatar 1988:17. And Touval 1963:12 documents the proportion of ethnic Somalis in the population of each as follows: Somali Republic 99 per cent, Djibouti 43 per cent, Ethiopia 4 per cent, Kenya 1 per cent.

The Somali People

[2] Laitin and Samatar 1987:xvi.
[3] For expansion of this point see Cassanelli 1982.
[4] Abdalla 1982:42; Touval 1963:13-14.
[5] Laitin and Samatar 1987:4, 22; Touval 1963:14.
[6] Cushite is a linguistic term referring to the division of the Afro-Asiatic language family to which Somali belongs. Other speakers of Cushitic languages include the Oromo of Ethiopia and Kenya and, less closely related, the Beja, inhabitants of the Red Sea littoral in Egypt and Sudan. Arabic (also Afro-Asiatic) was introduced to Africa with Islam, beginning in the seventh century A.D.; in contrast to such areas as Egypt and northern Sudan, where earlier languages have all but disappeared, Arabic in Somalia has never superseded Somali as the language of everyday use. Arabic loan words make up roughly 20 per cent of the present Somali vocabulary, however (Laitin 1977:25). In addition, pockets of Bantu-speakers live in southern Somalia, though they also speak Somali (Declich 1994).
[7] For summaries see Lewis 1961, 1988; Laitin and Samatar 1987.
[8] Possibly absorbing Bantu and Swahili farming populations already established there. See Lewis 1988:7, Laitin and Samatar 1987:7. See also the latter (pp. 171-172 n. 5) for other

sources.

9 Isaaq and Daarood. The four others are Hawiye, Dir, Digil, and Rahanwayn.

10 Cassanelli 1982:15-16; Touval 1963:10.

11 But see Lewis 1988:27-32 on Somali wars with the Oromo, who are locally known as "Galla".

12 See Abdi I. Samatar 1989; Pankhurst 1965.

13 Chittick (1969:110-11) maintains that Mogadishu in the thirteenth century was the most important town on the East African littoral; from inscriptions there we know that one of its leading families was Shirazi (from Shiraz, the capital of Fars [Persia]), and related to ruling families in coastal ports farther south along the coast.

14 This loosely governed "empire" was established during the seventeenth century in the Indian Ocean, and came to include the East African coast as far south as present Mozambique. Its authority over Somali towns was largely nominal for much of its existence.

15 See Touval 1963:32 ff.; Laitin and Samatar 1987, Chapter 1; Berg 1969; Lewis 1988:36 ff.

Colonial Intervention

16 Laitin and Samatar 1987:53.

17 As a result of a treaty between Britain and Ethiopia in 1897, shipments of arms intended for Ethiopia were allowed to pass through British

ports in Somaliland; some undoubtedly failed to reach their destination (Abdi I. Samatar 1989:34). And at the turn of the century the religious leader Sayyid Mohammad 'Abdille Hasan (below) was able to import guns and ammunition through Djibouti and Italian Somalia (*ibid.*:38).

18 See Cassanelli 1982 for a discussion of such arrangements.

19 S. Samatar (1991:15) citing indigenous testimony puts the number of livestock seized from Somalis between 1890 and 1897 at 100,000 head of cattle, 200,000 camels, and 500,000 sheep and goats.

20 See, in particular, S. Samatar (1982), also B. W. Andrzejewski and I. M. Lewis (1964), and B. W. Andrzejewski, "Translator's Introduction" (1982:xiii) to *Ignorance Is the Enemy of Love*, a novel by the Somali author Faarax M. J. Cawl, set in the period of the Dervish resistance.

21 From the Arabic *darwish*, plural *darawish* : Muslim ascetic.

Herding, Marriage, Family, Clan

22 See Lewis 1961, and Laitin and Samatar 1987.

23 Laitin and Samatar 1987:29.

24 Touval 1963:15. The term *clanfamily* was proposed by Lewis 1961.

25 Lewis 1961:4; Cassanelli 1982: 17 ff.

26 Lewis 1961:6.

27 *Diya* is the Arabic term, rendered as *dinyo* by Aman.

28 Laitin and Samatar 1987:29; Lewis

1961:6, 171 ff. The group is called a *mag* in Somali (Samatar 191:12), though Aman pronounces it *mek*.

29 Such groups are flexible, however, and may incorporate uterine or affinal kin (kin by marriage) under certain circumstances. Though derived principally from the Shafi'ite school of Islamic law, compensation amounts are determined by adult male members of the group and are subject to redefinition from time to time. These groups also periodically refine the rules of the contract by which they are bound. See Lewis (1961) for a detailed discussion.

30 But see Helander (1991:117), who notes that in the interriver zone of southern Somalia, where people engage in mixed farming and herding, marriage with father's brother's daughter or son is idealized, and marriages between other sorts of cousins are also frequent. Emulation of the Arab model has long been a statement of allegiance to Islam, particularly among those seeking to distance themselves from an "African", hence possibly slave background (Declich 1994). With regard to the northern pastoralists, Lewis (1961:5-6) suggests that members of a lineage are so well integrated that they "feel little need to supplement their already strong agnatic ties by subsidiary links through marriage"; hence the practice of lineage exogamy, through which they create ties with other groups. See also Cas-

sanelli 1982.

31 See Abdalla 1982; Lewis 1961, 1988; Laitin and Samatar 1987.

32 See Lewis 1961; Helander 1991.

33 See Boddy (1989) for a complementary case from northern Sudan.

34 For those unfamiliar with these terms the distinction between *family* and *descent group* may be confusing. *Family* typically includes relatives on both mother's and father's sides, and may include relatives by marriage, whereas a patrilineal *descent group* includes only those relatives on father's side who are related agnatically, through "blood".

35 See, for example, the incident with Abdi, fresh milk, and Aman's stepmother in Chapter 3. For her part, Aman's mother balks at the possibility of having to take care of her husband's children by wives he had divorced.

36 See Lewis 1961:141 on lineage-to-lineage ties.

37 Cassanelli 1982.

38 Lewis 1961:2.

39 The term *agnate* is useful, for it helps to avoid the confusion of patrilineal with paternal kin, as well as the popular misconception that women cannot be each other's patrilineal relatives. In Somalia, kin "on father's side" may belong to his and his children's lineage; some of them, such as his mother, will almost certainly not. Two women whose fathers are brothers having the same father and the same or different

mothers are agnatic kin. I give this example because agnatic ties between women exist so long as they can be traced exclusively *through* their male agnatic kin; here maternal links are irrelevant. The women's children by husbands who are not each other's agnates are not themselves agnatic kin. In Somalia, where all ethnic Somalis consider themselves members of one large tribe, ultimately everyone is an agnate; yet for practical purposes much finer distinctions are drawn.

40 Lewis 1961:135, Helander 1991:119.
41 Helander 1991.
42 The implications of this for women's status are dealt with in a later section.
43 However, families of Arab and Persian descent often fabricate genealogical links to the major clan-families so as to place themselves within the Somali system (Laitin and Samatar 1987:31).
44 Lewis 1961:7.
45 For a classic description of a segmentary lineage system see Evans-Pritchard (1940).
46 Laitin and Samatar 1987:31.
47 Throughout Somalia Islamic inheritance rules are often ignored where women are concerned. Sometimes, as with Aman's mother, daughters receive smaller stock and town property, but rarely are they allowed their rightful share of their father's camels. Their menfolk who comprise the core of the *diya*-group

have a corporate interest in these and prevent their dispersal among daughters, who are usually married to men from other lineages and reside elsewhere. Since the married woman's natal *diya*-group retains responsibility for her after her marriage, the retention of a kinswoman's inheritance is justified as a kind of trust. See Lewis 1961.

48 Laitin and Samatar 1987:31.
49 Lewis 1961:198. The council is called *shir*.
50 Lewis 1961:200-201.
51 Lewis 1961:241.
52 Luling 1971:180-91, cited in Laitin 1977:27.
53 See Lewis 1961; Luling 1971; Laitin 1977; Laitin and Samatar 1987.
54 Lewis 1961:25, *passim*; Laitin and Samatar 1987:28.
55 Abdalla 1982:43. Also Lewis 1961:151.
56 Laitin and Samatar 1987:30.
57 Abdalla 1982:54.
58 Andrzejewski and Lewis 1964:30-31
59 Lewis 1961:213 ff., also Abdi I. Samatar 1989:26-27.
60 Lewis 1961:56 ff.
61 Lewis 1961:83.
62 Lewis 1961:60.

Camels and Poets
63 Laitin 1977:21.
64 Cassanelli 1982:11.
65 Laitin and Samatar 1987:25.
66 Laitin and Samatar 1987:27.
67 Burton 1966 [1856]:92-93.
68 See also Abu Lughod 1986 on

Egyptian Bedouin poetry.

[69] Andrzejewski and Lewis 1964:4.

[70] Andrzejewski 1982:xiii.

[71] Laitin and Samatar 1987:36-40.

[72] The eminent Canadian novelist Margaret Laurence edited a collection of Somali verbal arts entitled *A Tree for Poverty* (1954). She lived in British Somaliland in the early 1950s with her husband, an engineer employed to sink permanent wells along the border with Ethiopia. In the memoir of her sojourn she wrote that Somali was "a language well suited to poetry...for so many of its words were of the portmanteau variety, containing a wealth of connotations. One word described a wind that blew across the desert, parching the skin and drying the membranes of the throat. Some words were particularly lyrical; some were acutely specific. A low bush with soft broad leaves and delicate purple flowers was called *wahharawallis*, which meant 'that which makes the little goats jump'. There was a word for anything tasting sweet, even the fresh air. The word expressing the state of well-being meant literally 'to have enough water in one's belly'. A risk or any dangerous situation was *saymo*, the net of God" (Laurence 1964:35). She describes a plant called *marooro* that "has an acid taste in the morning but tastes sweet in the evening", a term Somali men often used to refer to a woman (*ibid.*). Laitin writes: "A Somali proverb has

it that *af Somaaliga wa mergi*, 'the Somali language is sinuous,' because words can take on new and different shapes all the time" (1977:31).

[73] As observed in note 6, over a fifth of Somali vocabulary, including many personal names, consists of Arabic loan words (Laitin 1977:25).

The Position of Women: Gender, Honour, Female Circumcision

[74] Andrzejewski 1974:18, in his anthropological introduction to a play by the Somali writer Hasan Sheikh Mumin, *Leopard among the Women: Shabeelnaagood*.

[75] As Raqiya Abdalla (1982:33) notes: "Islam maintains that since absolute equality is never possible in all situations, basic equality remains in all man-woman relations. In addition, there are other customs reinforcing male domination which are widely interpreted as *Islamic* and *religious*, but supported by no specific Islamic text" (emphasis in the original). For a discussion not specifically focussed on Somali society see Mernissi 1991 and Ahmed 1992.

[76] Andrzejewski and Lewis 1964:20.

[77] Lewis 1961, 1969, Andrzejewski and Lewis 1964.

[78] Lewis 1961:122.

[79] Of course, the barriers to such a suit would be formidable, given the constraints of kinship and the need to be represented by a man.

[80] Lewis 1969, Andrzejewski

1982:xvii.

[81] Abdalla 1982:55.

[82] Andrzejewski and Lewis 1964:22.

[83] Abdalla 1982:55.

[84] Abdalla 1982:55, Andrzejewski and Lewis 1964:23.

[85] See Cawl 1982, and Andrzejewski's introduction to that book (1982).

[86] See Abdalla 1982; Laitin and Samatar 1987:95.

[87] Even so, Lewis (1961:138) reported a divorce rate of over 25 per cent among one nomadic group in northern Somalia. Some Somalis say that rates throughout the country may have been higher in the past than they are today.

[88] Abdalla 1982:45.

[89] The number of traditional bondsmen is small, being estimated at no more than 12,500 in the late 1950s out of a total population of just under four million. See Lewis 1961:14.

[90] Burton 1966:285.

[91] Lewis 1961:14; Touval 1963:18.

[92] Laitin and Samatar 1987:42.

[93] This discussion leans heavily on Abu-Lughod's insights into honour among the Egyptian Bedouin (1986: 79-108).

[94] See also Boddy 1989.

[95] Lewis 1969:195-96.

[96] Abu-Lughod 1986: 104.

[97] Abdalla 1982:43.

[98] See also Abu-Lughod 1986:124 ff.

[99] Abdalla 1982:43.

[100] In Abdalla 1982:46-8, with the following attribution: "Extracted from an article on 'Somali Tradi-

tional Marriage' by Musa Galaal, 1968."

[101] Lewis 1969:201.

[102] In Sudan, such spirits can either precipitate an illness or take advantage of an existing problem, causing it to be unduly prolonged. Specific types of symptoms, such as lassitude, insomnia, anxiety, are linked to spirit sickness.

[103] The zar cult is found in different forms in Egypt and Ethiopia as well as Somalia and Sudan. See Boddy 1988, 1989; Lewis 1969, 1971, 1986, 1989; and Lewis et al. 1991, which contain lengthy bibliographies. On the Somali zar, see also Luling 1991.

[104] The zar cult is far more complex than this brief sketch would lead the reader to assume. In Sudan, where I studied it, its ceremonies are elaborate satirical burlesques of established authorities and colonial powers; initiates speak a language that metaphorically plays with the meanings of everyday speech. See Boddy 1989.

[105] Abdalla 1982:35.

[106] See Hosken 1979 and McLean 1989 for the extent and variety of these practices.

[107] For one thing, morality is less strongly linked to agnation in Sudan than in Somalia. See Boddy 1982, 1988, 1989, 1991.

[108] Abdalla 1982:12,17. It has, of course, been condemned by Western activists and governments as well.

[109] Abdalla 1982:37.

343

110 Abdalla 1982:49.

111 Abdalla 1982:51.

112 Abdalla 1982:53, emphasis in the original.

113 See Laitin and Samatar 1987:86-87.

114 See Abdalla 1982:86-100; Laitin and Samatar 1987:86-87. As is the case in Sudan, those Somalis interviewed by Abdalla (1982) who want infibulation stopped do not advocate abandoning female circumcision altogether. Although the term *sunna* implies that the operation is religiously prescribed, whether this is the case is debated in the Muslim world. See El Dareer (1982) and other entries in the bibliography. According to Abdalla (1982:82-83), the Maliki legal code states that circumcision is *sunna* for men and an *embellishment* for women, whereas the Hanafi and Hanbali codes describe circumcision as *sunna* for men, and *ennobling* for women. She does not tell us the position of the Shafi'i code to which Somalis adhere. Muslim feminists in countries where the surgery is practised have worked tirelessly to eradicate it. McLean (1980:6) reports that in 1978, due to the efforts of the Somali Women's Democratic Organization, a commission to abolish infibulation was established in Somalia. Few countries apart from Sudan have legislated against it, and there the laws have met with mixed success (Boddy 1991, Sanderson 1981). Over 80 per

cent of Muslim Sudanese women are at present infibulated, despite the fact that the procedure became an indictable offence in 1946.

115 See Alice Walker's novel *Possessing the Secret of Joy* (1992) for a dramatic exploration of one link between anti-colonial politics and female circumcision.

116 For an example of this, see Boddy 1991. Other sources on female circumcision in Africa, including the "pharaonic" type described above, include Assaad 1980, Boddy 1982, 1988, 1989; Cloudsley 1983; El-Saadawi 1980; Giorgis 1981; Gordon 1991; Guenbaum 1982, 1988, 1991; Hosken 1980; Kennedy 1978; King 1890; Koso-Thomas 1987; Kouba and Muasher 1985; Lightfoot-Klein 1989; Morsy 1991; Otoo 1976; W.H.O. 1979. A better tactic, in my view, is to support the efforts of African women and organizations working towards eradicating the practice in their own societies.

117 Abdalla 1982:109-110.

118 Andrzejewski 1974:20-21. Though wanton use of a husband's divorce right was curtailed by the reforms of 1975, these are not fully enforced and the woman's position remains precarious.

119 Abdalla (1982:57-61) and Laitin and Samatar (1987:86-87) discuss the postrevolutionary regime's efforts to challenge sexual inequality. More opportunities for women have opened up in the workforce and education

since the 1970s, though most of the benefits have gone to those in the urban milieu.

120 Abdalla 1982:52.

121 S. Barnes 1990:259 ff.

Colonial and Postcolonial Somalia

122 This synopsis relies mainly on Lewis 1988 and Laitin and Samatar 1987.

123 Cassanelli 1988:321 ff.

124 Lewis 1988:98.

125 Lewis 1988:98.

126 Touval 1963:71.

127 Lewis 1988:108.

128 Touval 1963:72; Lewis 1988:110.

129 Lewis 1988:110.

130 Lewis 1988:111.

131 Laitin and Samatar 1987:62.

132 Lewis 1988:111.

133 Under the name of "Italian East Africa", which included Ethiopia and Eritrea as well.

134 Lewis 1988:118.

135 Lewis 1988:140.

136 Lewis 1988:140-41.

137 Touval 1963:12.

138 Abdi I. Samatar 1989:89.

139 Touval 1963:13.

140 Lewis 1988:173.

141 Laitin and Samatar 1987:75.

142 Laitin and Samatar 1987:74.

143 Lewis 1988; Laitin and Samatar 1987; S. Samatar 1991. But also see Lewis (1993:2), who points out that in the far north of Somalia a reversion to clan-structures during the recent troubles has revealed the positive side of traditional politics. Clan elders were able to make peace more effectively than the new secessionist government.

144 These included Siyaad Barre in the early years of his rule.

145 I am summarizing a persuasive argument by Abdi Ismail Samatar (1992), a Somali professor of geography who teaches in the United States. See also Ahmed I. Samatar 1988.

146 Abdi I. Samatar 1992.

147 Said Samatar 1991:17.

148 Abdi I. Samatar 1992:635.

149 Laitin and Samatar 1987:78.

150 Despite exaggerated government claims to have reduced the illiteracy rate from 95 per cent to 45 per cent by 1975, the gains were considerable, and resulted in a dramatic increase in school enrolment. See Laitin and Samatar 1987.

151 In fact the Majeerteen are a clan of the Darood clan-family to which Siyaad Barre's clan also belongs. Isaaq and Hawiye are clan-families.

152 S. Samatar 1991. Of Siyaad Barre, Said Samatar (1991:17) writes: "The personal rule and ascendancy that he established lasted for 21 years and in its final moments lurched towards a precipitous fall in a popular uprising which saw the streets of Mogadishu 'piling up with bodies'." Tragically, Faraax Cawl, the first Somali novelist, was one of the victims of this violence (S. Samatar 1991:5).

153 Omaar 1992:233.

References

ABDALLA, RAQIYA HAJI DUALEH. 1982. *Sisters in Affliction: Circumcision and Infibulation in Africa*. London: Zed.

ABU-LUGHOD, LILA. 1986. *Veiled Sentiments: Honor and Poetry in a Bedouin Society*. Berkeley: University of California Press.

———. 1993. *Writing Women's Worlds: Bedouin Stories*. Berkeley: University of California Press.

AHMED, LEILA. 1992. *Women and Gender in Islam: Historical Roots of a Modern Debate*. New Haven: Yale University Press.

ANDRZEJEWSKI, B. W. 1974. Introduction to *Leopard among the Women:* Shabeelnaa-good, by Hassan Sheikh Mumin. Transl. B. W. Andrzejewski. London: Oxford University Press.

———. 1982. Introduction to *Ignorance Is the Enemy of Love*, by Faarax M. J. Cawl (1974). London: Zed.

ANDRZEJEWSKI, B. W., AND LEWIS, I. M. 1964. *Somali Poetry: An Introduction*. Oxford: Clarendon.

ASSAAD, MARIE BASSILI. 1980. "Female Circumcision in Egypt: Social Implications, Current Research, and Prospects for Change". *Studies in Family Planning* 11(1):3-16.

BARNES, SANDRA T. 1990. "Women, Property, and Power". In *Beyond the Second Sex: New Directions in the Anthropology of Gender*. Eds. P. R. Sanday, R. G. Goodenough. Philadelphia: University of Pennsylvania Press.

BARNES, VIRGINIA LEE. 1989. "Coming of Age in East Africa: The Life History Process and Its Empowerment of a Somali Woman". Presented at Annual Meeting, American Anthropological Association, November, Washington.

BERG, F. J. 1969. The Coast from the Portuguese Invasion. In *Zamani: A Survey of East African History*. Eds. B. A. Ogot, J. A. Kieran. Nairobi: Longmans.

BODDY, JANICE. 1982. "Womb as Oasis: The Symbolic Context of Pharaonic

Circumcision in Northern Sudan". *American Ethnologist* 9(4):682-98.

———. 1988. "Spirits and Selves in Northern Sudan: The Cultural Therapeutics of Possession and Trance". *American Ethnologist* 15(1):4-27.

———. 1989. *Wombs and Alien Spirits: Women, Men, and the Zar Cult in Northern Sudan.* Madison: University of Wisconsin Press.

———. 1991. "Body Politics: Continuing the Anti-Circumcision Crusade". *Medical Anthropology Quarterly* 5(1):15-17.

———. 1992. "Bucking the Agnatic System: Status and Strategies in Rural Northern Sudan". In *In Her Prime: New Views of Middle-Aged Women.* Eds. V. Kerns, J. K. Brown. Chicago: University of Illinois Press.

———. 1994. "Managing Tradition: 'Superstition' and the Making of National Identity among Sudanese Women Refugees". In *Religious and Cultural Certainties.* Ed. Wendy James. London: Routledge. (Forthcoming.)

BURTON, SIR RICHARD. 1966. (1856) *First Footsteps in East Africa.* Ed. G. Waterfield. London: Routledge and Kegan Paul.

CASSANELLI, LEE V. 1982. *The Shaping of Somali Society.* Philadelphia: University of Pennsylvania Press.

———. 1988. "The Ending of Slavery in Italian Somalia: Liberty and the control of Labor, 1890-1935". In *The End of Slavery in Africa.* Eds. S. Miers, R. Roberts. Madison: University of Wisconsin Press.

CAWL, FAARAX M. J. 1982. *Ignorance Is the Enemy of Love.* (1974) Transl. B. W. Andrzejewski. London: Zed.

CHITTICK, NEVILLE. 1969. "The Coast Before the Arrival of the Portuguese". In *Zamani: A Survey of East African History.* Eds. B. A. Ogot, J. A. Kieran. Nairobi: Longmans.

CLOUDSLEY, ANNE. 1983. *Women of Omdurman: Life, Love and the Cult of Virginity.* London: Ethnographica.

DECLICH, FRANCESCA. 1994. "Identity, Dance and Islam among People with Bantu Origins in Riverine Areas of Somalia". In *The Invention of Somalia.* Ed. A. J. Ahmed. London: Red Sea Press. (Forthcoming.)

EL DAREER, ASMA. 1982. *Woman, Why do You Weep? Circumcision and Its Consequences.* London: Zed.

EL SADAAWI, NAWAL. 1980. *The Hidden Face of Eve.* Ed. and transl. Sharif Hetata. London: Zed.

EVANS-PRITCHARD, E. E. 1940. *The Nuer.* Oxford: Clarendon.

GIORGIS, BELKIS WOLDE. 1981. *Female Circumcision in Africa.* Addis Ababa: U.N. Economic Commission for Africa and Association of African Women for Research and Development.

GORDON, DANIEL. 1991. "Female Circumcision and Genital Operations in Egypt and the Sudan: A Dilemma for Medical Anthropology". *Medical Anthropology Quarterly* 5(1):3-14.

GRUENBAUM, ELLEN. 1982. "The Movement Against Clitoridectomy and Infibulation in Sudan: Public Health Policy and the Women's Movement". *Medical Anthropology Newsletter* 13(2):4-12.

———. 1988. "Reproductive Ritual and Social Reproduction: Female Circumcision and the Subordination of Women in the Sudan". In *Economy and Class in the Sudan*. Eds. N. O'Neil and J. O'Brien. Aldershot: Avebury.

———. 1991. "The Islamic Movement, Development, and Health Education: Recent Changes in the Health of Rural Women in Central Sudan". *Social Science and Medicine* 33(6):637-645.

HAYES, ROSE OLDFIELD. 1975. "Female Genital Mutilation, Fertility Control, Women's Roles, and the Patrilineage in Modern Sudan: A Functional Analysis". *American Ethnologist* 2:617-633.

HELANDER, BERNHARD. 1991. "Words, Worlds, and Wishes: The Aesthetics of Somali Kinship". *Cultural Anthropology* 6(1):113-120.

HOSKEN, FRAN P. 1979. *The Hosken Report: Genital and Sexual Mutilation of Females.* Women's International Network News.

———. 1980. *Female Sexual Mutilations: The Facts and Proposals for Action.* Lexington, MA: Women's International Network News.

KENNEDY, JOHN G., ed. 1978. *Nubian Ceremonial Life.* Berkeley: University of California Press.

KING, M. J. S. 1890. "On the Practice of Female Circumcision and Infibulation among the Somalis and Other Nations of North-East Africa". *Anthropological Society* (Bombay) 2:2-6.

KOSO-THOMAS, O. 1987. *The Circumcision of Women: A Strategy for Eradication.* London: Zed.

KOUBA, LEONARD J., AND MUASHER, JUDITH 1985. "Female Circumcision in Africa: An Overview". *African Studies Review* 28(1):95-110.

LAITIN, DAVID D. 1977. *Politics, Language, and Thought: The Somali Experience.* Chicago: University of Chicago Press.

LAITIN, DAVID D., AND SAMATAR, SAID S. 1987. *Somalia: Nation in Search of a State.* Boulder: Westview.

LAURENCE, MARGARET. 1963 *The Prophet's Camel Bell.* Toronto: McClelland and Stewart.

LAURENCE, MARGARET, collector and transl. 1970. (1954) *A Tree for Poverty: Somali Poetry and Prose.* Hamilton: McMaster University Library Press.

LEWIS, I. M. 1961. *A Pastoral Democracy: A Study of Pastoralism and Politics among the Northern Somali of the Horn of Africa.* London: Oxford University Press.

———. 1969. "Spirit Possession in Northern Somaliland". In *Spirit Mediumship and Society in Africa*. Eds. J. Beattie, J. Middleton. London: Routledge and Kegan Paul.

———. 1971. "Spirit Possession in North-East Africa". In *Sudan in Africa*. Ed. Y. F. Hasan. Khartoum: Khartoum University Press.

———. 1986. *Religion in Context: Cults and Charisma*. Cambridge: Cambridge University Press.

———. 1988. *The Modern History of Somaliland: From Nation to State*. Boulder: Westview. (Revised ed.)

———. 1989. *Ecstatic Religion: A Study of Shamanism and Spirit Possession*. London: Routledge. (Revised ed.)

———. 1993. "Misunderstanding the Somali Crisis". *Anthropology Today* 9(4):1-3.

LEWIS, I. M., AL-SAFI, A., AND HURREIZ, S., eds. 1991. *Women's Medicine: The Zar-Bori Cult in Africa and Beyond*. Edinburgh: Edinburgh University Press.

LIGHTFOOT-KLEIN, HANNI. 1989. *Prisoners of Ritual: An Odyssey into Female Genital Circumcision in Africa*. New York: Harrington Park.

LULING, VIRGINIA. 1971. *The Social Structure of Southern Somali Tribes*. Ph.D. dissertation, University of London.

———. 1991. "Some Possession Cults in Southern Somalia". In *Women's Medicine: The Zar-Bori Cult in Africa and Beyond*. Eds. I. M. Lewis, A. Al-Safi, S. Hurreiz. Edinburgh: Edinburgh University Press.

MCLEAN, SCILLA, ed. 1980. *Female Circumcision, Excision and Infibulation: The Facts and Proposals for Change*. London: Minority Rights Group Report.

MERNISSI, FATIMA. 1991. *The Veil and the Male Elite: A Feminist Interpretation of Women's Rights in Islam*. Reading, MA: Addison Wesley.

MORSY, SOHEIR. 1991. "Safeguarding Women's Bodies: The White Man's Burden Medicalized". *Medical Anthropology Quarterly* 5(1):19-23.

MUMIN, HASSAN SHEIKH. 1974. *Leopard among the Women*: Shabeelnaagood. Transl. B. W. Andrzejewski. London: Oxford University Press.

OMAAR, RAQIYA. 1992. "Somalia: At War with Itself". *Current History* 91(565):230-34.

OTOO, S. N. A. 1976. "Pharaonic Circumcision in Somalia". WHO/EMRO. Unpublished Report.

PANKHURST, RICHARD. 1965. "The Trade of the Gulf of Aden Ports of Africa in the Nineteenth and Early Twentieth Centuries". *Journal of Ethiopian Studies*. 3(1):36-82.

SAMATAR, ABDI ISMAIL. 1989. *The State and Rural Transformation in Northern Somalia 1884-1986*. Madison: University of Wisconsin Press.

———. 1992. "Destruction of State and Society in Somalia: Beyond the Tribal

Convention". *Journal of Modern African Studies* 30(4):625-641.

SAMATAR, AHMED. 1988. *Socialist Somalia: Rhetoric and Reality.* London: Zed.

SAMATAR, SAID S. 1982. *Oral Poetry and Somali Nationalism.* Cambridge: Cambridge University Press.

——. 1991. *Somalia: A Nation in Turmoil.* London: Minority Rights Group Report.

SANDERSON, LILIAN PASSMORE. 1981. *Against the Mutilation of Women: The Struggle to End Unnecessary Suffering.* London: Ithaca.

SHOSTAK, MARJORIE. 1981. *Nisa: The Life and Words of a !Kung Woman.* New York: Random House.

SMITH, MARY F. 1981. *Baba of Karo: A Woman of the Muslim Hausa.* Hew Haven: Yale University Press. (Reprint, 1954.)

TOUVAL, SAADIA. 1963. *Somali Nationalism: International Politics and the Drive for Unity in the Horn of Africa.* Cambridge, MA: Harvard University Press.

WALKER, ALICE. 1992. *Possessing the Secret of Joy.* New York: Harcourt Brace Jovanovich.

W. H. O. (WORLD HEALTH ORGANIZATION). 1979. *Pratiques traditionelles affectant la santé des femmes et des enfants.* Rapport d'un séminaire tenu à Khartoum du 10 au 15 février 1979. Alexandria: Eastern Mediterranean Office. (See WHO/EMRO Technical Publications 2 (1979), for English translation.)

ACKNOWLEDGEMENTS

I would like to thank Penny Orr, who didn't let the story die and who looked for people who could help us publish; John Middleton, who found Janice; Janice Boddy for bringing the book to Knopf Canada; Louise Dennys, David Kent, Rebecca Godfrey, Kathryn Gaizauskas, and everyone at Knopf Canada, for their work and time; and Sharifa, for all her help.

Aman

Many people have helped with this project and I am grateful to them all: on the home and literary fronts, my husband, Ronald Wright; at Knopf Canada, Louise Dennys, Rebecca Godfrey, Kathryn Gaizauskas, Catherine Yolles, and Susan Roxborough. A University of Toronto Social Sciences and Humanities Grant-in-Aid-of-Research made it possible for me to interview Aman in the summer of 1993. My thanks go also to Gamal Gulaid, Claudie Gosselin, Hilarie Kelly, Bella Pomer, Gena Gorrell, Audrey Glasbergen, Carole Tuck, Sharifa, Donya Peroff, John Middleton, Penny Orr, Martin Buss, Michael Lambek, Jacqueline Solway, Sharon Foster, Beverley Sotolov, members of the Somali community in Toronto, and my very patient students. Special thanks to Aman, for telling her story, and to Lee Barnes, for bringing it to the world.

Janice Boddy